THE AMERICAN NATION
A HISTORY

FROM ORIGINAL SOURCES BY ASSOCIATED SCHOLARS

EDITED BY
ALBERT BUSHNELL HART, LL.D.
PROFESSOR OF HISTORY IN HARVARD UNIVERSITY

ADVISED BY
VARIOUS HISTORICAL SOCIETIES

THE AMERICAN NATION
A HISTORY

LIST OF AUTHORS AND TITLES

GROUP I

FOUNDATIONS OF THE NATION

GROUP II

TRANSFORMATION INTO A NATION

COMMITTEES ORIGINALLY APPOINTED TO
ADVISE AND CONSULT WITH THE EDITOR

The Massachusetts Historical Society

Charles Francis Adams, LL.D., President
Samuel A. Green, M.D., Vice-President
James Ford Rhodes, LL.D., 2d Vice-President
Edward Channing, Ph.D., Prof. History Harvard
    University
Worthington C. Ford, Chief of Division of MSS.,
    Library of Congress

The Wisconsin Historical Society

Reuben G. Thwaites, LL.D., Secretary and Super-
    intendent
Frederick J. Turner, Ph.D., Prof. of American His-
    tory, Wisconsin University
James D. Butler, LL.D., formerly Prof. Wisconsin
    University
William W. Wight, President
Henry E. Legler, Curator

The Virginia Historical Society

William Gordon McCabe, Litt D., President
Lyon G. Tyler, LL.D., Pres. of William and Mary
    College
Judge David C. Richardson
J. A. C. Chandler, Professor Richmond College
Edward Wilson James

The Texas Historical Society

Judge John Henninger Reagan, President
George P. Garrison, Ph.D., Prof. of History, Univer-
    sity of Texas
Judge C. W. Raines
Judge Zachary T. Fullmore

BENJAMIN FRANKLIN

THE AMERICAN NATION: A HISTORY

VOLUME 6

PROVINCIAL AMERICA

1690–1740

BY

EVARTS BOUTELL GREENE, Ph.D.

PROFESSOR OF HISTORY IN ILLINOIS STATE UNIVERSITY

WITH MAPS

NEW YORK AND LONDON
HARPER & BROTHERS PUBLISHERS

TO
M. J. G. AND D. C. G.

CONTENTS

xiii

CONTENTS

MAPS

EDITOR'S INTRODUCTION

TO the period between 1689 and 1740 has been applied the term "The Forgotten Half-Century." Most of the writers on colonial history in detail give special attention to the seventeenth century, the period of upbuilding; and the general historians like Bancroft and Hildreth sweep rather lightly over the epoch between the English Revolution and the forerunnings of the American Revolution. In distributing the parts of *The American Nation*, this period has been selected for especial treatment, because within it are to be found the roots of many later institutions and experiences.

The external side of provincial history, especially in its relations with France, has been reserved for Thwaites's *France in America* (vol. VII. of this series), except so far as it affected the internal development of the colonies previous to 1713. Space is thus available for a constitutional treatment which shall bring out the general imperial system of Great Britain, the organs and methods of colonial control, and the principles of domestic government in America; and to put the subject in a proper relation with the economic and social life of the time.

The book begins with an account of imperial conditions in 1689 (chap. i.); the next four chapters are devoted to various phases of colonial government, and bring into relief the disposition of the English authorities to tighten the reins of colonial control. The establishment of the English Church in some of the colonies and the attempt to bring the colonies into the English "system," ecclesiastically as well as politically, is the theme of chapter vi.

Chapters vii. to x. summarize the military struggle in the colonies brought on by the world rivalry between France and England; but this war is treated in its relations with American colonial history, leaving out the extensions of Canada and Louisiana beyond the reach of the colonists, and also avoiding the European side of the story.

Chapters xi. to xiii. develop the changes in imperial and local government during the first third of the eighteenth century, and also deal with the important subject of the beginnings of political organization in America.

Chapters xiv. to xviii. are devoted to the social and economic development of the Continental colonies, including the movement of new masses and new race elements across the ocean; the filling-in of the settled area; and the pushing backward to the mountains, and southward to the southern boundary, of the new colony of Georgia. Special stress is laid upon the extension of the Navigation Acts to the West India and to over-sea trade, thus supplementing the treatment of that subject in Andrews's *Colonial Self-Government* (vol. V., chap. i.). Within the last chapter of text the author deals with the intellectual and literary life of the people. The Critical Essay on Authorities ranges in order the most valuable part of the confusing literature of the period.

The service of the book to the series is to build a bridge between the founding of the colonies, described in the fourth and fifth volumes of *The American Nation*, and the separation of the colonies, which is the subject of Howard's *Preliminaries of the Revolution* (vol. VIII.). Its theme is the essential difficulty of reconciling imperial control with the degree of local responsibility which had to be accorded to the colonists.

AUTHOR'S PREFACE

THE half-century of American history which follows the English revolution of 1689 presents peculiar difficulties of treatment. The historian must deal with the experience of thirteen different colonies which were, however, ultimately to become one nation, and which even then possessed important elements of unity. Within the limits of a single volume it is obviously impossible to tell the story of each individual colony, and at the same time to discuss the general movements of the time. It is the author's conviction that the most instructive method for the student of this period is to emphasize the general movements.

The history of this provincial era is comparatively deficient in dramatic incidents; and the interest lies rather in the aggregate of small transactions, constituting what are called general tendencies, which gradually and obscurely prepare the way for the more striking but not necessarily more important periods of decisive conflict and revolution.

First of all, this was a time of marked expansion: the seventeenth century stocks were reinforced by large numbers of immigrants; the areas of settlement were extended; and there was also an important development of industry and commerce. This material expansion led up gradually to the struggle for the mastery of the continent, which will be described in the next volume.

A second important feature of the time is the interaction of imperial and provincial interests. After the violent and radical movements of the years from 1684 to 1689, there was worked out for the first time a fairly complete system of imperial control. In the efforts of the colonists to preserve within that system the largest possible measure of self-government, principles were involved which were brought to more radical issues in the revolutionary era. In the political conflicts of this period such men as Thomas Hutchinson and Benjamin Franklin were trained for the larger posts assigned to them in later years.

Finally, with all due allowance for divisive forces, there was a growing unity in provincial life. Material expansion was gradually filling the wilderness spaces which divided the colonies; a broader, though still provincial, culture was increasing the points of intellectual contact; under various forms of government, the Americans of that time cherished common ideals of personal liberty and local autonomy.

Scholars generally agree that the subject-matter of this volume has never been adequately treated as a whole, though there are some good monographs and an almost bewildering mass of local and antiquarian publications. It is hardly possible even now to write a history which can be called in any sense definitive; certainly, no such claim is made for the present work. In the main, the author's purpose has been to state fairly, and to correlate, conclusions already familiar to special students in this field.

Mr. David M. Matteson prepared the preliminary sketches for the maps in this volume. The author desires also to express his more than usual obligations to the editor for helpful suggestions both as to matter and form.

EVARTS BOUTELL GREENE.

PROVINCIAL AMERICA

PROVINCIAL AMERICA

CHAPTER I

ENGLAND AND THE COLONIES

(1689)

THE revolution of 1689 was, in the first instance, a revolution of the English people. Through their representatives in the great convention they defended the Protestant establishment of the church, asserted the sovereignty of Parliament, defined certain fundamental rights of the individual, and, finally, placed these ancient rights under the protection of their new sovereigns, William and Mary. A few weeks later a similar convention in Scotland took similar action; and during the next two years the military campaigns of William and his officers re-established in the dependent principality of Ireland the authority of the English crown and the English church. These events, however, did not establish the "United Kingdom" of to-day. For a century longer Ireland maintained her separate though dependent Parliament; and the legislative

3

union of Scotland and England was not accomplished for nearly twenty years. From the standpoint of British law and administration, Scotchmen and Irishmen were still in large measure alien peoples, both in England and in the colonies.

These political movements in the British Isles were followed with close interest by large numbers of English subjects in the American hemisphere. They produced or made possible similar movements there, and radically changed the internal organization of the colonies as well as their relation to each other and to the mother-country. Notwithstanding the close causal connection between the revolutionary movements in the mother-country and in the colonies, there were important differences between them, due to peculiar conditions prevailing either in the colonies as a whole or in particular colonies or groups of colonies. The American movements cannot, therefore, be understood without some analysis of those conditions.[1]

The main body of the English colonists in 1689 occupied a narrow strip of territory stretching along the seaboard from the Kennebec River in Maine to the Ashley in South Carolina. Beyond the struggling English settlements in Maine, to the north and east, was a region in which English and French claims overlapped. In the south the Carolinas had been settled in defiance of the prior Spanish

[1] Compare the following discussion with Andrews, *Colonial Self-Government* (*Am. Nation*, V.), chaps. xviii, xix.

claims, and the new settlement of Charleston, in particular, was jealously watched by the Spanish garrison at St. Augustine. Everywhere the frontier line was drawn close to the sea. Here and there were interior posts in the wilderness, like the Massachusetts towns in the Connecticut Valley, and Schenectady on the Mohawk, but even towns within a few miles of Boston were still subject to Indian forays.

North of these permanent settlements on the main-land, were several remote trading-posts on the shores of Hudson Bay, maintained by the Hudson's Bay Company. A few small fishing settlements also existed on the eastern shore of Newfoundland, but the English claim to the island was challenged by a French fort on Placentia Bay.

To the south, England had already acquired a series of insular possessions, beginning with the Bermudas, and including in succession the Bahamas, the Leeward Islands, Barbadoes, and Jamaica. Commercial and social relations of considerable importance existed between the insular colonies and those of the mainland, and their political tendencies were in some respects much alike.

The population of these colonies can only be roughly estimated. New England, not counting Indians, may have numbered about eighty thousand, of whom about two-thirds were included in 1691 under the political jurisdiction of Massachusetts. New York, New Jersey, and Penn's colonies on the Delaware had together a population probably somewhat less than that of Massachusetts. Virginia was then the largest of the colonies, and the two Chesapeake provinces combined probably had a population slightly larger than that of New England. In the isolated Carolina settlements, there may have been in all five thousand people, including negroes.[1]

In these British dominions there was already a considerable variety of racial elements. The New England colonists were almost exclusively of English stock, and so for the most part were the white settlers of the south, though there was already a small French Huguenot colony in South Carolina. New York was a comparatively recent conquest, with the Dutch considerably outnumbering the English element and a smaller representation of other European stocks. In Pennsylvania the generous policy of Penn and his liberal advertisements in continental Europe had attracted some non-English immigrants to reinforce the early Swedish and Dutch settlers and the English Quakers. African and, to a lesser extent, Indian slavery existed throughout the continental colonies as well as in the islands; though in the former it was only beginning to assume an important position. In South Carolina, however, by the close of the century, the negroes outnumbered the whites.

The American colonists differed from each other

[1] Dexter, *Estimates of Population in the American Colonies.*

not merely in racial distinctions, but sometimes even more decisively in religion. New England as a whole was still dominated by the religious ideals of the Puritan founders of Massachusetts Bay. Dissenters could not, however, be absolutely excluded, as the Antinomians and the early Quakers had been in the days of Winthrop and Endicott. Rhode Island, with her ideal of religious toleration, still stood in marked antagonism to the old Puritan ecclesiasticism; and the royal government of the Andros régime had given the Episcopal church a foothold in Massachusetts. In the closing years of the seventeenth century the Anglican clergy and laymen of New England constituted a small but energetic minority which had to be reckoned with as a real political force.

The racial differences of the middle colonies were reflected in the field of religion. In New York, Calvinism was not so strongly intrenched nor so aggressive as in New England. Its adherents were in a decided majority, but were themselves divided into rival organizations, of which the most important were the old Dutch Reformed church, lately the established church of New Netherland, and the more loosely associated Congregational churches which had their strongholds on Long Island, thus bringing into New York politics the militant spirit of New England Puritanism. The Lutherans were also represented in the colony, and the Church of England had a bare foothold. Between these vari-

ous Protestant bodies, the early English governors
had maintained on the whole a fairly even balance.
The few Catholics of the province, protected from
persecution during the supremacy of James, the
Catholic proprietor and king, became in the revolution of 1689 the chief objects of popular hatred, and
were afterwards subjected to severe penalties. In
Pennsylvania the strongest influence was, of course,
that of the Quakers, but there were also Anglicans,
Lutherans, and other Protestants. In none of the
middle colonies was there a true state church, and
it is in them that the student finds the nearest ap-
proach to the freedom and diversity of our modern
American life.

Virginia, notwithstanding some jealousies between clergy and laity, held strongly to the Anglican establishment. In Maryland the Catholic proprietor had striven to keep the peace between
Catholics, Puritans, and Anglicans, but the violent
anti-Catholic spirit of the English revolution asserted itself here as in New York. Provincial politicians used this religious antagonism to overthrow
for a time the government of the proprietor, and
when the revolution was over the Anglican party
reaped the fruits of the Protestant victory in the
legal establishment of their own church. In the
Carolinas the early policy of the proprietors gave
rise to a religious diversity similar to that in the
middle colonies. The Anglicans were the strongest element among the early settlers of Charleston,

but there were also French Huguenots, Scotch and
Irish Presbyterians, and New England Puritans.
The obscure settlements of North Carolina could
hardly be said at this time to have any definite religious complexion. The Quaker missionaries exerted a considerable influence, but the general at-
mosphere was one of religious indifference.

The economic occupations and interests of the
colonies at the close of the seventeenth century
have been carefully examined in the preceding
volume of this series and require only a brief review here. In all the colonies agricultural interests
were predominant, but the specific character of
these interests varied widely. In Maryland and
Virginia the large plantation was becoming the
characteristic economic unit, and there were no
considerable centres of trade. Negro slavery had
gained a firm foothold, and the planters were almost wholly absorbed in the production of tobacco
for export. South Carolina was developing along
West Indian lines the plantation system in its
most extreme form; and she differed from the
Chesapeake colonies in possessing a commercial and
social centre at Charleston, which completely dominated also the political life of the colony throughout
its history.

In the middle colonies economic conditions were
more varied, and flourishing trading centres had
grown up at Philadelphia and New York, overshadowing others of less importance. The large

plantation existed here also to a limited extent, notably among the Hudson River people, but the small farmer was also an important factor throughout this region. The organization of agriculture in New England differed more sharply from that of the south. Here the farmers gathered in towns within easy reach of the meeting-house. Their outlying farms were small as compared with Virginia plantations, negro slavery was an almost negligible factor, and there were no great agricultural staples comparable with tobacco. Agriculture was supplemented by the important fishing industry and the Indian fur trade. The timber resources of New England had been used for ship-building on a considerable scale, and her vessels were engaged in a constantly widening intercolonial and foreign trade.

This developing industrial life of the colonies Parliament was now attempting to guide in certain legally established channels; but the navigation acts, with their restrictions on colonial shipping, imports, and exports, were imperfectly obeyed. For their really efficient enforcement a different governmental organization was necessary; and the attempt to secure such a system became one of the most important factors in the constitutional history of the later colonial era.

The governments of the American colonies were, at the close of the Stuart period, in a state of decidedly unstable equilibrium, due to the adoption by the English crown of a new and aggressive colonial policy. These new measures, however, cannot be appreciated without recalling certain leading principles of English colonial policy in its earlier phases.

The first is the leaving of responsibility, not merely for the economic development but for the government of new colonies, to private individuals, private associations, or corporations, acting either under the authority of royal charters, or, as sometimes happened in New England, simply by the sufferance of the crown. No one of the main-land colonies began its career under a royal or provincial government, and until 1684 only two were definitely so organized: Virginia, which became a royal government in 1624, after the charter of the Virginia Company had been annulled; and New Hampshire, which, after a varied experience at first under the nominal rule of a proprietor, and then as a part of Massachusetts, was finally, in 1679, organized as a separate royal province.[1]

Secondly, the tendency was, instead of concentrating governmental responsibility in a few hands, to authorize, or to permit, a large number of small governments. By 1684 there were on the mainland twelve distinct colonial governments: New Hampshire, Massachusetts, Plymouth, Rhode Island, Connecticut, New York, East New Jersey, West New Jersey, Pennsylvania with the "lower

[1] Compare on this subject, Tyler, *England in America*, passim; Andrews, *Colonial Self-Government*. chap. ii (*Am. Nation*, IV., V.).

counties," Virginia, Maryland, and Carolina, having,
for the most part, no political connection with each
other except their common subjection, slight and
intangible as that often was, to the English crown
and Parliament.

The greatest variety appeared in the character of
these governments, both as to the nature of their
relations with the home government and as to
their internal organization. In Virginia the constitution was in the main embodied in the royal
commission and instructions issued to each succeeding governor. In the more recently organized
proprietary governments the proprietor, though
given considerable freedom of action, was held in
check by such requirements as the allowing of appeals to the Privy Council or the submission of
colonial laws for the approval of the crown. There
were also quasi-independent governments like those
of Maryland, Massachusetts, and Connecticut, where
the crown had no effective check on colonial law and
administration. Under the royal charters, New
England had become the home of practically republican governments, where judges and executive officers as well as law-makers were chosen by the people
or their representatives. The Maryland proprietary
government may be described as a constitutional
monarchy of the conservative type, while Penn's
constitution was much more liberal. These governments, however, had one thing in common: the principle of popular representation had in some form or

other been conceded in all of them, sometimes freely, as in Pennsylvania, and sometimes tardily, or only temporarily, as in New York. Often, however, the privileges of these representative bodies were imperfectly defined and held on a somewhat precarious tenure.

A third striking characteristic of early colonial policy was the almost entire absence of parliamentary control. The English territories in America, whether acquired by discovery or by conquest, were the domains of the crown. The king determined the conditions under which they should be occupied, their trade carried on, and their governments organized. Not until the period of the Commonwealth did Parliament begin to concern itself actively in the affairs of the colonies; and at first its work was mainly confined to the assertion of principles, without providing adequate machinery for their enforcement.

During the second half of the seventeenth century there was in England greater interest in the problem of colonial government. The material resources and the industry of the colonies were to be exploited and made factors in the development of national power. By the navigation acts of the Commonwealth and Restoration governments, Parliament undertook to regulate the course of colonial enterprise. The trade of the colonies must be carried on in English ships and by English seamen. Many of their staple articles of export might be

sent to Europe only through English ports, and
their imports from Europe must come only by way
of England. The acts which asserted these general
principles were naturally followed by others which
were needed to settle doubtful questions of construction, and to secure a more effective enforcement.[1]

The primary motive of this legislation was financial or economic, but it had also important constitutional results. Since the existing colonial governments could not be relied upon to enforce thoroughly
the requirements of the navigation acts, a special
official service was organized in the colonies, charged
with this specific duty. Consequently, there soon
appeared side by side with the local governments
of individual colonies, whether provincial, proprietary, or republican, the surveyor-general and
the collectors of customs, as the representatives of
a new imperial control. These new officials in
turn were supervised and controlled by the Privy
Council with its Committee of Trade and Plantations.

Even these measures, however, were inadequate.
The thorough enforcement of the law required the
cordial co-operation of the colonial governor with
the royal agent, but instead of this there was
mutual suspicion and dislike. The governor was
influenced by the local sentiment of the colony or

[1] Cf. Andrews, *Colonial Self-Government* (*Am. Nation*, V.),
chaps. i., ii.

the personal interests of the proprietor, which were
often at variance with those of the crown. It was
natural enough, therefore, that such men as Edward Randolph, who looked at the problem from
the point of view of a royal official, should demand
a reorganization of the colonial governments themselves, in order to make them more effective agents
of imperial control. These general considerations,
with others of a more local character, gradually led
the English government to adopt new principles of
colonial administration.

The changed attitude of the crown towards the
proprietary governments was illustrated in the New
York patent of 1664, and still more in Penn's
charter of 1681. In both these provinces the right of
appeal to the Privy Council was expressly reserved
by the crown, and in Pennsylvania this check upon
provincial independence was reinforced by a number of new provisions, including a royal veto on
colonial laws. In 1684 came the revocation of the
Massachusetts charter, followed during the next
four years by the gradual incorporation in a single
province of eight hitherto distinct jurisdictions, including, besides all of New England, New York and
the Jerseys, all of which were covered by the royal
commission to Andros in 1688. Legal proceedings
were also ordered for the purpose of annulling the
proprietary authority in Delaware, Maryland, and
the Carolinas. It seems probable that if this policy
had not been interrupted by the revolution of 1689,

direct control by the crown would have been secured
in all, or nearly all, of the colonies.

Thus the later policy of the Stuarts embodied
these two leading principles: the substitution of
royal for proprietary or elective governments; and
the consolidation of numerous petty jurisdictions
into a smaller number of strong provinces. Such
a policy would probably in any case have provoked
sharp antagonism from the colonists, and from the
various proprietary interests which were thus as-
sailed. It was still further weakened by being associated with another form of restriction with which
it had no necessary connection: the colonies which
were successively incorporated in the "greater New
England" of 1688 were left without any general
representative assembly to take the place of the
various local bodies which had been superseded.
The extension of imperial control and the consolidation of governments may be regarded in some
aspects at least as measures of progress; the denial
of popular representation was distinctly reaction-
ary.

CHAPTER II

PROVINCIAL REORGANIZATION
(1689–1692)

WHEN the English revolution of 1689 opened the way for similar movements in America, the opposition gathered strength from various sources. The chartered colonies of New England desired their old local independence; their religious prejudices also were stirred by the support which the Andros régime had given to the Anglican church, and by its toleration of what seemed to them a looser morality. The Catholicism of James and some of his agents was a prime factor in enabling the revolutionists of New York to discredit his authority in the province. There and in New England stanch Anglicans were suspected as possible tools of a "Popish" conspiracy. In Maryland, however, this religious antagonism had precisely the opposite effect, and contributed towards the temporary overthrow of the proprietor and the extension of royal control.

One of the first acts of William III. was the appointment, in February, 1689, of a new Committee of the Privy Council on Trade and Plantations, including the leading ministers of state, both Whig

and Tory. In the early months of 1689 the general principles of colonial policy were discussed with
some care, and the new committee accepted, in
large measure, the policy of its predecessors.   Thus,
in April, 1689, before the uprising in New England
was known, the committee recommended the organization of such a government in New England,
New York, and the Jerseys, as would enable the
people to oppose the French with their united forces.
Here the military motive appears to reinforce the
commercial argument for closer control.   In May of
the same year the committee suggested as a proper
subject for consideration by Parliament whether
Maryland, the Carolinas, and Pennsylvania should
not be brought into closer dependence upon the
crown.   Pending the settlement of a definite policy,
the existing political arrangements in the colonies
were, in general, to be continued.[1]

In the mean time the colonists were taking matters into their own hands. Revolutionary movements in Massachusetts and New York overthrew
the Andros administration; the New England colonies resumed their chartered constitutions, and
in New York Leisler set up his revolutionary
government.   In Maryland the agitators of the
Protestant Association took advantage of religious
prejudices against the Catholic proprietor to overthrow his authority and organize a new government in the name of William and Mary.   Even in

[1] *Cal. of State Pap., Col.*, 1689–1692, pp. 6, 34, 39.

Virginia and the West Indian Islands considerable
uneasiness resulted from the political changes at
home.[1] The confusion was seriously increased in
many colonies by the outbreak of war with France
and by Indian incursions on the northern frontiers.
With these various and perplexing problems to be
dealt with, it is not surprising that the king and
his ministers were not able at once to restore order
and carry out a consistent policy; and it is a mark
of statesmanship that during the next two years
a fair solution of the problem was worked out in
most of the colonies.

The basis of this settlement was compromise.
Though the colonial policy of James II. was maintained in many of its essential features, it was considerably modified, and on one point was definitely
abandoned. The privilege of a representative assembly could hardly be denied by a government instituted for the protection of representative institutions in the mother-country; and it was now
restored in all the colonies.

The question still remained of restoring the old
charters, especially in New England. The colonists,
represented by skilful agents, and supported by influential politicians in England, claimed to stand
in defence of ancient privileges arbitrarily taken
from them by the now discredited government of
James II. The Puritan party had played an im-

[1] Cf. Andrews, *Colonial Self-Government* (*Am. Nation*, V.),
chap. xvii.

portant part in bringing about the English revolution also, and might reasonably claim some consideration for Puritan interests in America. Against these claims, however, were enlisted some powerful influences. Many of the new king's counsellors had had an active part in the administrations of the last two Stuart kings, and were hardly prepared to abandon altogether the old policy. The revolution also strengthened rather than weakened the influence of the merchants in the government; desiring, as they did, a strict observance of the navigation acts, and a steady assertion of British as against distinctively colonial interests, it was clearly their interest to extend the administrative control of the mother-country.

Lastly, the outbreak of war both in Europe and America served to emphasize the military point of view. It was urged again and again in the colonial correspondence that the ravages of the Indians on the frontier were largely the result of the political disintegration which followed the revolution. So long as the colonies were divided into petty independent jurisdictions, each pursuing selfishly its own immediate interests, there could be no effective co-operation for the defence of the empire as a whole.

The adjustment of colonial governments from 1689 to 1691 was a fair compromise between the antagonistic views which have just been described. The idea of a consolidated New England was abandoned; Connecticut and Rhode Island were allowed to resume their rights of government under the old charters which had never been definitely surrendered; and New Hampshire was to be governed, as before, as a separate royal province, though the proprietor of the soil, Samuel Allen, was given a governor's commission. The tendency towards consolidation appears, however, in the new charter of Massachusetts, which organized under a single royal government Massachusetts, Maine, and the old colony of Plymouth. The charter also included Acadia, recently conquered by Sir William Phips; but this clause was deprived of importance through the French reconquest of Port Royal in 1691.[1]

The Massachusetts charter was in itself a compromise. The interests of the crown were to be protected by a royal governor with a limited appointing power and the right of veto upon acts of the general court or assembly; there was also an ultimate royal veto on colonial statutes, and an express right of appeal from colonial courts to the Privy Council. These were serious deductions from the old colonial independence, but enough remained to give Massachusetts until the eve of the American Revolution several marked advantages among the royal provinces: the royal veto had to be exercised within a specified time; the executive council, which served also as the upper house of the legislature, was here alone an elective body,

[1] *Cal. of State Pap., Col.*, passim; cf. Andrews, *Colonial Self-Government (Am. Nation,* V.) chap. xvii.

annually chosen by joint ballot of the council and the house of representatives, though subject to the governor's veto.   The guarantee of annual elections, the right to exercise a considerable part of the appointing power, and the semi-popular character of the legislative upper house gave to the assembly a freedom of action and an influence in administration not to be found in any other royal province.[1]

In New York the revolutionary leaders had involved themselves in unnecessary antagonism with the new government in England and were set aside in the final settlement.   The province received a separate royal government of the ordinary type, but the representative principle was definitely recognized.

The problems of the proprietary governments were not settled in any consistent or logical fashion, but were largely affected by personal considerations. The pending proceedings against the proprietors of the Jerseys and of the Carolinas were not pushed, in spite of the disorderly conditions in those colonies. On the other hand, the proprietors of Pennsylvania and Maryland were prejudiced by their associations. The fact that Lord Baltimore was a Catholic had been emphasized by the unfortunate delay of his government in proclaiming the new sovereign, and was taken advantage of by the discontented elements within the province.   The friction between proprietary and royal officers during the preceding

---

[1] The Massachusetts charter, in Massachusetts Bay, *Acts and Resolves*, I., 1–20.

years injured him with the statesmen of the new government as well as with their predecessors. The result was a somewhat peculiar compromise; Baltimore remained technically in possession of his charter, and enjoyed certain rights as proprietor of the soil; while the king appointed the governor and council, and in general exercised the same political authority as in the normal royal province.

Penn's position was particularly vulnerable: his legal title to the lower counties was questioned; his officers were charged with laxity in the administration of the navigation laws; his intimacy with the late king made him an object of suspicion; and there was sharp criticism of the Quaker attitude towards imperial defence. In this crisis, however, Penn and his friends in the province showed a marked capacity for diplomacy and passive resistance. Except for a brief interruption in 1692–1694, during which Governor Fletcher, of New York, undertook to administer the province under a royal commission, Penn was able to hold his ground.

By the close of the year 1691, the two royal governments on the continent had been increased to five: New Hampshire; the three leading colonies of Virginia, Massachusetts, and Maryland; and New York, which occupied a position of pre-eminent strategic importance in the coming struggle with France. Taken together, the royal provinces now had perhaps two-thirds of the total population of the continental colonies. Thus the net result of

the decade which began with Penn's charter in
1681 and ended with the second Massachusetts
charter of 1691 was a marked extension of imperial
control.

Though the Stuart policy had been modified in
some respects, the Stuart traditions were still
strong at the court. Provincial officials who had
begun American service under Charles and James,
and were closely associated with the carrying out of
their policy, were retained in the service with every
indication of royal confidence. The charges against
Andros were dismissed, and he received afterwards
an appointment to the royal government of Virginia, the most important on the continent. Howard of Effingham, in spite of the vigorous opposition
in Virginia, was at first reappointed titular governor
of the province, with Francis Nicholson, Andros's
former associate in New York, as his lieutenant on
the ground. Usher, the new lieutenant-governor in
New Hampshire, belonged to the same party. Above
all, Edward Randolph, the unsparing critic of the
chartered governments, continued his colonial career
as surveyor-general of customs. From these and
others like them correspondence on colonial affairs
was constantly coming in to the secretaries of state
and the committee of trade, and impressing upon
them the desirability of pushing to its legitimate
conclusions the policy of imperial control.[1]

[1] *Cal. of State Pap., Col.*, 1689–1692, passim; cf. Andrews,
Colonial Self-Government (Am. Nation, V.), chap. xvii.

In Massachusetts the final establishment of even a modified provincial system was peculiarly painful, and it was associated with another event which gave to this constitutional change something of tragic dignity.

It is now well understood that the witchcraft delusion in Massachusetts was no unique incident in human history or in the Christian world of that time. The basis of the witchcraft idea was the belief in a personal devil who, through his agents, the witches, was constantly conspiring against the welfare of mankind. This dogma was almost universally held by the Christian church in its various branches for two centuries after the Protestant revolution, and was definitely recognized by the law of the land. In the Massachusetts Body of Liberties of 1641 witchcraft was made a capital offence, and in 1692 the general court enacted a law, taken almost verbatim from a statute of James I., imposing the same penalty for witchcraft in its more serious forms. During the sixteenth and seventeenth centuries many thousands of persons were executed as witches in England, and methods of procedure in such cases were carefully set forth in the legal treatises of the day.[1]

Before 1692 there were a few sporadic cases of conviction and execution for witchcraft. About ten years before the Salem outbreak, the ministers of

[1] Massachusetts Bay, *Acts and Resolves*, I., 55, 56, 90; 1 James I., chap. xii.; *Body of Liberties*, in MacDonald, *Select Charters*, 87.

Boston and vicinity undertook a serious investigation of the history of witchcraft in New England, and soon after Increase Mather described, in his *Illustrious Providences*, witchcraft and kindred phenomena. In 1688 the children of John Goodwin, of Boston, were supposed to have been bewitched by an Irish laundress, who was tried and executed. Cotton Mather, the son of Increase Mather, interested himself in this case, and applied to it his theory that the malign influences of the Evil One might be overcome by fasting and prayer. In the following year he published a book in which he insisted on the reality of devils and witches, and sharply criticised the sceptics. Richard Baxter, the famous English dissenter, thought the book so convincing " that he must be a very obdurate Sadducee that will not believe it." Both the Mathers recommended cautious methods of procedure in the trial of supposed witches, but probably their publications helped to develop a morbid interest in supernatural phenomena.[1]

In the mean time the colonists had been abnormally excited by experiences of other kinds. Their old charter had been taken from them, and serious men were anxious about the possibility of maintaining the old ideals under the changed conditions. Then, for several years, a peculiarly shocking warfare had been going on on the frontier with a savage people, whom it was easy to think of as fiendish

[1] Poole, in Winsor, *Memorial Hist. of Boston*, II., chap. iv.

allies of the Evil One. Thus, when the tales of witchcraft at Salem village began to come in, they found a more ready response than might have been given in calmer times.

The disturbance began with the strange actions of some young girls at Salem village (now Danvers). Friends and professional advisers were called in, and when they agreed that the girls had been bewitched there was great alarm, and public fasts were kept, not only in the immediate neighborhood, but in other parts of the colony. When questioned about the cause of their troubles, the "afflicted persons" named at first three women by whom they claimed to have been bewitched; then from time to time they made similar charges against other persons. In this way a large number of men and women, not only in Salem village but in neighboring towns, were examined and imprisoned, until finally, in May, 1692, the new governor, Sir William Phips, and his council organized a special court to try the witchcraft cases. During the following summer this court sat at Salem, and under its authority nineteen persons in all were convicted of witchcraft and executed. The majority of them were women, but one, George Burroughs, was a graduate of Harvard College and a prominent minister of the province. One man, Giles Corey, under a strict application of the old English law, was pressed to death for refusing to plead. Many others, overwrought by the cruel examinations which they had to undergo, and in order to save their own lives, made confessions implicating innocent persons.

These convictions were brought about in large measure by the acceptance of what was called "spectral" testimony. It was assumed by the court in accordance with some English precedents that the devil could not assume the form of an innocent person. When, therefore, the "afflicted persons" professed that they had been bewitched by the devil in the form of certain individuals whom they named, this was taken as conclusive evidence of guilt. The leading ministers, however, including the Mathers, condemned the use of spectral testimony, and insisted that the devil might assume the form of an innocent person. Finally, when an increasing number of people of high character and social standing, including Lady Phips, began to be accused, there was a strong revulsion of feeling. In the winter of 1692–1693 the special court was superseded by the newly organized superior court, which held a special session at Salem in January, 1693. About fifty persons were then tried; but only three were convicted, and they were reprieved by Governor Phips, who now ordered that the prosecutions should be stopped.[1]

Before many years had passed, the people of

[1] Upham, *Witchcraft in Salem Village*, II., passim; Hutchinson, *Hist. of Mass. Bay*, II., 22 et seq.; Woodward, *Records of Salem Witchcraft*, passim; *Cal. of State Pap., Col.*, 1689–1692, p. 720, 1693–1696, pp. 29, 30; Mather, *Magnalia Christi* (ed of 1853), I., 207–210, II., 471–479.

Massachusetts generally were convinced that great
wrong had been done to innocent people, and the
general court set apart a day of fasting and prayer
in recognition of the errors committed in the witchcraft proceedings. At that time Cotton Mather
expressed in his diary his anxiety lest the divine
displeasure might overtake his family "for my not
appearing with vigor enough to stop the proceedings of the judges when the inextricable storm
from the *Invisible World* assaulted the country."
A more memorable and impressive declaration is
that of Samuel Sewall, a councillor and a member
of the witchcraft court, in a paper which he caused
to be publicly read in his presence at church in
1697.   He manfully took upon himself a large share
of the "Guilt contracted" in the Salem proceedings,
"Asking pardon of men, And especially desiring
prayers that God, who has an Unlimited Authority,
would pardon that sin and all other his sins; . . .
and . . . Not Visit the sin of him, or of any other,
upon himself or any of his, nor upon the Land." [1]

[1] Extracts from Mather's diary, in Wendell, *Cotton Mather*,
122; Sewall, *Diary*, I., 445.

CHAPTER III

EXTENSION OF IMPERIAL CONTROL
(1689–1713)

IN the constitutional adjustments which took place in the colonies after the revolution of 1689, there had been a compromise between two contending forces, the spirit of particularism and colonial autonomy on the one side and the policy of consolidation and control on the other. This constitutional compromise was, however, satisfactory to neither party and could not be regarded as final. From the home government there came a series of measures, partly legislative and partly administrative, which limited the field of local autonomy. On the other hand, certain constitutional tendencies appeared in the colonies which were denounced as leading towards substantial independence.

The demand for closer imperial control was emphasized by the intercolonial wars, which showed clearly the need of concerted action, of having some authority in the colonies capable of directing military operations as a whole. Commercial considerations, too, were given a new emphasis during this period. The heavy burden of the continental wars hastened the development in England of a new and more complex financial system, including the beginnings of the national debt and the Bank of England. In these new departures the government needed more than ever the co-operation of the mercantile interests, and the strength of their influence is shown by the prominence of commercial considerations in foreign politics. When a great war, like that of the Spanish Succession, was fought largely in the interest of English trade, it was natural that the same interest should assert itself more strongly than ever in the field of colonial policy.

The war also brought out various irregularities in colonial trade which seemed to demand more effective control. There were frequent complaints of illicit trade with the enemy, and of privateering that passed easily into piracy. These, with the old charge of lax enforcement of the navigation acts, made up a formidable indictment, which was pressed with special vigor against the chartered governments, whether proprietary or elective.

Imperial control as a remedy for colonial ills was advocated, not merely by interested merchants and zealous officials in England; it was also urged by a small but energetic party in America, including certain officers of the British customs service. Edward Randolph, for instance, was again busily engaged in writing reports on the violation of the navigation acts in various colonies, and occasionally quarrelling with less zealous officials. Another important representative of the same class was Robert Quarry, for a time councillor and acting governor of South Carolina, afterwards an admiralty judge in the middle colonies, and finally surveyor-general of customs for North America. Quarry made himself particularly obnoxious to William Penn by his incessant complaints of misgovernment in Pennsylvania.[1]

Some of the royal governors also were conspicuous for their defence of imperial interests. Among them was Francis Nicholson, who, during the reigns of William and Anne, serving successively as lieutenant-governor of Virginia, governor of Maryland, governor of Virginia, and governor of Nova Scotia, showed a strong sense of the royal prerogative and a keen scent for irregularities of every kind, especially in the chartered colonies. Another was Richard, Earl of Bellomont, who, during the closing years of the seventeenth century, was at the same time governor of Massachusetts, New Hampshire, and New York. During the reign of Anne the most aggressive of the royal governors were Dudley of Massachusetts and New Hampshire, Hunter of New York, and Spotswood of Virginia. These men and others like them were constantly pointing out the evils of the existing situation, and urging upon their superiors at home a more

[1] *Randolph Papers*, passim; Ames, *Pa. and the English Govt.*, passim.

vigorous assertion of parliamentary or royal authority.

The imperialistic party in the colonies was not exclusively composed of royal governors and customs collectors. In the chartered colonies dissatisfied elements of various kinds saw their advantage in the extension of royal control. This was the case, for instance, with the comparatively small group of Church of England men in New England and Pennsylvania. In New Jersey and the Carolinas the inefficient or illiberal government of the proprietors led many of the colonists, at various times, to seek protection from the crown.

From all these various elements came complaints and proposals of reorganization which were reflected in "representations" by the Lords of Trade, in orders of the Privy Council, in resolutions of the House of Lords or the House of Commons, and sometimes even in acts of Parliament. Indeed, one of the striking features of colonial politics during this period is the constant suggestion of parliamentary action as the only means of dealing thoroughly with colonial problems.

The colonial statutes of William and Anne were intended first to secure a more effective enforcement of the system inaugurated by the navigation acts of Charles II., and, secondly, to enlarge the field in which its principles should be applied.

The first object is best illustrated by the navigation act of 1696, which was based clearly upon official experience of the defects of existing administration. The negligence of the governors, especially in the chartered colonies, led to the strengthening of the oath hitherto required of royal governors, which was now made unequivocally applicable to all governors of English colonies: any governor who failed either to take the oath or to perform the duties required by it was made liable to removal from office and to the forfeiture of £1000. Furthermore, the choice of governor in the chartered colonies was made subject to veto by the crown, although practically this clause was applied only in the proprietary governments. The naval officers appointed by colonial governors had also been found negligent, and were required, henceforth, to give security to the commissioner of customs in England. Complaints having been made of the unsatisfactory sureties accepted in the colonies, all sureties were thereafter to be persons of good financial standing, resident in the colonies. Randolph's correspondence had laid special stress upon the part taken by Scotchmen in the illegal trade: they were said to have used forged certificates, and to have escaped punishment for illegal acts through the sympathy of fellow-countrymen on the trial juries. More stringent measures were therefore adopted for the suppression of Scotch and other alien traders, and it was provided that jury service in cases arising under the trade and revenue laws should be limited to natives of England and Wales, Ireland, and the plantations. A few years later, however, the act of union placed Scotchmen on the same footing with Englishmen.[1]

The leading principle which underlies the various provisions of the act of 1696 is the bringing of colonial administration, so far as it affected the navigation acts, into harmony with the system of the mother-country. This principle was asserted as regards colonial legislation by the formal declaration that all colonial laws at variance with the navigation acts were null and void. Vessels in the colonies were subjected to the regulations, as to searches and seizures, which were already in force at home; and all vessels were to be identified by a uniform system of registration.[2]

The act of 1696 was thus mainly an administrative measure intended to make more effective the principles of previous legislation; but it also determined one important point of construction. The question had been raised whether the exporter of enumerated articles, who paid the prescribed duties at a colonial port, was then free to take his goods wherever he pleased. It was now definitely settled that a bond must in all cases be given not to take the enumerated articles elsewhere than to England, Wales, or Berwick-upon-Tweed, or to some other English colony. There was also one important

[1] 7 and 8 William III., chap. xxii.; 6 Anne, chap. xi., § 4; *Cal of State Pap., Col.*, 1689–1692, pp. 656–660.
[2] 7 and 8 William III., chap. xxii., §§ 5, 8, 16.

addition to the limitations imposed on colonial exports: the colonists were now forbidden to send even the non-enumerated articles to Ireland or Scotland, except after the payment of duties in England.[1]

In later statutes of William and Anne there was a real development of the commercial policy in principle as well as in administration. This is shown first by additions to the list of enumerated articles, especially in 1705, when three important classes of colonial products were first enumerated: rice, which had become one of the staple exports of South Carolina; molasses from the West Indies; and naval stores of various kinds, including ship timber, could now be shipped only to English ports.[2]

Another restrictive measure showed the growing jealousy of colonial manufactures, which was, of course, a logical result of the mercantilist system. In order to preserve colonial markets for English merchants, it was not enough to prevent the colonists from buying manufactured articles in foreign countries, they must also be prevented from supplying them to each other. During King William's War this subject was frequently referred to in the colonial correspondence; for instance, Governor Nicholson of Virginia pointed out the danger, that the continued interruption of trade by war would

---

[1] 7 and 8 William III., §§ 7, 13; cf. Beer, *Commercial Policy of England*, 40.
[2] 3 and 4 Anne, chap. iii., § 14, chap. ix., § 6.

compel the colonists to make their own clothing, as the New-Englanders were already doing to a considerable extent. The British point of view has hardly been better expressed than in the preamble of the woollens act of 1698, in which wool and its various manufactures were called "the greatest and most profitable Commodities of this Kingdom on which the Value of Lands and the Trade of the Nation do Chiefly depend." The development of this trade in Ireland and the colonies was tending, it was thought, "to sink the Value of Lands" and "to the ruine of the Trade and the Woollen Manufactures of this Realme," and hence the colonists were forbidden to carry wool or manufactures of wool from any one colony into any other.[1]

Not all commercial legislation of this period was restrictive. Colonial officials were constantly trying to find means of diverting the colonists from industrial enterprises injurious to the mother-country by encouraging others which were thought to be beneficial. Thus a statute of Queen Anne encouraged colonial shipping by exempting colonial seamen from impressment in the royal navy.[2] The industry, however, which the English government most desired to encourage was the production of naval stores, including hemp, pitch, tar, and masts;

[1] *Cal. of State Pap.*, *Col.*, 1689–1692, pp. 568, 569; Weeden, *Econ. and Soc. Hist. of New England*, I., 303–307, 387–394; 10 William III., chap. xvi.

[2] Commission to Board of Trade, in *N. Y. Docs. Rel. to Col. Hist.*, IV., 145–148; 6 Anne, chap. lxiv., § 9.

and this interest was stimulated by the wars of William and Anne, in which the sea power was so important a factor. Hitherto, the Baltic countries had been the important source of supply for naval stores, but this trade was now being conducted on unfavorable terms and was at best precarious. The resources of the colonies were therefore carefully inquired into; and finally, after a long period of discussion, Parliament took definite action in the statute of 1705. This act, as has been noted, restricted the export of naval stores by listing them among the enumerated articles; it also reserved trees of a certain size for the royal navy, with severe penalties for cutting by unauthorized persons. These restrictions were offset, however, by bounties on the importation of naval stores produced in the colonies, and this encouragement of colonial industry became a settled part of British policy.[1]

The measures already noted may all be regarded as logical developments from the earlier acts of trade; a few others deserve attention because they show the broadening scope of parliamentary legislation for the colonies—especially the piracy act of 1700, the currency act of 1707, and the post-office act of 1710.

The piracy act was an attempt to remedy a serious evil which it was felt had not been prop-

[1] 3 and 4 Anne, chap. ix.; Lord, *Industrial Experiments in the Engl. Cols.*, pt. ii.

erly dealt with by the colonies, and for which the old statute of Henry VIII. was no longer found adequate. The colonial governments, especially those which still retained their charters, were criticised for failure to enact suitable legislation and for their toleration of pirates within their jurisdiction. Under these circumstances, the act of 1700 provided that in the future piracy and other felonies on the high seas might be tried in the colonies by special courts constituted by commissions from the crown. If any governor refused to comply with the provisions of this act, such a refusal was to constitute a forfeiture of the chartered rights of the government to which he belonged.[1]

The conditions which gave rise to the currency act of 1707 can be only briefly considered here. During the reign of William III. the problems of coinage and currency were conspicuous in the politics both of the mother-country and the colonies. The colonial situation was especially difficult, for coin of any kind was scarce, and English sterling money was hardly current at all. The most common coins in the colonies were the Spanish "pieces of eight," which have been called "the original of the American 'dollar.'" The "piece of eight" was not, however, a fixed standard either in weight or commercial value as measured in sterling money

---

[1] *Cal. of State Pap., Col.*, 1689–1692, pp. 674; 1693–1696, p. 114; Report of Board of Trade, in *Penn-Logan Correspondence*, I., 380; 11 William III., chap. vii.

One of the charges made against the chartered colonies was that by raising and lowering the value of coins, as well as by various other methods, they tended "greatly to the undermining the trade of the other plantations." William Penn, in his *Suggestions Respecting the Plantations*, presented to the home government in 1700, said that the value of pieces of eight varied from 4s. 6d., in Maryland, to 7s. 8d., in the neighboring colony of Pennsylvania, and he urged the desirability of a single fixed standard.[1]

Such a standard was attempted in 1704 through a proclamation of Queen Anne, which fixed within certain limits the ratio between standard foreign coins and sterling. This royal order proved ineffective, and in 1707 Parliament gave to the proclamation the force of a statute, imposing penalties on persons who took foreign coins at a rate exceeding the legal ratio; and this act was specifically declared applicable to the chartered colonies as well as to the royal governments.[2]

In the case of the post-office also, there was, first, a period of separate colonial action, followed by the exercise of prerogative, and finally by the intervention of Parliament. Before the revolution of 1689 postal arrangements in the colonies had been left to the colonists themselves, and the results

---

[1] Weeden, *Econ. and Soc. Hist. of New England*, I., 383–387; *Penn-Logan Correspondence*, I., 380; *N. Y. Docs. Rel. to Col. Hist.*, IV., 757.   [2] 6 Anne, chap. lvii.

were meagre.   In 1692, Thomas Neale received
from William and Mary a patent authorizing him
to establish post-offices in the American colonies;
and he proceeded to appoint Andrew Hamilton, a
New Jersey colonist, as his deputy in America.
Hamilton then secured the co-operation of several
of the colonial assemblies, which passed laws regulating the rates of postage.   His patent, however,
was to expire in twenty-one years, and by that time
Parliament was ready to take action.   The act of
1710 provided for "Chief Offices" in New York
and elsewhere; fixed the rates of postage within the
colonies, as well as in the mother-country; and, with
a few exceptions, limited the carrying of mails to the
postmaster - general and his deputies.   Under the
operation of this law postal facilities were gradually extended from New England and the middle
colonies into the south.[1]

One of the declared purposes of the new law was
to raise a war revenue, and it was therefore enacted
that a weekly payment of £700 should be turned into
the royal treasury.   The New-Englanders seem to
have made no public objection to the revenue feature of the law, and though some Virginians at first
objected on the ground that Parliament could not
tax them without the consent of the general assembly, the opposition soon died away.[2]

[1] Woolley, *Early Hist. of the Col. Post-Office;* 9 Anne, chap. xi.
[2] Palfrey, *New England*, IV., 327–332; Spotswood, *Official Letters*, II., 280.

The constitutional significance of the colonial statutes of William and Anne may easily be overlooked if they are considered individually. In the main, they took the form of restrictions upon colonial enterprise, but sometimes, as in the bounties on naval stores, they aimed to stimulate it when directed along acceptable lines. Taken as a whole, they mark the increasing importance in colonial life of the political control exercised by the mother-country.

CHAPTER IV

ADMINISTRATIVE CONTROL OF THE PROVINCES
(1689–1713)

EVERY step in the extension of legislative control increased the importance of administrative organization. Existing agencies were strengthened and new ones developed, until, finally, a radical reorganization of the colonial constitutions was demanded, which could only be accomplished by the action of Parliament itself.

In the shaping of administrative policy the personal action of King William and Queen Anne seems, on the whole, a factor of minor importance. William III. was much absorbed in the politics of continental Europe, and had little time for colonial affairs, though his influence was in general exerted to uphold the royal prerogative. He consented reluctantly to triennial parliaments at home, and he opposed the triennial election of assemblies in America. In one instance, when Parliament attempted to organize a council of trade under its own control, the king exerted himself to defeat the project.[1] Queen Anne's policy was still more large-

---

[1] Chalmers, *Revolt*, I., 294, *n.*; Cobbett, *Parliamentary History*, V., 977.

ly that of her ministers, though her colonial appointments were sometimes influenced by personal preferences. William Penn was a man of experience in such matters, and he wrote to his secretary in 1703 warning him not to submit even to royal orders when at variance with law, adding, "Queens never read, as well as Kings, what they sign; they are signed upon the credit of committees or secretaries." [1]

In general, then, the colonial policy of the crown was the policy of its official advisers. Matters of importance were determined by the Privy Council, composed, for practical purposes, of the king's ministers of state. Details were managed by individual ministers, by subordinate officials, or by administrative committees or boards. Government by homogeneous party ministries was not yet established, and the ministries were usually composite, including both Whigs and Tories, so that one of the secretaries of state might be a Tory and the other a Whig. Generally, one party or the other had a preponderance, but sometimes the attempt was made to keep an even balance. In the minds of party politicians colonial politics took a subordinate place, and it could rarely be said that any particular ministry had its own distinctive colonial policy. In the main, the ministries of this period seem to have accepted the traditions of colonial administration as they found them.

[1] *Penn-Logan Correspondence*, I., 247, 248.

The ministers most steadily concerned with colonial affairs were the two secretaries of state, with
whom the colonial governors were expected to cor-
respond.   At first there was no definite assignment
of colonial business to either one of them, but during the reign of William III. one secretary usually,
at any given time, gave special attention to colonial
correspondence.   Two of these secretaries were the
Duke of Shrewsbury, a Whig, and the Earl of Not-
tingham, a Tory, both statesmen of great prominence and influence.

During the reign of Anne, and afterwards, American affairs were regularly transacted by the secretary of state for the southern department, an
office held, during by far the larger part of that
reign, by prominent Tories.   Harley, Earl of Oxford, served for three years, and St. John, Viscount
Bolingbroke, during his service of about four years,
took a considerable interest in American affairs.
None of these ministers can, however, be credited
with such an influence in the development of colonial policy as has been ascribed to Clarendon and
Shaftesbury during the reign of Charles II.

The most important work in colonial administration was done by executive boards, some of
which were restricted to specific departments of
colonial administration: thus the commissioners of
customs were specially charged with the enforcement of the navigation acts; and the commissioners
of admiralty transacted a considerable amount of

colonial business, especially in time of war. Much
the most important executive boards, however,
were the Committee of the Privy Council on Trade
and Plantations, and its successor, the Board of
Commissioners for Trade and Plantations, or, more
briefly, the Board of Trade.

In 1689 the old Committee of Trade and Plantations, instituted during the reign of Charles II., was
reorganized by a new commission, still composed
of the leading ministers of state, many of whom had
been in the service of Charles II., and who were, in
general, disposed to adhere to the colonial policies
of that reign. This committee shaped in large measure the constitutional adjustments in the colonies
after the revolution; and the navigation act of 1696
was in full harmony with their views. Among the
merchants, however, there was a strong feeling that
the government was not adequately protecting their
interests, and in the parliamentary session of 1695–
1696 it was proposed to organize a new board whose
members should be nominated by Parliament. The
attempt failed, and in May, 1696, the king himself
organized the Board of Commissioners for Trade
and Plantations. The new board was not a mere
committee of the Privy Council, for, though the
chief ministers of state were *ex officio* members,
they were not expected to give regular attendance;
the real work was generally done, as was intended,
by a small group of non-ministerial members. In
the first commission the number of such members

was eight, including John Locke, who had been long and prominently associated with colonial affairs, and William Blathwayte, who had been secretary of the Committee of Trade during the later years of its history.[1]

The work of the new board was similar to that of the old committee; they were expected first of all to guard the commercial interests of the mother-country; colonial trade and government were to be closely investigated, and means were to be devised for guiding colonial enterprise in channels beneficial to the mother-country. During the earlier years of its history the Board of Trade carried on investigations with energy, reporting from time to time to the king, and occasionally also to the houses of Parliament; their reports or "representations" contained statements of fact, and also proposed new lines of policy, legislative as well as administrative. They draughted the instructions to the royal governors, suggesting from time to time desirable changes; they made nominations to fill vacancies in the colonial service, and were entitled to receive regular reports from the various royal governments. Colonial legislation and the administration of justice and finance were also carefully supervised. In performing their functions they were entitled to the

[1] Commission in *N. Y. Docs. Rel. to Col. Hist.* IV., 145–148; Chalmers, *Revolt*, I., chap. xviii; Cobbett, *Parliamentary History*, 977; cf. Andrews, *Colonial Self-Government* (*Am. Nation*, V.), chaps. ii., xvii.

legal advice of the king's counsel, and could compel the attendance of witnesses.

Their actual authority, however, was comparatively slight. In matters of real importance, they could make "representations," not final decisions; they could nominate officers, but not appoint them; they could remonstrate with delinquent governors, but could not finally remove or control them. Under these circumstances, the real influence of the board depended on maintaining vital relations with the leading ministers, especially the secretaries of state. During the period of William and Anne, the board undoubtedly influenced to a considerable extent the policy of the government, but even then many important recommendations were not carried out.[1]

Some administrative supervision was also exercised by the House of Commons and the House of Lords through formal inquiries, and by recommendations to the executive authorities. Two instances of intervention by the House of Lords during this period are noteworthy. After the passage of the navigation act of 1696, courts of admiralty were established in the colonies by the king soon after they had been recommended by the House of Lords. In 1706 the peers called upon the queen to protect the dissenters of South Carolina from a provincial law requiring an ecclesiastical test for mem-

[1] Egerton, *Short Hist. of Col. Policy*, 116; Report of Board of Trade (1721), in *N. Y. Docs. Rel. to Col. Hist.*, V., 627-630.

bership in the assembly, and a royal order was
issued accordingly. The revolution of 1689 had
greatly strengthened the parliamentary element in
the constitution, and the proposed formation of a
council of commerce to be nominated by Parliament shows a tendency to encroach even upon the
field of naturally executive functions.[1]

An important method of control during this
period was the supervision of colonial legislation.
In the royal governments the right of the crown
to disallow provincial laws had been recognized
from the outset; but fifty years elapsed after the
revocation of the Virginia charter before another
royal province was fully organized on the continent.
In the mean time a large number of charters had
been issued to proprietary and self-governing colonies
without any provision for a royal veto; but in 1681
the Pennsylvania charter showed the development
of an imperialistic conception by requiring even
that proprietary province to submit its legislation
for royal approval. During the reign of James II.,
imperial control of legislation was carried to a violent extreme by the abolition of assemblies in the
new royal provinces, and it was not until after the
revolution that the royal veto became a normal
factor in the colonial system. By 1692 the right
of disallowance existed in the five royal provinces
of Massachusetts, New Hampshire, New York,
Maryland, and Virginia, and in the proprietary

[1] Chalmers, *Revolt*, I., 273; *N. C. Col. Records*, I., 642.

province of Pennsylvania. In 1702 New Jersey
became a royal government and was subjected to
the same restriction. Attempts were made to apply
the principle in other colonies also : Rhode Island
laws were sent over for examination; in 1705 a
Connecticut law banishing Quakers was disallowed;
and in 1706 a royal order in council annulled two
South Carolina statutes. The legality of the royal
orders in these cases was doubtful, and the right
to veto Connecticut laws was subsequently dis-
claimed by the law-officers of the crown; but the
earlier action is important as showing the general
trend of colonial policy.[1]

The rules regarding the exercise of the royal
veto were not the same in all the colonies. Under
the Massachusetts and Pennsylvania charters, the
action of the crown had to be declared within a
limited period. In the royal provinces, generally,
it might be declared at any time. Colonial laws
sent over by the governors were examined by the
Board of Trade, which frequently took the advice
of the attorney and solicitor general. Acts disapproved by the board were ordinarily repealed by
the Privy Council.[2]

During the decade immediately following the
English revolution the prerogative of disallowance
was vigorously exercised. In Massachusetts an

[1] *R. I. Records*, III., 388; *Conn. Col. Records*, IV., 546; Chalmers, *Opinions* (ed. of 1858), 339.
[2] Cf. Massachusetts Bay, *Acts and Resolves*, I., passim.

elective assembly found itself obliged for the first
time to accept the constitutional limitations of a
royal province. Public sentiment in the colony
demanded the retention, so far as possible, of usages
which had developed during the era of self-government. On the other hand, the home government
desired to limit closely the concessions granted in
the new charter, and to bring colonial institutions into harmony with imperial policy and English law. This conflict is well illustrated by the
action of the home government on the legislation
of 1692, the first enacted under the new charter,
including a number of what may be called fundamental statutes. One was a law continuing in general terms the local laws of the colony; another provided for the organization of a judicial system; and
a third took the form of a bill of rights. These and
twelve others were disallowed by the crown in
1695, sometimes for lack of definiteness and sometimes because of supposed encroachment on the
rights of the crown or conflict with the laws of
England. During the next five years the struggle
continued. The general court made some unsuccessful efforts to adjust their measures to the views
of the Board of Trade, but there was no year of
legislation from 1692 to 1699 in which one or more
acts were not ultimately disallowed. In the end,
a practical adjustment seems to have been reached
and disallowance became less frequent.[1]

[1] Massachusetts Bay, *Acts and Resolves*, I., passim.

The treatment of New York was somewhat like that of Massachusetts, but less drastic. The first assembly passed, in 1691, a general declaration of constitutional rights and privileges, which was disallowed in 1697 on the recommendation of the Board of Trade, one reason being that undue privileges were given to the assembly. In the first year of Queen Anne, six New York acts were disallowed almost immediately after their passage, and several others were vetoed during the later years of the reign.[1]

In Pennsylvania the proprietary government was severely criticised for its failure to transmit laws for approval, but during the early years of Queen Anne a large number of acts were received by the Board of Trade. About fifty of these, covering a wide range of subjects, were disallowed by order in council in 1706, though Penn congratulated himself that many others had received the royal approval. In Virginia and Maryland, also, a number of acts were disallowed.[2]

The reasons assigned for disallowance vary widely. In general, however, the prerogative was used to keep the legislation of the colony in harmony with somewhat conservative views of the royal prerogative; with the English common law; with the stat-

[1] *N. Y. Colonial Laws*, I., 244, 476; *N. Y. Docs. Rel. to Col. Hist.*, IV., 263.
[2] Pa., *Statutes at Large*, II., passim; *Penn-Logan Correspondence*, II., 110; *Cal. of State Pap., Col.*, 1693–1696, pp. 31, 38; Hening, *Statutes*, III., 344, 404, 502.

utes applicable to the colonies; and, lastly, with British economic interests. To a certain extent the right of disallowance was evaded, as, for example, by the passage of temporary laws, but this practice was forbidden by royal instructions. Indeed, one striking result of the experience of the Board of Trade with objectionable statutes was the gradual increase, in the governor's instructions, of articles forbidding his approval of certain kinds of laws. Some acts could only be passed with a so-called suspending clause postponing enforcement until the law had been approved by the crown.[1]

The harmony of English and colonial law depended very much in practice on the maintenance of some system of judicial control. During the reign of William III. this control was extended partly by the creation of new courts in America, acting under royal commissions and including within their jurisdiction chartered colonies as well as the royal governments. The piracy courts organized under the act of 1700 have already been noted. Soon after the passage of the navigation act of 1696 courts of admiralty were instituted in order to secure a stricter enforcement of the laws of trade than could be expected from the colonial courts and juries. Admiralty judges were appointed for various colonies or groups of colonies,

[1] Instructions to Hunter (N. Y., 1709), in *N. Y. Docs. Rel. to Col. Hist.*, V., 124–143; cf. with instructions to Sloughter (1690), *ibid.*, III., 685–691.

some of whom were men of strongly imperial views, notably Robert Quarry, one of the first appointed in the middle colonies. The new courts were exceedingly unpopular; their trial of cases without juries was offensive, and they were also charged with encroaching upon the jurisdiction of the common-law courts. Notwithstanding the colonial opposition, the new policy was maintained.[1]

The home government also sought to control the administration of justice by securing to individuals in the colonies the right of appeal to the Privy Council. This right was not specifically provided for in the earlier charters, but it appears in the Duke of York's patent of 1664 and in Penn's charter of 1681. Like the royal veto, it first assumed importance in the closing years of the seventeenth century.[2] The instructions to the royal governors insisted upon the allowance of appeals to the Privy Council, and the proprietary colonies were sharply criticised for refusing to permit them. The right was asserted even in colonies where it was not specifically secured by charter. During the reign of William III., the Privy Council, after being informed that their right of appeal had been denied by a Connecticut court, declared that it was "the inherent right" of the crown "to receive and determine ap-

[1] Chalmers, *Revolt*, I., 273, 284–288; Palfrey, *New England*, IV., 163; *Penn-Logan Correspondence*, I., 35, 66; Smith, *South Carolina*, 147–156; Chalmers, *Opinions* (ed. of 1858), 500–502.
[2] Cf. Osgood, *Am. Cols. in the Seventeenth Century*, II., 10, 293.

peals" from all the colonies in America. In later years several Rhode Island and Connecticut cases were heard on appeal by the Privy Council. There was some difficulty in enforcing this right even in the royal provinces, and some provincial statutes were disallowed for failure to secure it fully.[1]

During this period special provision was made for the trial of governors guilty of misconduct in office. In 1699 an act of Parliament was passed, declaring that colonial governors who had hitherto considered themselves legally accountable neither in their provinces nor at home, might be tried in the Court of King's Bench.[2]

These measures of administrative control brought out more sharply the abnormal position of the chartered colonies. Their legal exemption from control in most matters made it difficult for the crown to exercise even that authority to which it was fairly entitled. Especially was this true in the self-governing colonies, where every department of government was controlled by the people themselves. Governors chosen from year to year served more zealously the people who elected them than a distant authority whose control was somewhat fitful. It was thought also that the irregularities and ex-

---

[1] *N. Y. Docs. Rel to Col. Hist.*, III., 688; *Penn-Logan Correspondence*, I., 25, 379; Hazeltine, *Appeals from Colonial Courts* (Am. Hist. Assoc., *Report*, 1894, pp. 299–350); *N. C. Col. Records*, II., 161 et seq.; Massachusetts Bay, *Acts and Resolves*, I., 144.   [2] 11 William III., chap. xii.

ceptional privileges of the chartered colonies tended
to demoralize the people of the royal governments.
There was consequently almost constant agitation
on the part of the official party in America and
England for the resumption or regulation of the
charters.[1]

During King William's War special emphasis was
laid upon consolidation for military purposes. The
royal governors of Massachusetts and New York
were authorized to command the militia in Rhode
Island, Connecticut, and the Jerseys, but these commissions were vigorously resisted; and the crown
finally accepted a compromise which asserted in substance simply the right to exact certain quotas of
men when needed for the common defence, authorizing command of the militia as a whole only in
case of threatened invasion. In 1696 the Board of
Trade recommended the appointment of a captain-
general with the right to command the militia of all
the colonies; but the war ended without the project
being carried fully into effect, though a step was
taken in that direction by the commission to the Earl
of Bellomont in 1697. Bellomont was made governor in each of the three royal provinces of Massachusetts, New Hampshire, and New York, and was
also given the command of the militia in Connecticut
and Rhode Island. This was not, however, a real
consolidation of provinces, for each province retained
its distinct administration, and there were still three

[1] Letter of Quarry, in Ames, *Pa. and the English Govt.*, 8–14.

assemblies to be reckoned with. The combination proved unwieldy and soon fell apart, but the policy was not wholly abandoned. During the first third of the eighteenth century the two royal governments of New England had the same governor; and the governors of New York also held commissions for New Jersey.[1]

The need of consolidation and union was recognized by many serious students of colonial problems. William Penn submitted, about 1697, his famous proposal for a colonial congress consisting of representatives from each province; and a little later Robert Livingston, of New York, proposed the consolidation of the colonies into three provinces, and a meeting of commissioners from each province at Albany to provide for the common defence. For projects of this kind, however, the colonists in general were not yet ready.[2]

During this period royal control of the proprietary governors was somewhat strengthened. The navigation act of 1696 required that proprietary governors should be approved by the crown, and after some delay the rule was enforced. The Board of Trade also insisted that security should be given for their observance of the navigation acts. Thus the proprietary governors became in a measure royal officers. Such regulations could not, however, be

[1] *N. Y. Docs. Rel. to Col. Hist.*, IV., 29-31, 69-73, 106, 227-230, 266; *R. I. Col. Records*, III., 288-292.
[2] *N. Y. Docs. Rel. to Col. Hist.*, IV., 296, 874.

enforced upon the annually elected governors of Connecticut and Rhode Island.[1]

The most ardent advocates of imperial control could be content only with the final overthrow of all the chartered governments. In 1691 Governor Nicholson expressed his hope that "their Majesties will send their own Governors to all the colonies," and royal agents like Randolph and Quarry made similar recommendations. Finally, the policy was definitely adopted by the Board of Trade.[2]

Of all the proprietary colonies, the most vulnerable were the Jerseys, in which the rights of government had never any foundation in strict law.[3] On the eve of the revolution the proprietors agreed to surrender them to the crown, and the Jerseys were included in the "greater New England" of 1688. After the revolution the proprietors of East and West Jersey resumed their governments, but they were weakened, not merely by the hostile criticism of royal officers, but by dissatisfaction among the colonists. In 1702 the rights of government were again surrendered; the transfer was now accepted, and in the same year Governor Cornbury, of New

[1] Rivers, *South Carolina*, 443; *Randolph Papers*, 284; *Penn-Logan Correspondence*, I., 25, 270; *N. C. Col. Records*, I., 476, 557.

[2] *Cal of State Pap., Col.*, 1689–1692, p. 568; *Randolph Papers*, V., 263–273; Ames, *Pa. and the English Govt.*; *Penn-Logan Correspondence*, I., 380.

[3] Cf. Osgood, *Am. Cols. in the Seventeenth Century*, II., 169–173.

York, received his commission as the first royal governor of the reunited province of New Jersey.[1]

Elsewhere chartered privileges were more vigorously defended. During the early years of William III. there was some uncertainty as to the right of the crown to appoint governors in chartered colonies without a judicial abrogation of the charter. Chief-Justice Holt gave his opinion, in 1690, that the king might do so in case of "necessity," and a royal government was accordingly inaugurated in Maryland.[2] A similar course was taken in 1692 when Governor Fletcher received a royal commission as governor of Pennsylvania, but Penn was determined not to submit to action which seemed to him illegal. He sent his warning to Fletcher, and encouraged his followers in the province to keep up a kind of passive resistance. The result was his restoration, in 1694, to the exercise of his proprietary rights, although the attacks on his government continued. Rhode Island and Connecticut were severely criticised by the royal governors for tolerating irregularities of various kinds, and it was proposed during Queen Anne's reign to send royal governors to each of these colonies, at least during the war; but though the attorney-general and the

[1] N. J. Docs. Rel. to Col. Hist., I., 26, 369–373, 398–403, 448, 452–461, 489; N. Y. Docs. Rel. to Col. Hist., III., 537.
[2] Chalmers, Opinions (ed. of 1858), 65; N. Y. Docs. Rel. to Col. Hist., III., 856; IV., 33, 110.

solicitor-general gave a favorable opinion, the proposition came to nothing.[1]

The same lawyers declared, in 1706, that two recent acts of the South Carolina assembly, if definitely approved by the proprietors, constituted a forfeiture of the charter, which might be annulled by judicial proceedings. Though the acts were annulled, the attack on the charter was dropped, partly because some of the proprietors were peers of the realm, whose privileges had to be cautiously handled.[2]

After several years of discussion, the Board of Trade having become convinced that legislation was necessary, prepared, in 1701, careful reports to the king and the House of Commons, reciting all the familiar charges against the chartered governments, and recommending that all the charters "should be resumed to the Crown." They added their belief that "this cannot otherwise be well effected than by the legislative power of this kingdom." A bill was accordingly introduced into the House of Lords for the revocation of the colonial charters and the institution of royal governments in their place; but the bill, though read twice, was never passed. Immediately after the accession of Queen Anne the proposal was renewed by the board, but without result. In 1706 a bill was introduced in the House of Commons "for the better Regulation"

[1] *R. I. Col. Records*, III., 385–388; IV., 12–16.
[2] *N. C. Col. Records*, I., 642–644.

of the charter governments, and after the Tory ministry came into power, in 1710, the problem was again seriously considered, especially by St. John, as secretary for the southern department.[1]

It is difficult to explain wholly the failure of these attempts in the face of such vigorous recommendations from the Board of Trade. In some instances, the demands of other public business seem to have prevented action; apparently even among English ministers there was some scepticism as to the desirability of the policy. The colonists themselves, through their agents, vigorously resisted the proposed measures, and were able to bring some strong influences to bear against them. This was particularly true of Penn, who for a time also acted as agent for Rhode Island. In the winter of 1704–1705, he wrote that by his interest alone he had been able to prevent "a scheme drawn to new model the colonies." The high spirit which characterized him at his best, comes out in another letter urging his secretary, Logan, to defend the rights of the province against encroachments: "I desire you to pluck up that English and Christian courage, to not suffer yourselves to be thus treated and put upon."

Yet Penn himself was so much harassed by opposition in the province and by his financial troubles

---

[1] Ames, *Pa. and the English Govt.*, 21,; *Penn-Logan Correspondence*, I., 78, 87, 380; *N. Y. Docs. Rel. to Col. Hist.*, V., 255; *N. C. Col. Records*, I., 552–554; Kellogg, *Am. Colonial Charter* (Am. Hist. Assoc., *Report*, 1903, I.), chap. iv.

that he was prepared to surrender his government on condition of obtaining satisfactory compensation for himself and some safeguards for his fellow-Quakers in the colony. In February, 1712, the Board of Trade recommended the acceptance of such an offer, and a bill for that purpose was introduced in the House of Commons. The bill failed, however, and Penn's heirs finally determined to hold the government.[1]

The net result of twenty years' warfare on the colonial charters was, therefore, comparatively slight. The royal province of New Jersey had taken the place of two proprietary governments, but those of Pennsylvania, Delaware, and the Carolinas remained, together with the self-governing colonies of Connecticut and Rhode Island.

Notwithstanding the limitations and failures of the imperialist movement, important results were accomplished: the legislative control of Parliament over the colonies was largely extended; provincial legislation was subjected to serious restraints; a system of appeals to the crown was organized; and new courts were instituted independent of local control. Thus the great majority of the American colonists were brought under the control of a provincial system which thirty years before had been distinctly exceptional.

[1] Chalmers, *Revolt*, I., 380; *Penn-Logan Correspondence*, I., 73, 112, 248, 354; *R. I. Col. Records*, IV., 64; Shepherd, *Proprietary Government in Pa.*, 540–544.

CHAPTER V

CONSTITUTIONAL TENDENCIES IN THE COLONIES
(1689–1713)

AMERICAN colonial life at the close of the seventeenth century shows a striking tendency towards uniformity in political thought and action. In the earlier period two strong influences had been at work to produce variation rather than uniformity; the first was the policy of proprietary or chartered colonization, which gave to each proprietor and each group of self-governing colonists the opportunity to modify the common English tradition according to their special needs and ideals; the second was the geographical isolation of the various groups of settlers, which checked their interchange of ideas and experiences with each other and with the mother - country. Great differences had resulted in institutions and in political issues. The practical politics of Massachusetts under its theocratic-republican constitution had little in common with that of Virginia under the rule of Governor Berkeley or that of Maryland under the proprietary system.

Gradually, however, the extension of imperial control limited the opportunity for political experiment. The provincial system was established in half of the colonies and the proprietary governors themselves were held to a stricter accountability to the crown. Only the two small governments of Connecticut and Rhode Island remained wholly outside of the provincial system, and even they were troubled with appeals to the crown and acts of Parliament restraining their trade. The physical obstacles to colonial intercourse were still serious, but even these had been lessened. New settlements were gradually filling the intervening spaces, intercolonial trade was developing, and an intercolonial postal system had been begun. The common dangers of border warfare also forced the colonies into a rather grudging co-operation, and brought their leaders into more frequent contact with one another. Thus there arose a degree of uniformity which makes it possible to speak, not merely of the politics of Massachusetts or Virginia, but of certain common tendencies which appear in the political life of the colonies as a whole, or at least of that large majority of them which had been brought under the provincial system.

These general principles of colonial politics cannot be understood without a study of the provincial constitution, using the term in its broadest sense to include proprietary as well as royal governments. The essential feature of this system was a governor appointed either by the king or by a proprietor,

except in those comparatively rare cases in which
the proprietor governed the province in person. In
any case, the governor represented the principle of
external control, an authority outside of the community itself. His powers and duties were defined
by his commission and instructions, issued by this
same external authority and revocable at will. By
his side stood the councillors, who, except in Massachusetts, derived their powers from the king or
proprietor, and thus like him represented the principle of external control. Generally speaking, the
home government took the governor's advice in the
appointment and dismissal of councillors, so that he
could depend upon their political support. There
were, however, frequent exceptions, and often, as in
Virginia, the councillors belonged to a kind of local
aristocracy whose point of view differed from that
of the governor.

The only royal province in which councillors
were not appointed by the crown was Massachusetts.
There they were annually chosen by joint ballot of
the representatives and councillors, but the governor had the right of veto, which was frequently
exercised during the first twenty years of royal government. Aggressive leaders of the popular party
were thus kept out of the council, and members
once elected were disposed to conciliate the governor.

The governor, either independently or with the
council, was intrusted with the ordinary executive

powers of appointment, military command, financial control, and, with some limitations, that of pardon. The governor and councillors also influenced the administration of justice through their appointment of judges and the direct exercise of certain judicial functions. These functions were not the same in all the provinces, but in the ordinary royal governments the governor and council served as a court of appeal in civil cases. Generally speaking, then, the executive and judicial powers were intrusted to representatives of external authority.

In the legislative department alone was the principle of popular representation generally recognized by the authorities in England. By the close of the seventeenth century every province had its representative assembly, known by different names in different colonies. In Virginia, it was the house of burgesses; in South Carolina, the commons house of assembly; and in Massachusetts, the house of representatives. These different names, however, stood for essentially the same thing, an assembly of representatives, not of the whole people, but of the owners of property. The policy of the crown was to restrict representation to freeholders, as in the English counties, but this was not generally done.[1]

After a long period of controversy, two rights had been finally conceded to these representative

[1] Bishop, *Elections in the Colonies*, 69 et seq.

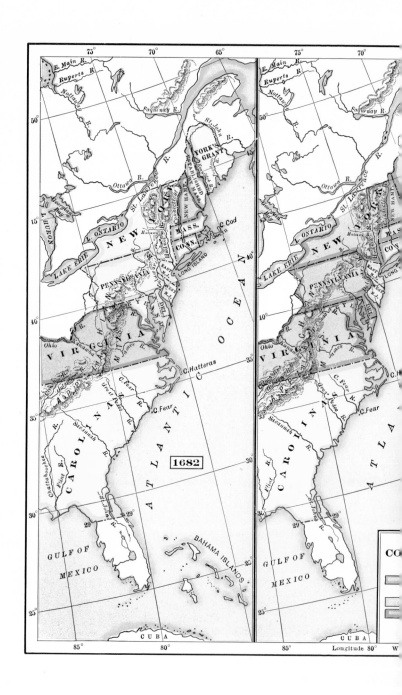

1682

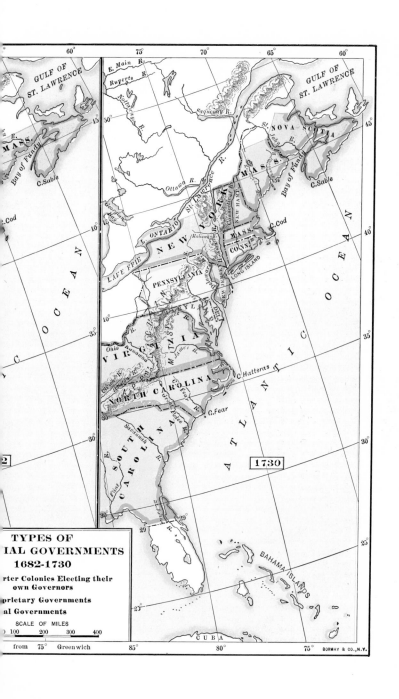

GULF OF
ST. LAWRENCE

E. Main R.
Ruperts R.
Nottaway R.
Saguenay R.

GULF OF
ST. LAWRENCE

St. NOVA SCOTIA

MASS.

Bay of Fundy
C.Sable

Bay of Fundy
C.Sable

C.Cod

Ottawa R.

St. Lawrence R.

L. ONTARIO

Georgian
Bay

NEW YORK

NEW HAMP.

MASS.

C.Cod

Mohawk R.

CONN.

LAKE ERIE

LONG ISLAND

PENNSYLVANIA

NEW JERSEY

MARYLAND

DEL.

Ohio

Kanawha

VIRGINIA

James R.

OCEAN

C.Hatteras

NORTH CAROLINA

Cape Fear R.

C.Fear

SOUTH CAROLINA

Savannah R.

ATLANTIC

1730

OCEAN

Flint R.

St. John R.

30°

29°

BAHAMA ISLANDS

CUBA

TYPES OF
IAL GOVERNMENTS
1682-1730

rter Colonies Electing their
own Governors

prietary Governments

al Governments

SCALE OF MILES
0 100   200   300   400

from   75°   Greenwich   85°   80°   75°   BORMAY & CO., N.Y.

60°   75°   70°   65°   60°
50°
45°

40°

35°

30°

25°

bodies. They had a right, shared with the council, to initiate legislation; and no taxes could be laid by any other department of the provincial government without their consent. The legislative power of the representatives was, however, seriously limited by at least two checks: in all the provinces (except Pennsylvania after 1701) measures enacted by the representatives required the consent of the council acting as an upper house; in proprietary provinces acts had to be further approved by the proprietors or their representatives. In the royal governments acts without a suspending clause became law on the approval of the governor, though still subject to disallowance by the crown, a condition which, as already observed, was also required in Pennsylvania.

The fundamental fact of provincial politics after the revolution of 1689 is the conflict between the provincial governor and the representative assembly. The governor represented, first, the monarchical idea of prerogative, and, secondly, the principle of imperial control, whether exercised by king or Parliament. The assembly, on the other hand, stood not merely for the representative principle in government, but also for distinctly local interests. The policy of the colonial assemblies at its worst expressed a narrow and particularistic spirit, disregarding sound considerations of national or imperial policy; at its best it stood for the vital principle of local self-government, and for the pro-

tection of legitimate American interests as against
a narrow British policy.

The popular party in America was stimulated by
the course of politics in the mother - country.   In
1689 the representative principle triumphed over
prerogative, and the transfer of the crown was followed by the enactment of great fundamental statutes like the Bill of Rights and the Act of Settlement, which secured more completely than ever
before the privileges of Parliament and the personal
liberty of the subject.   Among other measures at
first rejected by William III., but finally forced
upon him, were the triennial election of parliaments
and the exclusion of office-holders from the House
of Commons.   The Commons also asserted more
strictly their control of the national finances at the
expense both of the king and the House of Lords.
Large sums were given for the conduct of the foreign war, but the objects of expenditure were defined in detail; and, as already noted, an unsuccessful effort was made to establish a parliamentary
council of trade.   On the whole, the reigns of
William and Anne show a clear though uneven advance towards the modern system of cabinet government, which practically enables a committee of
the House of Commons to exercise the most important powers of the crown.

The provincial governments reproduced on a
smaller scale the constitution of the mother-country.
As the governor felt the responsibility of maintain-

ing within the province the prerogative of the crown, so the assembly found support for its privileges and encouragement for its aspirations in the example of the English House of Commons. The colonial journals reproduce in surprising detail the parliamentary conflicts of the mother - country. Nevertheless, these ambitions of the colonial assemblies met with little sympathy from British statesmen of either school; the colonial prerogatives of the crown were identified with the political supremacy of England, and therefore had the support of English Whigs as well as English Tories.

Another influence favorable to the popular party in America was the experience of the chartered colonies: where, as in Massachusetts, a royal government was established over colonists who had been accustomed to almost complete independence, the freer practice of the earlier days established precedents which the crown could not wholly disregard. In provinces without exceptional privileges of self-government, the example of the chartered colonies exerted a strong and, from the royalist point of view, a demoralizing influence. In the surviving proprietary colonies the active hostility of the home government contributed to weaken the authority of the governors as against the popular party. This was notably the case in South Carolina, where the colonists appealed successfully to the crown against obnoxious measures of the proprietors. In 1702 the secretary of Pennsylvania

wrote that the surrender of the Jerseys, taken together with other difficulties, had made "this government too precarious to be called one." From
such governments it was comparatively easy for
the assemblies to extort concessions. Nowhere was
the spirit of self-government so strongly intrenched
as in New England and Pennsylvania, and during
the eighteenth century their example was especially
dreaded by the prerogative party. Thus the distinctly American traditions of the self-governing
colonies combined with the parliamentary usages of
the mother-country to strengthen the representative element in the provincial constitution.[1]

Among the most interesting illustrations of the
similarity of English and colonial politics after the
revolution are the statutes or charters proposed in
the principal royal governments. Thus, in 1691,
the Virginia assembly instructed its agent in England to secure, if possible, a new charter confirm-
ing that of Charles II. and all previous charters
of liberties and privileges. The burgesses asked,
among other things, specific recognition of the exclusive right of the assembly to levy taxes, and of
the "ancient method" of allowing appeals from the
general judicial court to the general assembly. In
the same year the New York assembly passed an act
stating "the Rights and Priviledges of their Majesties Subjects inhabiting within their Province of New
York." This act set forth certain privileges of the

[1] *Penn-Logan Correspondence*, I., 121.

representative assembly and certain securities for
personal and property rights.[1] A year later, the first
provincial assembly of Massachusetts passed an act
"setting forth general privileges;" and in 1694 a sup-
plementary act with special reference to the constitutional privileges of the house of representatives.
Under these acts the people of the province were
declared exempt from all taxes except those levied
by the general court, and the house of representatives was declared to have "an undoubted right
to all the liberties and priviledges of an English
assembly." The Maryland assembly took a somewhat similar course by inserting in the church act
of 1696 a clause asserting that the people of the
province "shall enjoy all their Rights and Liberties
according to the Laws and Statutes of the Kingdom of England" on all points on which there was
no provision in provincial statutes. Besides these
general declarations, a number of acts were passed
in the colonies affirming particular rights of the
subject. Thus Massachusetts and South Carolina
specifically asserted the privileges of the writ of
habeas corpus.[2]

The attitude of the home government towards
these colonial imitations of the English Bill of
Rights is remarkable. All of the acts which have

[1] *Cal of State Pap.*, *Col.*, 1689–1692, pp. 453, 454; *N. Y.*
Colonial Laws, I., 244.

[2] Massachusetts Bay, *Acts and Resolves*, I., 40, 95–99, 170;
Mereness, *Maryland*, 438; McCrady, *South Carolina under Pro-*
prietary Government, 247.

been mentioned were disallowed. In one instance, there was a minor and somewhat technical defect; in another, the act was declared unnecessary; and in another, the objections were not clearly stated. Two disallowances were particularly noteworthy: the New York act of 1691 was similar to that of 1683, which had been disallowed by James II., and the reasons given in the two cases were much alike. The later act was condemned by the Board of Trade, because it gave to the representatives "too great and unreasonable privileges"; because the exemption from the quartering of soldiers contained "several large and doubtful expressions." The Massachusetts act for the prevention of illegal imprisonment was set aside on the ground that the privileges of the habeas corpus act of Charles II. had not as yet been granted in any of his majesty's plantations.

The colonial assemblies resembled the English House of Commons in desiring greater freedom from executive control and influence, and hence measures resembling the acts for triennial parliaments and the exclusion of office-holders from the Commons were more or less successfully advocated in the colonies. In Massachusetts the charter of 1691 permitted annual elections; Penn granted the same privilege to his colonists in his "charter" of 1701; and in both the Carolinas acts were passed for holding biennial elections; the Virginia assembly asked that assemblies might be held at least once in two years; and in New Jersey, which under the proprietors had been accustomed to frequent elections, the king was urged, though without success, to provide for triennial assemblies. So far as such acts were passed, they limited the power which the provincial governors generally possessed of summoning, proroguing, and dissolving assemblies.

Another parliamentary privilege jealously guarded by the colonists was that of judging elections; the Virginia burgesses declared, in 1692, that the house was the sole judge of the capacity or incapacity of its members; sheriffs who attempted to determine such questions were declared guilty of a breach of privilege, and two of them were ordered under arrest.[1]

The assemblies were not, however, content with securing their freedom in the exercise of legislative privileges. They desired also to strengthen their control over the provincial executive, and their chief instrument for this purpose was the power to grant or withhold taxes. Of all the royal provinces, the most aggressive in this respect was Massachusetts, where the colonists under the old charter had been accustomed to almost entire independence. Even the new charter allowed them privileges unusual in a royal province, including the right to appoint many administrative officers. There was, more-

[1] Poore, *Charters and Constitutions*, II., 1536; Cooper, *Statutes of S. C.*, II., 79; *N. C. Col. Records*, II., 213; *Cal. of State Pap., Col.*, 1689–1692, pp. 454, 617; Chalmers, *Revolt*, I., 294, *n.*

over, in the province a strong radical party under
the leadership of Elisha Cooke, one of the most
aggressive members of the radical party which had
been unwilling to accept the compromise charter
of 1691. Cooke was repeatedly elected to the council, though several times excluded by the vetoes of
Governor Phips and Governor Dudley. It appears
to have been his policy to secure for the colony the
largest measure of independence possible under the
new charter.[1]

The programme of the popular party in Massachusetts is partially set forth in an act passed by
the general court in 1694, but soon after disallowed by the crown, claiming for the assembly the
right to appoint all civil officers not particularly
designated in the charter, besides a complete control
of public expenditures. All official salaries were
to be fixed by the assembly; whenever revenue was
to be raised, the house should be apprised of the
purpose for which it was to be used; and no money
was to be expended except for the objects specified by law. Except in the case of contingent
charges, every warrant must indicate the specific
service for which the money was used and the law
by which it had been authorized. The disallowance
of the act did not prevent the assembly from carrying out substantially the policy here indicated;
for in the face of constant protests from royal governors and the home government, the assembly

[1] Hutchinson, *Hist. of Mass. Bay* (ed. of 1795), II., 70, 125, 137.

steadily refused to make permanent provision for the civil list. The governor's salary was voted from year to year, expenditures were controlled by detailed appropriations, and the province treasurer was appointed by act of assembly.[1]

This radical programme was not fully carried out in the other provinces, but nearly every feature of it may be found in one or more of the royal or proprietary governments. In Virginia, where the assembly had granted a standing appropriation before the revolution, a fixed salary was secured to the governor; but permanent grants were refused in nearly all of the other colonies. There was also a growing tendency to appropriate money in detail and for limited periods of time, a method particularly objectionable to the home government because it enabled the assembly to exert pressure upon the governor for the purpose of carrying distinctively popular measures.

The claim of the assembly to control the finances came more and more to mean control by the representative house. Even before the English revolution, the Virginia burgesses refused to allow the council to act with them in laying the levy; and elsewhere the council was denied the right to amend money bills. This claim of the representative was resisted by the home government and was not always made good, though it was in

[1] Massachusetts Bay, *Acts and Resolves*, I., 170, 174, 188, 394, 437; VII., 24, 376, passim.

accordance with the usage of the House of Commons.[1]

In one respect the constitutional development of the colonies outstripped that of the mother-country. In England the formal appointment of ministers of state has remained to the present time in the hands of the crown, and, until the accession of the Hanoverians, Parliament had only an imperfect control. On the other hand, the appointment of administrative officers by the provincial assemblies became common soon after the English revolution, as a natural result of their theory of financial control. The money raised by public taxation belonged to the people, and their representatives had, therefore, the right to determine how it should be spent, and to provide the necessary safeguards for such expenditure.

The most important application of this theory was the appointment of the province treasurer by the assembly. In 1691 the governor of Barbadoes complained that the treasurer was appointed by act of assembly, and that the lower house claimed the nomination as "absolutely its own." In 1693 the Virginia council refused to accept a bill from the burgesses for appointing a treasurer; but after 1704 the treasurer of that province was regularly appointed by act of assembly. In New York the same policy was adopted during the early years of

[1] Cf. Osgood, *Am. Cols. in the Seventeenth Century*, chap. xiv.; Greene, *Provincial Governor*, 121–124, 169–174.

the eighteenth century, after the passage of resolutions referring to previous misapplication of funds;
and in 1715 the governor was convinced that resistance to that method of appointment was no
longer practicable. Similar appointments by the
assembly were made in the proprietary governments of Pennsylvania, the Jerseys, and South
Carolina, and for a time at least in the temporary
royal province of Maryland. In South Carolina
the public receiver or treasurer had been appointed
by act of assembly at least as early as 1691, and in
1707 the governor approved an act which gave the
exclusive right of nomination to the "House of
Commons." [1]   Thus, by the close of Queen Anne's
reign, the colonial assemblies were, with few exceptions, enforcing their claim not merely to lay
taxes and determine expenditures, but also to appoint the chief financial officer of the province.

Royal officers in the colonies and the Board of
Trade in England often pointed out the marked
tendency towards autonomy in provincial administration and sought to check it. In 1703 the board
attempted to make a stand upon the salary question, and Governor Dudley urged repeatedly upon
the Massachusetts assembly the establishment of a
fixed salary; but the house answered his arguments

[1] *Cal. of State Pap., Col.*, 1689–1692, pp. 371, 373, 405, 1693–
1696, p. 66; Greene, *Provincial Governor*, 182–186; Chalmers,
Opinions, 179; Smith, *South Carolina*, 15–17; cf. Osgood, *Am.
Cols. in the Seventeenth Century*, II., 372–374.

by insisting on "the native right and privilege" of English subjects, "from time to time to raise and dispose such sum and sums of money as the present exigency of affairs calls for." Hunter, in New York, was equally aggressive, but the best he could do was to secure a civil list for a fixed term of years. In 1711 the Board of Trade suggested that the New-Yorkers might be brought to terms by threatening the intervention of Parliament; but the ministry, as a whole, was not then ready for such thorough-going measures.[1]

While engaged in these constitutional controversies, the colonists came to appreciate the necessity of having their interests guarded by agents in the mother-country. Until the latter part of the seventeenth century such agents, though occasionally appointed, were intended to meet special emergencies of some kind. After the revolution it gradually became the general custom to maintain standing agencies in London, in charge of the interests of the particular province. At first these agents were usually appointed by act of assembly, requiring the consent of the governor, council, and representatives; but sometimes, as in Massachusetts, the choice was practically that of the house; they were also instructed from time to time by the assembly.[2]

[1] Address of council and representatives, quoted in Palfrey, *New England*, IV., 297, *n.; N. Y. Docs. Rel. to Col Hist.*, V., 191.

[2] *Cal. of State Pap., Col.*, 1689–1692, pp. 453, 458, 632, 710; Sewall, *Diary*, II., 284; Tanner, "Colonial Agencies," in *Political Science Quarterly*, XVI., 24–49.

Through these agencies, and by various other methods, the colonists came to have considerable influence in London. Money was used to some extent to promote colonial interests, and there was an impression in the colonies that men of influence might be won by the use of it. In 1693, Governor Fletcher represented some of the colonists as thinking that "anything may be Effected at Whitehall for mony."[1] A few years later William Penn, after a considerable experience in English politics, was trying to secure the attorney-general's approval of the Pennsylvania laws. He noted some objection which the latter had made, but added his opinion that "a good fee would go a great way to clear the scruple, if I had it to give him."[2] The history of this colonial diplomacy in London has not yet been adequately studied; such a study should throw new light on the failure of the Board of Trade to repress the independent tendencies in colonial politics.

The preceding survey seems to show that the practical effect of the imperialistic movement was counteracted by strong independent tendencies within the colonies, so that it is hard to avoid the paradoxical conclusion that a period characterized by the extension of imperial control was also one of growing independence on the part of the colonies. The explanation may be stated briefly thus: whereas,

[1] *N. Y. Docs. Rel. to Col. Hist.*, IV., 73; cf. Bassett, *Writings of Colonel William Byrd*, chaps. xxiv., xxv.
[2] *Penn-Logan Correspondence*, I., 297.

during the larger part of the seventeenth century,
the colonists were left almost wholly to themselves
or their proprietary governors, a measure of imperial control was, thereafter, gradually extended
over them, and a majority were brought under the
influence of the provincial system. When, however, that new status was extended over communities hitherto accustomed to freer action, important
concessions became necessary; and as the colonies
were brought into closer relations with each other,
modifications of that system which had been found
necessary in one colony tended to become general.
The influence of English precedents also contributed
to this result. The provincial constitution was
modelled closely on that of England, without its
strong aristocratic upper house; and the colonial
assemblies shared the aspirations of the Mother of
Parliaments. Thus we have, at the same time, an
extension of the provincial system and a vigorous
development within that system of the self-governing spirit.

By some contemporary observers the colonists
were charged with cherishing the ideal of ultimate
independence, and much was made of their violation
of acts of Parliament, especially those relating to
trade. Here and there, particularly in New England, men were said to dispute the validity of parliamentary statutes. Zealous royal officials were
easily led to identify opposition to their own authority with disloyalty to the crown, and that

charge was most frequently and naturally brought against New England, where the old independent Puritan ideals clashed most sharply with the prevailing English system in church and state. This charge of disloyalty to the mother-country was, however, vigorously repelled by the New-Englanders, who pointed to their sacrifices in the intercolonial wars and emphasized important elements of common feeling underlying their political and ecclesiastical differences.[1]

Yet the charges of British officials had undoubtedly a certain basis. The political horizon of the colonists was hemmed in by the physical barriers which separated them from their fellow-subjects, so that they often displayed a lack of that broader loyalty which leads men to make sacrifices for objects not directly affecting their own interests or safety. It is true also that with this lack of interest in matters of more than pure y local concern, there existed an intense desire to manage their provincial interests in their own way. This insistence on local autonomy was not peculiar to any group of colonies. It attracted most attention in New England; but it may be found also among the Quakers of Pennsylvania, the tobacco planters of Virginia, and the little slave-holding oligarchies of Barbadoes and South Carolina. Royal governors

[1] Chalmers, *Revolt*, I., 225, 315–317, 369; Penhallow, *Wars of New England*, 72–74; Dummer, *Defence of the New England Charters;* see also below, p. 188.

like Hunter pointed out the inherent inconsistency between this spirit of autonomy and the authority of the mother-country as understood by colonial administrators in England. The danger of independence which they sought to avert, though **not** immediate, was not altogether imaginary.[1]

[1] Cf. *N. Y. Docs. Rel. to Col. Hist.*, V., 330, 340.

CHAPTER VI

PURITANS AND ANGLICANS

(1689–1714)

FOR a quarter-century after the revolution of 1689 English and colonial politics were largely influenced by the conflict of ecclesiastical parties. In England, and at one time or another in most of her colonies, church and state were united, and religion and politics were constantly reacting upon each other. In the ecclesiastical politics of the colonies during this period three phases are of prime historical importance: first, the gradual relaxation of the Puritan system in New England, particularly in Massachusetts; secondly, the effort of the aggressive Anglican party to extend over the colonies the ecclesiastical system of the mother-country, with its financial support of the established church and its discrimination against dissenters; and, finally, the conflict between clergy and laity within the ranks of the established church.

At the close of the seventeenth century the old Puritan order was still strongly intrenched in New England. Except in Rhode Island, the Congregational churches were generally recognized as entitled to public support; churches were built and ministers paid by taxes which were exacted from dissenters as well as from adherents or members. The church-membership qualification for voters had, indeed, been superseded by property qualifications, but the Puritan clergy still exerted a strong influence on the conduct of public affairs. Their advice was still asked on questions of policy; and the law, both in its making and in its administration, still expressed in large measure the opinions and ideals of the Puritan founders.

These general propositions are well illustrated in the history of Massachusetts in the years immediately following the revolution. The most important agent in securing the new charter and in determining the personnel of the new government was Increase Mather, a Congregational minister in active service. Phips, the first governor, had been recently received into a Congregational church. The lieutenant-governor, Stoughton, and most of his associates in the council, were thorough-going Puritans, who, after the recall of Phips, were charged for several years with the administration of the provincial government. The next governor, Bellomont, though himself an Anglican, thought it wise to attend one service weekly in a Congregational church. The Church of England had gained a foothold; but, from the Puritan point of view, it was still a peculiarly odious, dissenting sect.

One of the most marked characteristics of the

old Puritan life was its strong belief in the presence
and concrete manifestation in human affairs of
supernatural forces. This intense supernaturalism
was, of course, not peculiar to the Puritan; it was
equally characteristic of the mediæval church, and
in seventeenth - century Europe the conventional acceptance of supernatural theories was almost
universal. Yet among the English Protestants of
that day it was the Puritan sects with whom the
conventional dogma was most likely to become a
vital factor in the conduct of life.   It was the per-
sistence of this conviction which, at the beginning
of the provincial era, made possible that great
tragedy of New England history, the Salem witchcraft.[1]

It is not easy to determine the effect which this
tragedy and the part taken in it by the conservative
leaders may have had upon the religious thought
of New England.   Yet it is certain that while Massachusetts was being brought into closer commercial
and political relations with the outside world the
exclusive supremacy of Puritan ideals was being seriously shaken.   This can be seen first in lax or liberal movements within the church itself.   The conditions of church-membership were relaxed so that the
church could be entered without that thorough
spiritual examination which the fathers had thought
necessary.   In Boston the new Brattle Street Church,
organized in 1699, though accepting the substance

[1] See above, chap. ii.

of the old theology, adopted certain usages which
the conservatives regarded as highly objectionable.
The Scriptures might be read in the Anglican fashion,
without comment; members might be admitted
without any public statement of their experiences;
and persons who were not full members of the
church might be allowed to vote in the choice of a
new minister.   There was a long controversy between the leaders of this new movement and the
conservatives represented by Increase and Cotton
Mather.

Both parties were anxious to control the government of Harvard College, and Cotton Mather, finding that the liberals had gained the upper hand,
began to interest himself in the new Connecticut
college.   Such men as Sewall and the Mathers frequently expressed misgivings regarding religious
and social tendencies at variance with the old
Puritan standards.   In his *Magnalia Christi*, Cotton
Mather recorded his opinion that, "The *old spirit*
of New England hath been sensibly going out of
the world, as the *old saints* in whom it was have
gone; and instead thereof the *spirit of the world*,
with a lamentable neglect of *strict piety*, has crept
in upon the rising generation." [1]

In those times of declining spiritual vigor the
established churches of New England had to meet
the growing activity of the dissenting bodies.   Of

[1] Winsor, *Memorial Hist. of Boston*, II., chap. vi.; Mather,
Magnalia Christi (ed. of 1853), II., 334; cf. below, chap. xviii.

these the most important were the Quakers, the
Baptists, and the Anglicans. By the close of the
seventeenth century each of these denominations
was represented by a regularly organized church in
Boston. In Rhode Island the Quakers and Baptists were probably the strongest bodies. Elsewhere in New England their numbers were relatively small, and they had to contend with strong
prejudices. During the reign of Queen Anne, both
the Connecticut and Massachusetts governments
were complained of for unfriendly treatment of the
Quakers. When, in 1708, the Quakers of Boston
petitioned for leave to build a wooden meeting-
house, Sewall opposed it, saying that he "would
not have a hand in setting up their Devil Worship."[1]

Sewall and his contemporaries watched with particular anxiety the growth of the Anglican congre-
gation worshipping at King's Chapel. This church
had gained a foothold in Boston after the overthrow of the first charter; and after the revolution
it grew pretty steadily, until during the first quarter
of the eighteenth century it came to number several
hundred adherents and a second church became
necessary. Some of the rectors of King's Chapel
were prominent figures in Boston life, and it gained
some prestige from the special patronage of the
crown. Lord Bellomont was a member of this con-
gregation; and his successor, Dudley, though maintaining some relationship with the Congregation-

[1] Sewall, *Diary*, II., 232.

alists, also frequented the Anglican services, and
for a time at least was thought to be in special
sympathy with them. From time to time there
were funerals of prominent social personages, at
which Puritan sensibílities were disturbed by the
use of the English burial service. The religious
observance of Christmas was another Anglican
usage against which Sewall repeatedly recorded his
protest. In Rhode Island, especially in Newport,
the Episcopal church gained considerable strength,
and Connecticut had a small but aggressive Episcopal element, especially in the western counties.

One of the most dramatic incidents in the long-
drawn-out struggle between Puritans and Anglicans
in New England was the libel case of John Checkley, an Anglican bookseller in Boston, who in 1724
was tried by the superior court of Massachusetts,
convicted of seditious libel, and sentenced to pay
a heavy fine for an argumentative publication asserting the exclusive Episcopal authority as against
Congregational ordination. This seems to have
been the last attempt to check dissenting publications by legal process.

The most serious practical grievance of the dissenters in New England was the obligation imposed
upon them of paying the town taxes for the support of the Congregational worship. This was the
general rule outside of Rhode Island at the beginning of the eighteenth century; but some concessions had been made by Massachusetts In the

town of Swansea, annexed to Massachusetts in
1691 with other towns of the Plymouth Colony,
the Baptists were in control and continued as before to appropriate their church taxes to the support of their own minister: this course was, however, distinctly exceptional. During Queen Anne's
reign efforts were made by Anglicans to secure
exemption from this obligation to support another
communion, and they seem to have had some encouragement from Governor Dudley. In 1713 one
of the Puritan ministers of Boston spoke "very
fiercely against the Govr. and Council's meddling with
suspension of Laws, respecting Church of England
men not paying Taxes to the dissenting Ministers."
In this particular instance, an Episcopal resident
of Braintree had refused to pay his church tax,
and the matter ended by the levy of an execution
on his property. The Quakers also presented re-
peated complaints of the injustice done them in
New England by "priest's rates." In 1723 the
Privy Council took action upon a case in which
Quaker town officers had been imprisoned because
of their refusal to collect taxes for a Congregational
minister; the decision of the Massachusetts authorities was reversed, and it was ordered that the tax
should be remitted and the assessors released.[1]

During this decade a number of events contributed

[1] Backus, *New England*, I., chaps. x., xi.; Sewall, *Diary*, I.,
430, 493; II., 58, 59, 233, 337, 379, 387; Slafter, *John Checkley*,
passim, especially the *Memoir* (Prince Society, *Publications*).

to enhance the prestige of the Anglican party. In 1722, Timothy Cutler, president of Yale College, and some other prominent Congregational ministers of Connecticut, announced their conversion to the Church of England, and soon after Cutler became the rector of one of the Episcopal churches in Boston. In 1725, when the Massachusetts Congregationalists proposed to hold a synod, they met with a protest from the Anglican party, which was sustained by the bishop of London and by the law-officers of the crown. By the close of the decade special acts were passed, both in Massachusetts and Connecticut, partially relieving the Anglicans, Quakers, and Baptists from the necessity of contributing to the Congregational churches. The obligation still continued for Anglicans who had no local church of their own; but wherever an Episcopal church had been organized those who attended its services were entitled to reclaim for their minister their share of the local church taxes. The separation of church and state and the equal rights of all religious bodies did not receive complete recognition until long after the War of Independence, but the old Puritan ideal of a single church imposing its fixed standards upon the community had been hopelessly broken down.[1]

Once fairly established, the Anglican clergy and

[1] Massachusetts Bay, *Acts and Resolves*, II., 461, 494, 619, 783, 1022; *Talcott Papers*, I., 53, 65; cf. Cobb, *Religious Liberty in America*, 269–271.

laity became an important factor in New England
politics. In Connecticut and Massachusetts they
formed a small but aggressive loyalist group, who,
as members of the state Church of England, valued
also their political connection with the mother-
country. When hard pressed by the dominant
church of their new home, they looked for encouragement and support to the crown and its official representatives in America, with whom they
felt it their duty to stand for order in church and
state. In 1724 the Anglicans of Newport united
in a declaration to the king which, though perhaps
too extreme to be wholly representative, does fairly
illustrate the political tendencies of their fellow-
churchmen in New England. They assured the
king that, "The religious and loyal principles of
obedience and non-resistance are upon all suitable
occasions strongly asserted and inculcated upon
your Majesty's good subjects of this Church." [1]

Nowhere except in New England did the established Church of England have to struggle for bare
tolerance or equal rights at the hands of a rival
church supported by colonial law. Elsewhere the
Anglicans were more ambitious in their demands;
their ideal was the legal establishment of their
church in the various provinces, and, ultimately,
the close adjustment of this provincial church to
the English diocesan system.

Before 1689 the Church of England was not defi-

[1] Memorial quoted in Palfrey, *New England*, IV., 470.

nitely established by law in any of the continental colonies, except Virginia, though there were some Anglican churches in Maryland and a strong Anglican element in South Carolina. In North Carolina and the northern proprietary provinces, the field was almost exclusively occupied by various sects of Protestant dissenters. During the next twenty-five years, however, there was a marked extension of Anglican influence in all of these colonies.

One of the important leaders in this movement was Henry Compton, who was bishop of London for nearly forty years, beginning his official career under Charles II. and dying near the close of Queen Anne's reign. At his accession to office there was a well-recognized tradition that the colonies were under the special guardianship of the bishop of London, and in the royal province of Virginia no minister could be preferred to any benefice without his certificate. This responsibility for the colonies was expressly asserted by Compton soon after his accession; and in 1685 he secured a modification of the instructions to the royal governors by which his episcopal authority was to take effect "as far as conveniently may be," reserving to the governor the rights of collation to benefices, issuing of marriage licenses, and the probate of wills. Henceforth, also, no school-master coming from England was to keep a school without the bishop's license.[1]

[1] Cross, *Anglican Episcopate and the Am. Cols.*, chaps. i., ii.; Anderson, *Church of England in the Cols.*, II., 341.

During the reign of James II., Compton's independent course in English affairs led to his suspension; but after the revolution he resumed his office and at once became a member of the Committee of Trade and Plantations. In the same year he inaugurated an important new policy by appointing James Blair as his representative or commissary in Virginia. The commissary had a small part of the episcopal authority; he was to act as counsellor for the clergy of the province and to hold visitations or inquiries into the conduct of ministers, and in rare instances he might suspend a delinquent clergyman. Blair was an aggressive Scotchman of some ability and learning, who had already been in Virginia for several years. He took an active interest in politics as well as in religion, and quarrelled with the successive governors of the province. Yet he undoubtedly advanced the interests of the church by working for reform in the manners of the clergy, though he was conservative in the exercise of disciplinary authority, making only two suspensions in thirty-five years. Under his influence the supply of ministers was increased also, so that vacancies became much less common. Blair's greatest work was the founding, in 1693, of William and Mary College, which he looked upon as an important agency for the religious as well as the intellectual welfare of the province.[1]

[1] Motley, *Commissary James Blair* (*Johns Hopkins University Studies*, XIX., No. 10).

A more important figure than Blair in the annals of the colonial church was Thomas Bray, appointed by Compton as commissary for Maryland on the request of the provincial clergy. Before assuming the duties of this office Bray interested himself in the establishment of parochial libraries for the colonies, and though he made only a short visit to Maryland he had an important influence in securing the legal establishment of the Church of England in that province.[1]

During the eighteenth century commissaries were sent to several of the colonies, but none of them deserve to rank with these first two holders of that office. They frequently became involved in serious conflicts with the civil authorities, and were rarely able to maintain an effective discipline over the clergy.

Probably the most important and best - known single agency for promoting the interests of the Anglican church in America was the Society for the Propagation of the Gospel in Foreign Parts. This organization came into existence largely through the efforts of Dr. Bray, who had previously been interested in a similar organization known as the Society for Promoting Christian Knowledge. The Society for the Propagation of the Gospel, often called the Venerable Society, was chartered in 1701, with the patronage and active co-operation of the bishop of London and other prominent prelates.

---

[1] Mereness, *Maryland*, 438.

The new organization entered at once upon active missionary work in America. During the years 1702–1704 two of its agents, George Keith, a former Quaker, and John Talbot, made a long tour of the colonies, beginning at Boston and going as far south as North Carolina. The missionaries sent out by the society varied greatly in character and efficiency. Some of them were lacking in tact, and some brought scandal upon the church by gross personal misconduct, as, for instance, in North Carolina. Others were men of marked ability and fine Christian spirit.[1]

Another important influence at work for the Church of England in the colonies was that of the provincial governors and other royal officers in the colonies. The aggressive royal governors of this period — such men as Nicholson, Fletcher, Bellomont, and Spotswood — were also strong churchmen. Nicholson in particular was widely known as a zealous and disinterested friend of the church, to which he contributed considerable sums of money. The same thing was true of such royal agents as Randolph and Quarry. Conversely, the aggressive churchmen were usually advocates of closer imperial control.

Under these favoring circumstances, there was naturally a decided increase in the number of

---

[1] Anderson, *Church of England in the Cols.*, II., 550–578, III., 24–76, 220–234; Prot. Episc. Hist. Soc., *Collections*, I., especially Keith, *Journal*.

Anglican churches and adherents in nearly all the
colonies. For the first time there appeared regularly organized Episcopal churches in New York
and New Jersey. In 1695 the first Episcopal
church was built in Philadelphia, and soon assumed
an important place in the life of the Quaker colony.
In North Carolina there had been no Episcopal
ministers or churches before 1700, but in the next
decade the Anglican party was able for a time to
shape the ecclesiastical policy of the province.[1]

With increased numbers and a growing sense of
power, there came in several colonies a strong movement for the legal establishment of the English
church. The movement was least successful in the
middle colonies where the dissenting Protestant
sects were in a large majority. In New York,
however, Governor Fletcher secured from the assembly an act under which a few Episcopal churches
were supported by public taxation.[2]

In the south the new movement towards establishment was general and in form at least successful. The first to act was Maryland. Here the
proprietary governments had before the revolution
been called upon to provide a tax for the support
of the Anglican clergy. In reply the proprietor
declared that at least three-fourths of the popula-

[1] Anderson, *Church of England in the Cols.*, II., 434–441;
Weeks, *Religious Development in N. C. (Johns Hopkins University Studies*, X., Nos. 5, 6).
[2] *Ecclesiastical Records, New York*, II., 1073–1079; *N. Y. Docs.
Rel. to Col. Hist.*, V., 334.

tion were Protestant dissenters of various sects and
that a tax on them for the support of another
worship would be unfair. The first assembly under
the royal government took a different view. By
a statute of 1692 the Church of England was established and the vestries were authorized to levy
taxes for the support of their ministers. Another act
of 1696, which superseded the earlier legislation,
having been opposed by the Quakers and Catholics,
was disallowed by the crown, ostensibly because it
contained some irrelevant matter. During his short
visit to the province in 1700, Bray secured the
passage of a new establishment act, which, however,
contained an extreme clause requiring the use of the
common prayer in every place of public worship.
This act also was antagonized by the Quakers and
Catholics; in anticipation of another royal veto, a
new bill, without the objectionable clauses, was accepted by the Maryland assembly and became law
in 1702. Under this law the Anglican church retained its position as an establishment until the
American Revolution.[1]

The Anglicans of North Carolina had been almost
entirely passive until 1699, when Henderson Walker
took office as deputy governor of the province.
Walker was an aggressive churchman, and under his
leadership the church party, by "a great deal of
care and management," secured control of the
assembly. In 1701 an act was passed establishing

[1] Mereness, *Maryland*, 130, 436–441.

the church and authorizing the levy of a poll-tax
for the support of the clergy, and under its provisions three churches were built; but the next
assembly was controlled by the Quakers and their
allies, and shortly afterwards the establishment act
was disallowed by the proprietors. For the next
twelve years there was a constant conflict between
churchmen and dissenters, culminating in the petty
civil war known as the Cary rebellion.   The vestry
act of 1715 settled the issue nominally in favor of the
establishment; but the results attained were small,
and many years later a governor of the province
complained to the assembly that there were "but
two places where divine service is regularly performed." [1]

In South Carolina the Anglican influence was
stronger than in the northern colony, and as early
as 1698 provision was made by the assembly for
the support of an Episcopal minister in Charleston.
In 1702, Sir Nathaniel Johnson, a former governor of
the Leeward Islands, who on the accession of William
and Mary had proved his loyalty to the Stuarts
by resigning his post, was appointed governor by
the proprietors.   Like most high Tories of that day,
whether in England or America, Johnson was also an
extreme churchman, and under his leadership a
church act was passed in 1704 which divided the

[1] Weeks, *Religious Development in N. C.*, and his *Church and
State in N. C.* (*Johns Hopkins University Studies*, X., Nos. 5, 6,
and XI., Nos. 5, 6).

province into six parishes, and allowed the minister of each parish a salary of £50 out of the public treasury. A provision of this act regarding the discipline of the clergy was objectionable to the bishop of London, and in 1706 it was annulled by the crown; but in the same year a new establishment act was passed without the obnoxious clause and became the permanent law of the province.[1]

The simple establishment of the Anglican church was not enough to satisfy its more zealous adherents. In some instances they followed the example of the English Tories and demanded legislation still further discriminating against the dissenters. Even in the revolution settlement of 1689 the English dissenters had only been granted a bare toleration, and they were still excluded from public offices, except so far as they chose to qualify themselves by occasionally receiving the sacrament according to the Anglican rites. During the reign of Queen Anne the high-church party was particularly aggressive, and after some unsuccessful attempts finally carried, in 1711, the Occasional Conformity Act, imposing heavy penalties on dissenters who attempted to evade the legal tests. Three years later the so-called Schism Act was passed, imposing severe penalties upon any one, with a few clearly defined exceptions, who should keep a school

[1] McCrady, *South Carolina under Proprietary Government*, chaps. xiv., xviii., xix.

or engage in teaching without a bishop's license and
an agreement to conform to the Church of England.[1]

With this intolerant spirit prevailing in the
church at home, it is not strange that similar
measures were attempted in the colonies. In 1707,
Governor Cornbury, of New York, undertook to
punish two Presbyterian ministers for preaching
without a license; but in this case the ministers were
protected by the jury.[2] The unsuccessful attempt
of the Maryland assembly to compel the use of the
English prayer-book has already been noted.

The controversy in the Carolinas took on a much
more serious character, and nearly resulted in the
overthrow of the proprietary government. In the
same year, 1704, in which the first general church
act was passed for South Carolina, the high-church
party obtained a law providing that no one should
sit in the assembly without having received the
sacrament according to the Anglican rite. This
measure was conceived in the same spirit as the
religious tests at home, and it was brought forward
in America just at the time when the occasional
conformity bill was being urged in Parliament.
It is at least possible that a similar measure was
enacted in North Carolina, though the evidence is
incomplete. At any rate, the dissenters in both
the Carolinas were now thoroughly aroused, agents
were sent to England, and through the influence of

[1] 10 Anne, chaps. v., vi.; 13 Anne, chap. vii.
[2] *N. Y. Docs. Rel. to Col. Hist.*, IV., 1186.

the House of Lords, where the extreme churchmen
were still in the minority, the law was annulled.[1]

In the Quaker colony of Pennsylvania the church
party was not in a position to secure an establishment and it remained always in a small minority.
Yet at times this minority was a decidedly aggressive
and important element in provincial politics. At
the beginning of the eighteenth century its leaders
were hostile to the proprietary government, and did
what they could to discredit it by bringing out
sharply two points which caused special embarrassment to the responsible Quaker leaders: one was the
unwillingness of the Quakers to provide adequate
measures for defence; the other was their refusal
either to take or administer oaths. Harassed by
these attacks, moderate Quakers were even ready
to consider the possible advantage of leaving the
government in the hands of moderate churchmen.
Penn himself held the bishop of London largely
responsible for the agitation on the question of
oaths, and referred to him as "the great blower-up
of these coals." Thus in the middle as well as in
the southern colonies the antagonism of churchmen
and dissenters became an important phase of
provincial politics.[2]

The adherents of the Anglican church were by no
means free from dissensions within their own ranks.
In church as well as in state the spirit of local

[1] See above, p. 60.
[2] *Penn-Logan Correspondence*, I., 278, 282; II., 276, 420.

antagonism asserted itself against external authority, and the Old-World jealousy between laity
and clergy appeared also in the American provinces,
especially in the colonies where the Church of
England was established. Sometimes, on the question of financial support for the clergy, indifferent
Anglicans would even join hands with the dissenters. Two of the most practical of these subjects of
controversy were the method of engaging ministers
and the maintenance of discipline over the clergy.

The general rule in an Anglican province like
Virginia was that the parishioners had the right of
selecting or *presenting* a minister, who should then
be formally *inducted* into his office. A clergyman
once presented and inducted was established for
life and could not be removed by his parishioners.
This arrangement was unsatisfactory to the people,
who preferred to keep the matter under their control; and therefore, instead of regularly presenting
a minister, they preferred to enter into yearly
agreements with him regarding his service and his
compensation. By the end of the seventeenth
century this usage had developed into a serious
abuse, at least from the clerical point of view.[1]

The question of ecclesiastical discipline, especially
in the case of ministers regularly inducted, was
peculiarly difficult in the colonies, because there was
no resident bishop and the disciplinary authority

[1] Perry, *Papers Relating to the Church in Virginia*, 127, 132;
cf. Jones, *Present State of Virginia*, 104.

of the commissaries was generally ineffective. This led to various efforts on the part of the laity to take the matter into their own hands. Thus, in Virginia, the governor and council were constituted a court for the trial of ecclesiastical offences. Generally, however, proposals of this kind were vigorously and successfully resisted by the clergy. In Maryland there were serious complaints of the immorality of the clergy; and during Queen Anne's reign the assembly passed a bill establishing a lay court for the trial of delinquent ministers, who, in case of conviction, could be removed from office. The bill was condemned by the clergy as tending to the "Presbyterian form of ministers and lay elders," and the governor withheld his consent. The project was not, however, abandoned: in 1714 the governor refused the request of the vestries to discipline a delinquent clergyman; a bill to recognize the authority of the bishop's commissaries was then defeated, and a few years later another bill was introduced for the organization of a lay court. Again, however, the clerical influence prevailed, and no real settlement of the question was reached until near the close of the colonial era. Reference has been made to a similar attempt in South Carolina at the very height of the high‑church movement, which was defeated by the opposition of the bishop of London.[1]

[1] Hening, *Statutes*, III., 289; Mereness, *Maryland*, 441 et seq.; cf. Cross, *Anglican Episcopate and the Am. Cols.*, 71 et seq.

By the beginning of the eighteenth century the
opinion was widely held both in England and
America that the true solution for the problem of
the colonial church would be found in the appointment of resident American bishops. There are a
few earlier references to the subject, but the most
earnest advocates of the plan were the members
and missionaries of the Society for the Propagation
of the Gospel, including Thomas Bray. In 1705 a
petition from Burlington, New Jersey, signed by
fourteen clergymen asked for the appointment of a
suffragan bishop, and this proposal was approved by
Bishop Compton. Governor Hunter, of New York,
was interested in the project, and in 1712 the Society
went so far as to provide a house for a bishop of
Burlington. At about this time an effort was made
to gauge colonial sentiment on the subject. Bishop
Kennett, for instance, wrote to Colman, a Congregational minister in Massachusetts, expressing the
hope that "your Churches would not be jealous,"
"they being out of our Line, and therefore beyond
the Cognizance of any Overseers to be sent from
hence."

At the close of Queen Anne's reign there seemed
some reason to expect that the project might be
carried out. The queen expressed her approval, and
shortly before her death a bill was draughted for the
organization of a colonial episcopate. The new
king, George I., was soon asked by the Venerable
Society to establish four colonial dioceses, two for

the islands and two for the continental colonies, the seats of the latter to be respectively at Burlington, in New Jersey, and Williamsburg, in Virginia. Nothing came of the proposal, though the general idea of a colonial episcopate was discussed at intervals during the remainder of the colonial era. In the later stages of this discussion, on the eve of the Revolution, there was some anxiety, especially in New England, lest a colonial bishop might not content himself with a purely spiritual jurisdiction over the churches of his own communion. This ecclesiastical controversy became finally one of the minor factors in the alienation of the American colonists from the mother-country.[1]

Thus the period of William and Anne shows, on the whole, a marked relaxation of the old Puritan system in Massachusetts and a general advance on the part of the Anglicans. Nevertheless, the self-governing instinct of the colonists showed itself in the conduct of the church as well as of the state, and the attempt to organize an effective episcopal jurisdiction in America failed, partly, perhaps, because of colonial jealousy, but more probably because of the apathy of the home government.

[1] Cross, *Anglican Episcopate and the Am. Cols.*, chap. iv.; *N. Y. Docs. Rel. to Col. Hist.*, V., 310, 316, 473; Anderson, *Church of England in the Cols.*, III., 74; Jones, *Present State of Virginia* (ed. of 1865), 110; cf. Howard, *Preliminaries of the Revolution* (*Am. Nation*, VIII.), chap. xii.

CHAPTER VII

FRENCH AND ENGLISH INTERESTS IN AMERICA
(1689)

THE revolution of 1689 was not merely an important event in the constitutional history of the British Isles and of the English colonies; it also exerted a decisive influence on their international relations. Under the later Stuarts the foreign policy of the English government had been shifting and uncertain. The aggressive measures of Louis XIV. had awakened anxiety for the balance of power in Europe, and his harsh treatment of his Huguenot subjects was resented by the strongly Protestant spirit of the English nation; the spirit of commercial rivalry was also growing. These considerations would naturally have led to an English alliance with the Hapsburg monarchies of Spain and Austria on the one side, and the northern Protestant states on the other, against the expanding and menacing power of France; and such a policy seemed to be indicated by the Triple Alliance of 1668, when England combined with Holland and Sweden to defend the Spanish Netherlands against French aggression.

The consistent carrying out of this policy was prevented chiefly by two considerations: the first was the commercial jealousy between England and Holland, which still interfered somewhat with their political co-operation; the second was the peculiar relation which existed between the last two Stuarts and the king of France. Charles and James were both Catholics, and both desired for the old faith—first, toleration, and after that, if possible, the supremacy in England. Politically in accord with the traditions of their family, they desired also to secure for themselves, not perhaps absolute power, but at least greater freedom from parliamentary restraints. Both in their political and in their ecclesiastical policies they counted upon the support of Louis XIV.; and the influence of these sympathies was shown in the secret treaty of Dover in 1670 and the English co-operation with France against the Dutch in 1672.

The accession of William and Mary to the English throne brought a decided change of foreign policy. William III. was the head of the European alliance against Louis XIV. in the new continental war; and though the English people were less interested than their king in the continental question of the balance of power, Louis XIV. virtually forced them to join the alliance when he championed the cause of their exiled king. The substitution of William and Mary for James II., intended to secure parliamentary liberties and the Protestant faith, was now challenged by a foreign king, who represented precisely those tendencies in religion and politics which the nation had rejected. Not only was Louis XIV. the most striking embodiment of absolute monarchy, but he was also regarded since the revocation of the Edict of Nantes as the arch-enemy of the Protestant cause. He now contributed his money, his fleets, and his soldiers to bring about the restoration to the English throne of the Catholic Stuart king. The eight years of war which followed meant, therefore, a real struggle for national independence against foreign interference.

The breach between England and France in the Old World brought into direct conflict their subjects in America. During the previous decade the rival colonies had attempted local wars, from which they had been held back by the conservative influence of their respective governments at home. James II. was sincerely desirous of defending English interests in the New World, but opposed to aggressive measures which might disturb his friendly relations with Louis XIV. Nevertheless, Englishmen and Frenchmen had already come to blows, and each suspected the other of instigating Indian attacks upon the frontiers. Thus the American war, though partly a result of the European conflict, was also in large measure the natural outgrowth of American conditions. A brief survey of these conditions is therefore essential.

The French and the English came into contact
and competition at a large number of widely scattered points. To the far north the rights of the
British Hudson's Bay Company were disputed by
the French; and in 1686, three years before the
formal declaration of war, a French party captured
three of the British posts. In Newfoundland the
settlements of English fishermen had an offset in
the French post of Placentia. Similar close con-
tacts were to be found in the West Indies: among
the small islands of the Leeward group, Nevis,
Antigua, and Montserrat were British, and St.
Christopher partly French and partly English; in
the Windward group, Barbadoes was British and
Martinique French; and the new British colony of
Jamaica was exposed to the attacks of French
marauders from the neighboring islands. The
French islands were few and small, but they became important centres for privateering and piratical enterprise.[1]

For the present - day student of the American
nation, the chief interest of these international
rivalries lies in the contest for supremacy on the
continent of North America, which, in the closing
years of the seventeenth century, took place chiefly
on the frontiers of New England and New York.

[1] Parkman, *Frontenac* (ed. of 1878), 132–134; *N. Y. Docs. Rel.
to Col. Hist.*, IX., 801; *Cal. of State Pap.,Col.*, 1689–1692, p. 108;
for a discussion of this subject from the point of view of French
colonization, see Thwaites, *France in America* (*Am. Nation*,
VII.), chaps. iii., vi.

The boundary between Acadia and New England had never been accurately defined. The English establishments in 1688 extended eastward a little beyond the Kennebec to the frontier fort of Pemaquid; but a few miles away, at the mouth of the Penobscot, was the half-savage establishment of the French Baron de St. Castin. Farther to the north and east were French trading-posts and settlements on the St. John's River and the Bay of Fundy. The competition here was quite as much for Indian trade as for territory. Each party tried to conciliate the tribes who occupied the upper courses of the rivers. On the whole, the French were more successful, chiefly through their political agents the Jesuit missionaries, although they owed something also to the blunders of their English rivals.

At the outbreak of the revolution of 1689, these Abenakis, or "Eastern Indians," were bitterly hostile to the English, and had already made a number of raids on the frontier. Such an Indian war was particularly dangerous to the northern villages of Maine and New Hampshire, but there were few places even in the old Massachusetts Bay colony which could count themselves entirely safe. Since the Indian raids were thought to be largely instigated by French missionaries, no permanent solution seemed possible without the expulsion of the French from Acadia and Canada.[1]

[1] Cal. of State Pap., Col., 1689–1692, pp. 45–47; Sewall, Diary, I., 223–227.

On the New York frontier the situation was quite different. Though Dutch and English settlements had spread beyond Albany to Schenectady on the Mohawk, they were still distinctly outposts at a long distance from any other considerable places. North of Albany the English were separated from the French by a great expanse of wilderness extending to the St. Lawrence. The chief difficulty here arose from the western ambitions of the two nations, and especially their competition for the fur trade. From the beginning of French colonization in America the westward movement had been one of its most marked characteristics; French missionaries and traders early made their way by the Ottawa River to the Great Lakes, and established trading-posts and missions at the Straits of Mackinac and on the Illinois River. In 1673 Fort Frontenac was built at the outlet of Lake Ontario to strengthen the French interest in the west, especially as against the Iroquois.[1]

Before the English conquest of the Hudson valley, what the French had to fear in this quarter was not so much European rivalry as the hostility of the Iroquois, who lived in the Mohawk valley and in the region south of the lower lakes. Alienated

[1] Schuyler, *Colonial New York*, I., 426–428; *N. Y. Docs. Rel. to Col. Hist.*, IX., 95–114; cf. Tyler, *England in America*, chap. xviii., and Thwaites, *France in America*, chap. iv. (*Am. Nation.* IV. and VII.).

from the French as early as 1609, they soon formed an alliance with the Dutch, with whom they carried on an important trade, especially in fire-arms. With these European weapons the Iroquois soon became the most formidable of the Indian tribes; they nearly exterminated some of their neighbors, and extended their ravages among the tribes of the upper lakes and the Mississippi valley, many of whom were the allies of the French.

The hostile attitude of the Iroquois blocked effectually French movement south of the lower lakes, and disturbed trade with the western Indians; vigorous efforts were therefore made to conciliate or overawe these formidable antagonists. Here, as in Acadia, their most effective political agents were Jesuit missionaries, by whose efforts some of the Iroquois were converted to the Catholic faith and placed in settlements on the St. Lawrence under French protection. From time to time military expeditions were undertaken to punish and overawe the hostile members of the league, but they failed to produce permanent results.[1]

In November, 1686, the kings of France and England agreed to the so-called treaty of neutrality for America, and the governors on both sides were exhorted to refrain from hostile measures. Commissioners were appointed to adjust the pending boundary disputes, but no final agreement was reached. Even James II., with all his desire for

[1] Parkman, *Frontenac*, passim.

friendly relations with France, insisted that the Five Nations were British subjects and entitled to his protection.[1]

Hence the English governors of New York made active efforts to maintain and strengthen their hold upon the Iroquois, especially the aggressive Governor Thomas Dongan, the Irish Catholic representative of the Duke of York from 1683 to 1688. Some of the Iroquois had been induced to acknowledge themselves as under the protection of the Duke of York and King Charles, and the Five Nations as a whole were claimed as British subjects. The English tried also to develop their trade with the western Indians, and with so much prospect of success that the French were thoroughly alarmed. An angry correspondence took place on these subjects between the rival governors, and in 1687 two trading parties sent out by Dongan were attacked and captured by the commandant of the French fort at Mackinac. In the same year Denonville commanded a Canadian expedition against the Senecas, which was denounced by Dongan as an invasion of British jurisdiction. Some Indian villages were destroyed, but the chief practical result was to provoke the Iroquois to measures of savage retaliation.[2]

Such in brief was the situation in America when

[1] *N. Y. Docs. Rel. to Col. Hist.*, III., 503; IX., 330, 416; *Mémoires des Commissaires* (Paris, 1755), II., 81–89.

[2] Parkman, *Frontenac* (ed. of 1878), 92; Colden, *Five Indian Nations*, pt. i., chap. iii., *N. Y. Docs. Rel. to Col. Hist.*, III., 347, 363, 436, 520, IX., 318, 336, 357–369, 405.

in April, 1689, the formal outbreak of war in Europe closed the unsatisfactory chapter of diplomatic controversy and brought the rival nations to the trial of arms.   In the war of the Grand Alliance, France stood almost alone against a formidable combination, including not merely the Protestant states of England, Holland, and Germany, but also the Hapsburg monarchies of Spain and Austria.   Two of England's allies, the Dutch and the Spaniards, had also possessions in America.   There was little practical co-operation between them in the American war, but it was worth something to the Carolina settlers to be relieved from the fear of Spanish invasions.

The great resources of France enabled Louis XIV. to meet the allies on equal terms; and indeed the military advantages at the outset were on his side, for during the first two years of the war the English government was handicapped by disturbances in Scotland and Ireland.   The first important naval engagement, the battle of Beachy Head in 1690, seemed also to indicate the superiority of the French on the sea, even against a combination of Dutch and English fleets.   It was not until 1692 that the English naval victory at La Hogue turned the scales in favor of England, and even then the English preponderance was not decisive.   The long-continued wars also imposed upon the English people unaccustomed financial burdens and strained their resources to the utmost.

The pressure of the European war seriously

limited England's efficiency in defence of its American interests. British fleets were, indeed, sent to the West Indies, to co-operate in their protection and in offensive operations against the French, but they accomplished little of real importance. A few British regulars were stationed in the West Indies and in New York, and from time to time money and military supplies were sent. On the whole, however, the action of the British government upon the military situation in America was ineffective and of subordinate importance. The most important enterprise of the war in North America, the attack on Quebec in 1690, was undertaken by inexperienced colonists without assistance from the home government.

A comparison of the resources of the rival colonies themselves seems at first sight to show a decisive advantage on the side of the English. In population and in wealth they far exceeded their French competitors. Even if we include only the colonies of New England and New York, which were most directly affected by the war, the English still had a decided preponderance. The comparatively large proportion of regular soldiers sent to Canada did not offset the English advantage in population.

Yet on some points the French showed decided superiority: they had better trained and more efficient leaders, a more effective because more centralized political administration, and more capacity for co-operation with their Indian allies. On the outbreak of the war the French government again sent out, to replace Denonville in the government of Canada, the famous Count Frontenac, a trained soldier and a daring commander, yet not reckless of his military resources. His previous service gave him a good knowledge of Canadian conditions, and he was remarkably effective in his dealings with the Indians. The increased prestige with which he now assumed office made him somewhat more independent of local antagonisms and more nearly master of the situation. No British representative on the continent could be compared with him for a moment in the essential qualities of leadership. He had also some able subordinates, such as his successor, Callières, then governor of Montreal, and such effective partisan leaders as Villieu and Iberville. To oppose this chieftain and his lieutenants the English had plenty of daring and energetic men, but no able general, and few officers really trained to lead in the serious enterprises of war.[1]

Even if a leader like Frontenac had appeared on the English side, he would have been seriously hampered by the loose political organization of the colonies. During the first two years of the war, New England and New York, which had to bear the brunt of the French attack, were without definitely settled governments, and suffered from the confusion incident to radical changes in govern-

[1] Parkman, *Frontenac;* Lorin, *Le Comte de Frontenac.*

ment. In New York the situation was particularly
serious; at Albany the local civil and military officers organized themselves in a convention which for
several months maintained its independence of the
Leisler government at New York.[1]

After the new constitutional arrangements of
1689–1692 were worked out, there was still no effective concentration of military authority, though
some efforts were made in that direction. Sir William Phips received a commission, not only as governor of Massachusetts, but as commander-in-chief
of all the New England militia; and Governor
Fletcher, of New York, was given a similar authority in Connecticut and the Jerseys, besides holding
for two years the king's commission as governor
of Pennsylvania. Both governors met with resistance in the colonies and were unable to enforce the
authority thus conferred. At different times during
the war other methods of securing co-operation were
attempted. In 1690 a convention of the northern colonies was held in New York and plans were made for
what proved to be an unsuccessful movement against
Canada. In 1693, Governor Fletcher called a meeting of commissioners from the different colonies to
meet at New York, but it was poorly attended. It
called upon the various colonial governments to
contribute definite sums of money or quotas of
militia. A few contributions were received; but the
final results were unsatisfactory and Fletcher de-

[1] *Doc. Hist. of N. Y.*, II., 80, 147.

clared that the English colonies were as badly divided as Christian and Turk.[1]

Under these conditions decisive operations were hardly to be expected on either side. The resources of Canada, though on the whole efficiently organized, were insufficient for large offensive operations, and the English failed to use effectively their advantages in population and wealth. A few large operations were planned on both sides, some of which were seriously attempted, only to end in humiliating failure; others were abandoned almost at the outset as impracticable. The military enterprises of this war were, therefore, generally on a small scale, taking the form of mere raids on the enemy's frontier, with the help usually of Indian allies.

[1] *Cal. of State Pap., Col.*, 1689–1692, p. 572, 1693–1696, pp. 28, 63; *N. Y. Docs. Rel. to Col. Hist.*, III., 855–860; IV., 29–227, passim; *Doc. Hist. of N. Y.*, II., 239.

CHAPTER VIII

KING WILLIAM'S WAR

(1689–1701)

WAR was formally declared between England and France in April, 1689, but in some of the colonies it was not proclaimed until several months later, and the most important operations of that year were in the West Indies. There the advantage was temporarily with the French, and in the summer of 1689 they seized the English part of St. Christopher. Urgent appeals were made by the islanders for an English fleet, but none could be sent out until the following year. Fortunately, the new governor of the Leeward Islands, Sir Christopher Codrington, a man of unusual ability, made an energetic defence, and no further losses followed.[1]

On the North American main-land the chief feature of the year was a series of Indian raids on the New England frontier, where, during the previous winter, Andros had sent an expedition against the Maine Indians. He established a number of frontier posts extending as far north as Pemaquid; but on the fall of his government these garrisons were

---

[1] *Cal. of State Pap., Col.*, 1689–1692, pp. 21, 111, 118–123.

either recalled altogether or reduced, and the Indians were encouraged to renew their raids. In June they attacked and ruined the village of Cocheco, near Dover, New Hampshire, killing or capturing a large number of the inhabitants. In August an Indian party, led by the French Baron de St. Castin, captured the fort at Pemaquid and massacred the inhabitants of the adjacent village. These disasters aroused the government of Massachusetts. A considerable force was raised and sent to the frontier, Casco (Portland) was relieved from a siege by the Indians, and an unsuccessful retaliating expedition was undertaken by the well-known Indian fighter Benjamin Church.[1]

The French also suffered seriously from Indian attacks. The Iroquois, thoroughly exasperated by Denonville's attacks, made a succession of raids on the French settlements of the upper St. Lawrence. At Lachine, in the immediate vicinity of Montreal, several hundred persons were butchered by the Indians or carried into captivity. When Frontenac arrived in the province, two months later, he reported that the colonists were still terrified and dejected by the blow. Meanwhile, Callières, the governor of Montreal, proposed an elaborate plan for the conquest of New York by a land expedition from Montreal co-operating with a naval force sent

[1] Drake, *Border Wars of New England*, chaps. ii.–v.; *Andros Tracts*, III., 21–38; *N. Y. Docs. Rel. to Col. Hist.*, IX., 440; Church, *History of the Eastern Expeditions* (ed. of 1867), 1–37.

out from France. This plan, though accepted in substance by the king and embodied in instructions to Frontenac, was found impracticable at that time.

Frontenac now undertook to bring the Iroquois to terms by a vigorous show of force, and to check the English offensive through a series of border raids. In the winter and spring of 1690 three war parties were sent out against the English frontier, each composed of Canadians and Indians and led by French officers. The first blow fell on Schenectady in February, 1690, and the capture of the post was followed by a wholesale butchery of the inhabitants. The sense of horror which this outrage produced in the neighboring town of Albany was strongly expressed a few days later by Mayor Peter Schuyler: "The Cruelties committed at said Place no Penn can write nor Tongue expresse: the women bigg with Childe rip'd up and the Children alive throwne into the flames, and there heads dash'd in pieces against the Doors and windows." The two other parties attacked and destroyed the village of Salmon Falls, in New Hampshire, and the fort and village at Casco (Portland) on the Maine coast. From various points on the long, exposed frontier news of similar disasters were sent to the government at Boston.[1]

---

[1] *N. Y. Docs. Rel. to Col. Hist.*, IX., 408–435, 466–473; *Andros Tracts*, III., 114; Sewall, *Diary*, I., 311–321; *Cal. of State Pap., Col.*, 1689–1692, p. 240; on this war, see also Thwaites, *France in America* (*Am. Nation*, VII.), chaps. ii., vi.

These losses by land, accompanied by others on the sea, suffered by New England merchantmen at the hands of French privateers, soon made evident the necessity of more aggressive measures. The first important offensive movement on the English side was undertaken by the New-Englanders. During the winter and early spring of 1690 they had been preparing an expedition against Port Royal, which was a base for French privateering operations as well as for raids against the English frontier. For this purpose a fleet of about seven vessels was collected and an infantry force of about four hundred and fifty men. The command was given to Sir William Phips, himself a native of the Maine frontier, a daring and adventurous sea-captain, but without special fitness for military command. The fleet sailed from Boston, April 28, entered Port Royal harbor about ten days later, and the French commander yielded almost at once. The settlement was plundered, and the Puritan feeling showed itself in some wanton destruction of Catholic church property. The inhabitants of Port Royal and the surrounding country were then compelled to take the oath of allegiance to William and Mary.[1]

This conquest of Acadia was a comparatively simple matter, but before Phips's return to Boston the colonists had planned the far more serious en-

[1] Parkman, *Frontenac* (ed. of 1878), 236–243; *N. Y. Docs. Rel. to Col. Hist.*, IX., 474; *Cal. of State Pap., Col.*, 1689–1692, pp. 240, 275.

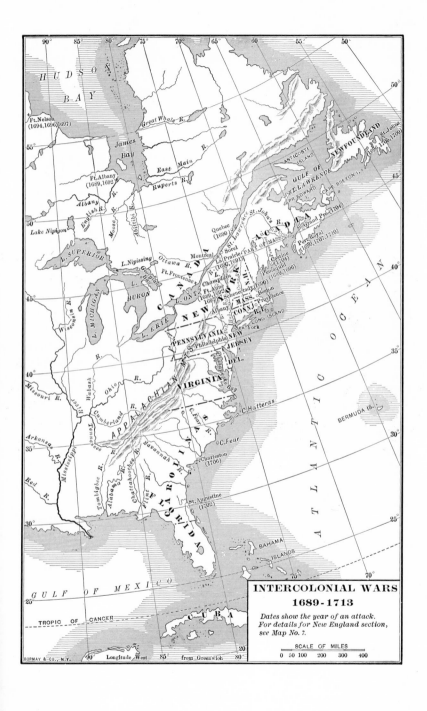

INTERCOLONIAL WARS
1689 - 1713

Dates show the year of an attack.
For details for New England section,
see Map No. 7.

SCALE OF MILES

0 50 100   200   300   400

terprise of taking Quebec and completely expelling
the French from Canada. At the congress in New
York in the spring of 1690 representatives of New
York, Massachusetts, Plymouth, and Connecticut
arranged for a land force to move northward by way
of Lake Champlain against Montreal. To the proposed movement by sea, the Massachusetts dele-
gates would not pledge their colony; but after the
capture of Port Royal it was determined to carry
out that part of the plan also.

Definite quotas for the land expedition were assigned to Massachusetts, Connecticut, Plymouth,
Maryland, and to New York, which was held responsible for about half of the total. After considerable
disagreement, Fitz-John Winthrop, of Connecticut,
was appointed by Leisler to command the expedition. When, however, the time came for the advance, it was found that the quotas had not been
filled; the Iroquois allies also failed to perform their
part; and the main expedition was finally abandoned, though a small volunteer force, under John
Schuyler, gave some annoyance to Frontenac by
attacking the French settlement of La Prairie, opposite Montreal.[1]

In the mean time preparations had been going
forward at Boston for the expedition against Quebec, and Phips's easy success at Port Royal led to
his selection for this larger responsibility. The re-

[1] *Doc. Hist. of N. Y.*, II., 237–288; *N. Y. Docs. Rel. to Col.
Hist.*, IV., 193–196.

sources of the colony were strained to provide the necessary men and supplies. The fleet was composed of merchantmen and fishing-vessels, and the officers were generally untrained men. An unsuccessful effort was made to secure the co-operation of the home government, and finally, after numerous delays, the fleet left Boston harbor on August 9, 1690. No pilot had been provided for the St. Lawrence, and there was another long delay in the river, so that the fleet did not appear before Quebec until the middle of October. Phips at once sent a demand for immediate surrender, but the golden moment had passed.[1]

Less than a week earlier Frontenac had received, at Montreal, his first intimation of a possible English attack on Quebec. Acting with a promptness and decision which appear in marked contrast with the conduct of the enemy, he hastened to Quebec, giving orders for the despatch of reinforcements. The defences of the city were strengthened, and when the messengers from Phips arrived, Frontenac treated the summons with studied contempt. In accordance with their plan for a joint attack, the English then landed about twelve hundred men a little below the city, but the expected co-operation of the fleet was not given; and in the mean time the garrison of Quebec was strengthened by the arrival

---

[1] Parkman, *Frontenac*, chap. xii.; Hutchinson, *Hist. of Mass. Bay*, I., App.; *Cal. of State Pap., Col.*, 1689–1692, pp. 240, 385, 415.

of several hundred men from Montreal.   After some
indecisive skirmishing on land and an ineffective
bombardment by the fleet, the landing force returned in confusion to the ships.   After some hesitation it was decided to abandon the siege and return to Boston.   The losses in action had been small
on both sides, but the New - Englanders suffered
severely from disease.[1]

The expedition had involved Massachusetts in
heavy loss, both of men and money, and the chief
officers were severely criticised.   Major Walley, the
commander of the land forces, prepared a brief defence, naming the following reasons for the disappointment: "The land army's failing, the enemy's
too timely intelligence, lyeing 3 weeks within 3
days' sail of the place, by reason whereof they
had the opportunity to bring in the whole strength
of their country, the shortness of our ammunition,
our late setting out, our long passidge, and many
sick in the army." [2]

Frontenac appealed to his king for more aggressive measures.   He suggested the employment of
the royal navy in "punishing the insolence of these
veritable and old parliamentarians of Boston; in
storming them, as well as those of Manath [New
York] in their dens, and conquering these two
towns whereby would be secured the entire coast."

---

[1] Parkman, *Frontenac*, chap. xiii.; *Cal. of State Pap., Col.*, 1689–
1692, pp. 377, 385, 415; *N. Y. Docs. Rel. to Col. Hist.*, IX., 455–
461.   [2] *Journal*, in Hutchinson, *Hist. of Mass. Bay.*, I., App.

For large enterprises of this kind, however, Louis XIV. was not then prepared.[1]

While preparations were being made in Boston for the unsuccessful expedition against Quebec, the British had won a substantial success in the West Indies. With the help of an English fleet St. Christopher was retaken, in 1690, and the French driven altogether from the island. The colonists hoped for the complete expulsion of the French from the West Indies, but the later years of the war were almost wholly lacking in events of decisive importance.[2]

On the New England frontier the war consisted mainly of French and Indian raids like those of 1689 and 1690, and some rather ineffective retaliatory expeditions by the New-Englanders. In 1691 a new French governor, Villebon, was sent to Acadia; he easily recovered Port Royal and established himself at Naxouat, on the St. John's River. With the help of the Jesuits the Abenaki Indians were again aroused and led against the Maine frontier. York was destroyed in February, 1692, and a determined but unsuccessful attack was made upon Wells. There was also a series of small raids on the towns of central Massachusetts.[3]

---

[1] N. Y. Docs. Rel. to Col. Hist., IX., 461, 494.
[2] Cal. of State Pap., Col., 1689–1692, pp. 186–195, 278, 291–294, 303, 712, 1693–1696, pp. 39–43, 79, 86, 92.
[3] Ibid., 1689–1692, 560; N. Y. Docs. Rel. to Col. Hist., IX., 526; Parkman, Frontenac, 347–356; Drake, Border Wars of New England, chaps. viii., ix.

In 1692, Phips returned from England with a commission under the new charter as governor of the enlarged province of Massachusetts. For the kind of military service now required he was better fitted than for the larger enterprise of 1690. Acting under royal instructions, he rebuilt the fort of Pemaquid, and in 1693 made a treaty there with representatives of the Abenaki Indians. Nevertheless, through the efforts of the daring French officer Villieu and the Jesuit missionary Thury, the warlike faction among the Indians regained the ascendency and the war began again. The Oyster River settlement, in New Hampshire, was destroyed in 1694, and a raid on Groton, about thirty miles from Boston, brought the war still nearer home to the people of Massachusetts.

In 1696, after a few minor raids on the Maine and New Hampshire borders, a French expedition commanded by Le Moyne d'Iberville again destroyed Pemaquid, and the New England fisheries were seriously depressed by Iberville's destruction of the English settlements on the eastern shore of Newfoundland. English attempts at retaliation were only partially successful: an expedition under Church plundered and burned the French settlement of Beaubassin at the head of the Bay of Fundy, but a subsequent attack on the French at Naxouat was repulsed. Massachusetts was so much discouraged by the situation in Acadia that the general court asked that the province be re-

lieved from further expense in defence of Port
Royal or the St. John's River. The closing months
of the war were marked by murderous forays on the
interior towns of Massachusetts. In March, 1697,
occurred the Haverhill raid, made famous in colonial annals by the capture of Hannah Dustin
and her subsequent escape by the killing of her
captors. In February, 1698, several months after
peace had been proclaimed in London, the Indians made another raid as far south as Ando-
ver. Taken individually, these French and Indian
forays seem unimportant, but in the aggregate
they constituted a serious check on the expansion of the colonies beyond the older settled
areas.[1]

From time to time more ambitious enterprises
were discussed on both sides. Phips was not discouraged by his failure at Quebec, and continued
to urge the conquest of Canada. In the summer of
1693 a fleet under Sir Francis Wheeler arrived at Boston from the West Indies, under orders to co-operate
with the Massachusetts government in another attack on Quebec, but its effective force had been
much reduced by disease, and Phips argued that
it was now too late to prepare for an attack that
year. The plan was therefore abandoned, and

[1] Sewall, *Diary*, I., 391; *Cal. of State Pap., Col.*, 1693–1696,
pp. 149, 157; Drake, *Border Wars of New England*, chaps., xi.–
xiv.; Parkman, *Frontenac*, 361–391; Hutchinson, *Hist. of Mass.
Bay* (ed. of 1795), II., 88–104; *N. Y. Docs. Rel. to Col. Hist.*,
IX., 664.

during the remaining years of the war Quebec was not seriously threatened.[1]

On the French side, the idea of a naval attack on Boston and New York repeatedly appears in the official correspondence, but without definite action, until the last year of the war, when a detailed plan was worked out for a strong fleet from France, under the command of the Marquis de Nesmond, to be joined on the Maine coast by a force of Indians and fifteen hundred troops from Canada. It was thought that Boston could be easily captured, and it was proposed afterwards to destroy the leading towns to the northward. The fleet actually set sail from France, but arrived too late to accomplish its purpose.[2]

On the New York frontiers the contest was quite as much diplomatic as military. The English wished to keep the Iroquois aggressively on their side and to enforce their view that these tribes were dependent on the English crown. On the other hand, the French were constantly seeking to detach the Iroquois from the English alliance and compel them to a separate peace. The western Indians, especially those of the lake region, also formed a factor in the problem. Their trade was essential to the prosperity of Quebec, and the French

---

[1] *Cal. of State Pap., Col.*, 1693–1696, pp. 13, 31, 124.
[2] Charlevoix, *History of New France* (Shea's trans.), V., 69–73; *N. Y. Docs. Rel. to Col. Hist.*, IX., 659–661; Parkman, *Frontenac*, 382–384.

therefore desired not only to protect them against Iroquois attacks, but also to prevent their reaching an understanding with the Five Nations which might result in the diversion of the western trade to the English.

In this peculiar contest of diplomacy and Indian warfare, the chief figure on the French side was, of course, Frontenac. He found on his return to Canada that the French prestige, even among the western Indians, had been seriously impaired. Just before his arrival the danger from the Iroquois had been emphasized by the fearful massacre of Lachine, and the western trade was almost cut off. Frontenac first undertook to secure peace by negotiations with the Five Nations; and when that failed, to revive French prestige by striking a series of severe blows against the English and their Iroquois allies. Until the Iroquois could be forced to terms, the breach between them and the western Indians was, if possible, to be kept open.[1]

The chief representatives of the English interest in New York were the successive governors of the province, especially Fletcher, and an able Dutchman, Peter Schuyler. Fletcher was afterwards severely censured for misconduct in other matters;[2] but in the management of French and Indian affairs he showed considerable energy, and made, for a time at least, a favorable impression upon the Iro-

---

[1] Lorin, *Le Comte de Frontenac*, pt. ii., chap. iv., pt. iii., chap. i.
[2] *N. Y. Docs. Rel. to Col Hist.*, IV., 479–486.

quois. It is difficult to say what he would have accomplished with larger resources within his own province and heartier co-operation from the neighboring colonies. The most important work on the frontier was done by a little group of Dutch colonists at Albany, of whom the most conspicuous was Peter Schuyler, who began his official career under Governor Dongan. He became the first mayor of Albany, and chairman of the board of commissioners of Indian affairs. Under the Leisler government he was out of favor, but in the later years of the war the value of his services was recognized by making him a councillor in the provincial government and its chief agent and adviser on the northern frontier.[1]

After the fiasco of 1690 the New York government undertook no serious military movement, though the desirability of an attack on Canada was strongly urged by the Iroquois and was recognized by Governor Fletcher. The resources of the province were considered inadequate to such an undertaking without the effective co-operation of the home government and the neighboring colonies, and such co-operation was not to be had. During the last six years of the war the burden fell almost wholly on the Iroquois.[2]

While the English remained comparatively inactive, the Five Nations were being gradually weakened by the aggressive measures of Frontenac. In

---

[1] Schuyler, *Colonial New York*, I., 302 et seq.
[2] *N. Y. Docs. Rel. to Col. Hist.*, IV., 23, 32, 74.

1693 a force of several hundred French and Indians attacked and destroyed three Mohawk villages. In the same year an expedition to Mackinac strengthened the French influence among the western Indians and revived their trade with Montreal. These reverses and the inactivity of the English seriously weakened the Iroquois alliance. In 1694, conferences were held by some of the Iroquois with the French, but Frontenac refused to accept any peace which did not include his Indian allies, and insisted that the English should not be considered in the negotiations. The English influence was still strong enough to prevent a peace on these terms, and the war continued.[1]

In 1696 the French prestige in the west was strengthened by two aggressive measures. One was the re-establishment of Fort Frontenac, which had been abandoned by Denonville, but which Frontenac considered of great importance for the defence of French interests in the west. The other was a formidable expedition against the Iroquois, composed of French regulars, Canadian militia, and several hundred Indians, with Frontenac himself in command. The Onondagas, who were the special object of attack, retired before this superior force, so that the French had to content themselves with the destruction of food and of the growing crops. Though this expedition, standing by itself, was in-

[1] N. Y. Docs., Rel. to Col. Hist., IV., 118, IX., 550-555, 577-584; cf. Parkman, Frontenac, chap. xiv.

decisive, the long continuance of the war had so seriously impaired the fighting strength of the Five Nations that, according to an official report made in 1698 by order of the English governor, the number of their men had been reduced by one-half.[1]

The operations of the American war were, on the whole, indecisive, though the French could count some considerable strokes against the enemy during the closing months. In the west, French prestige was notably higher than at the beginning of hostilities. On the seaboard, Pemaquid had been taken and the fishing interests of New England had been seriously depressed by Iberville's operations in Newfoundland. Finally, the French had gained an important advantage in the Hudson Bay region through Iberville's capture of Fort Nelson in 1697.[2] These military operations were, nevertheless, too small to affect negotiations for peace, and the American provisions of the treaty of Ryswick were only minor incidents in the general European settlement between Louis XIV. and the allies.

In America, as in Europe, the treaty of Ryswick, in 1697, brought no real settlement of the questions at issue. It was agreed that the two contending parties should retain the possessions which they held at the beginning of the war; but the boundary disputes then existing were not adjusted, although

[1] N. Y. Docs. Rel. to Col. Hist., IV., 337, IX., 640–659.
[2] Parkman, Frontenac, 391–394; Lorin, Le Comte de Frontenac, 464–467.

commissioners were to be appointed by the two governments.[1]

Before peace could be definitely established in America, both sides were obliged to negotiate with the Indians. On the New England border the war was closed by a treaty between the government of Massachusetts and the Abenaki Indians at Casco Bay in January, 1699.[2] The position of the Iroquois was quite different from that of the eastern Indians, for the English assumed that the Five Nations were dependent upon the English crown, and hence included in the peace between France and England. Acting on this assumption, the Earl of Bellomont, the new governor of New York and Massachusetts, demanded of Frontenac the surrender of all prisoners in his hands, including the Iroquois as well as the English, promising in return the release of French prisoners held by the Iroquois. Frontenac rejected the theory of English sovereignty over the Iroquois, and insisted upon separate negotiations with them. There was an angry correspondence between the two governors, and when Frontenac died, in 1698, the controversy was still unsettled. The English used all their efforts to prevent the Iroquois from conferring with the French; but they suffered a serious diplomatic defeat when, in 1701, under the auspices of the French

[1] Treaty in *Mémoires des Commissaires* (Paris, 1755), II., 92–108.
[2] Drake, *Border Wars of New England*, chap. xiv.; Hutchinson, *Hist. of Mass. Bay* (ed. of 1795), II., 104.

governor Callières, a general peace was concluded
between the French and their Indian allies on the
one side and the Iroquois on the other.[1]

[1] Parkman, *Frontenac*, 423–426, 438–452; *N. Y. Docs. Rel. to
Col. Hist.*, IV., passim., esp. 564–573, IX., 690–695, 715–725.

CHAPTER IX

QUEEN ANNE'S WAR

(1700–1709)

THE treaty of Ryswick failed to bring, either in Europe or America, a settlement of the essential issues. The problem of the Spanish succession, which had troubled the statesmen of Europe for a generation, remained unsolved. Charles II., the reigning king of Spain, was an invalid and childless, and the succession was contested by the two leading dynasties of continental Europe; both the Austrian Hapsburgs and the Bourbons of France had claims based upon intermarriage with Spanish princesses. The complete triumph of either would have produced a political combination more serious than any in Europe since the days of Charles V., but the union of France and Spain seemed particularly dangerous to those who wished to defend the balance of power.

The treaty of Ryswick was followed by prolonged negotiations in which Louis XIV., William III., and the Hapsburg emperor were the chief participants. A compromise which gave the Spanish crown to a minor personage, the electoral prince of Bavaria, and

allowed certain concessions of territory to the French
and Austrian claimants, was soon nullified by the
death of the young Bavarian prince. Renewed
negotiations between the English and Dutch governments on the one side, and Louis XIV. on the
other, resulted in the second partition treaty of
1700, by which Spain, with the Spanish Netherlands and the colonies, was assigned to an Austrian
prince and the important possessions in Italy to
the French Dauphin. Again, however, the work
of diplomacy was undone; for in the same year
Charles II. died, leaving by will all the Spanish
dominions to Philip of Anjou, a younger grandson
of Louis XIV. Louis accepted the will, and with
his support Philip established himself on the Spanish
throne.[1]

This Bourbon succession was at once contested
by the Austrians, but it was at first doubtful whether
they would receive general support. To William
III. the desirability of resistance was clear, but his
English subjects were not yet convinced that their
own interests were at stake. Again, as in 1689,
this conviction was forced on them by the French
king himself. Their anxiety was first aroused by
his occupation of border fortresses in the Spanish
Netherlands, previously secured by Dutch garrisons.
In September, 1701, there came news of French
edicts excluding British manufactures. The French
seemed also to be reaching after a monopoly of the

---

[1] Von Noorden, *Spanische Erbfolge-Krieg*, I., 97–118.

Spanish-American trade, to the serious detriment of English interests. Finally, in the same year, Louis XIV. again challenged the national spirit of the English people by acknowledging, on the death of James II., his son, "the Pretender," as James III., king of England. There was soon a decided change of feeling in England, and the newly elected Parliament gave its cordial support to the king's war policy. Before war was actually declared, King William died, but the accession of Anne and the choice of new ministers brought no change in the foreign policy of the government. Under the leadership of Marlborough, England became more than ever the predominant partner in the coalition against France.[1]

Aside from the sentiment of national independence challenged by Louis' acknowledgment of the Pretender, the primary interest of England in the War of the Spanish Succession was to prevent the close union of France and Spain which seemed likely if Philip V. were allowed to keep his crown. This was not merely a question of continental European politics, but even more largely one of commercial competition. During the later years of the Spanish Hapsburgs the English and the Dutch had, lawfully or unlawfully, secured for themselves an important part of the Spanish trade, including

---

[1] Von Noorden, *Spanische Erbfolge-Krieg*, I., 119–121, 125–139, 172–179; Stanhope, *England, 1701–1713* (ed. of 1870), 11; Grimblot, *Letters of William III. and Louis XIV.*, II., 477–479.

that of the American colonies. There was reason
to suppose that under a Bourbon prince stricter
regulations would be enforced, that special privilege enjoyed by the English would be withdrawn,
and that the French would use their political power
to exploit the Spanish trade.

This emphasis on commercial interests, and especially upon colonial trade, appears repeatedly in
the diplomatic representations of the British government, from the foundation of the coalition until
the final settlement. Thus, in the secret treaty between England, the Netherlands, and the Austrian
emperor in 1701, there were included as indispensable conditions of a settlement with France, not
only the exclusion of the French from the trade of
the Spanish Indies, but also the securing to English
and Dutch merchants of all the commercial privileges enjoyed by them under the late king. The
same treaty reserved to the Dutch and the English
the right to make conquests in the Spanish Indies.
Similar views were expressed in the English treaty
with the Austrian claimant in 1706, and in the
preliminary articles proposed by England in the
peace negotiations of 1709 and 1711. Thus one of
the leading issues of the war was in part, at least,
American.[1]

---

[1] Von Noorden, *Spanische Erbfolge-Krieg*, I., 46–51, 162, II.,
224, III., 504; Stanhope, *England, 1701–1713*, p. 490; Bolingbroke, *Letters and Correspondence*, I., 374–381, notes; cf. Mahan,
Sea Power, 203.

In the preceding wars the resources of Spain were, in a measure at least, at the service of the coalition. In 1702, however, its government was in the hands of the French party and the authority of Philip V. was recognized at once in the American colonies. For the first time the English in North America had to face an alliance of the two great Latin powers; and for South Carolina and the British West Indies this was a serious danger.

The great engagements of this war were fought on the continent of Europe, and the victories of Marlborough and Prince Eugene were probably the most important factors in forcing France to terms. Yet one of the most marked features of the struggle was the steady decline in the naval power of France and the steady advance in that of England. England gained at the expense of the Dutch as well as of the French, and by the close of the war had become unquestionably the leading maritime power. This naval superiority produced, however, no marked results in the American war. Though the French navy declined because of official neglect, English colonial trade suffered severely at the hands of French privateers, especially from the West India Islands.[1]

As the European conflict approached, it was probably not materially hastened by any crisis in North America. In fact, there was a strong disposition among the French to maintain peace in

[1] Mahan, *Sea Power*, 217–231.

America. A French state paper of 1701 contains
an elaborate project for the conquest of the northern
English colonies, but ends with the opinion that,
after all, the neutrality of North America would
be preferable to war and would be "infinitely more
advantageous for Canada." Proposals for neutrality
were afterwards made by Governor Dudley, of
Massachusetts, and accepted in principle, not only
by Governor Vaudreuil at Quebec, but by the
French authorities at home. Upon the precise
terms, however, the two governors could not agree.[1]

On the New York frontier the peculiar position
of the Iroquois resulted in a sort of partial neutrality which was maintained during the greater
part of the war. Since, after a long and harassing
conflict, the Canadian government had just brought
the Five Nations into peaceable treaty relations,
it was considered very important that these relations should be maintained. Conferences were held
with the Iroquois and assurances of neutrality were
secured. In view, however, of the close relations
which had long existed between these Indians and
the authorities at Albany, it seemed doubtful
whether, in case of actual war between the French
and the English, the Iroquois could be prevented
from taking sides with the latter. For this reason
the French refrained from attacking New York.
The English and Dutch of New York found it almost equally their interest to preserve the peace.

[1] *N. Y. Docs. Rel. to Col. Hist.*, IX., 725–728, 770–776, 779.

Thus for several years New York was protected from Indian incursions and the Indian trade was freely continued both with Albany and Montreal.[1]

The attitude of the French towards New England was quite different. The Indians of that region had been under Jesuit influence and closely allied with the French, but there was some anxiety lest they might be reconciled with the English and take sides with them. The Marquis de Vaudreuil, who in 1703 became governor of New France, argued that the English and the Abenakis must be kept "irreconcilable enemies," and he therefore instigated these Indians to attacks on the New England frontier, in which the converted Iroquois of the French mission were also engaged. The government in France expressed some misgivings with regard to this policy at first, but its opposition does not seem to have been serious.[2]

The peculiar neutral attitude of New York, while the New England settlements were exposed to the horrors of border warfare, provoked sharp criticism. The New-Englanders suspected that their own safety was being sacrificed in order that the men at Albany might carry on a profitable trade. From time to time they attempted to secure the help of the Iroquois in their war with the eastern Indians,

[1] N. Y. Docs. Rel. to Col. Hist., V., 42, IX., 736–739, 742–745; Schuyler, Colonial New York, II., 13–26; Parkman, Half-Century of Conflict, I., 11–14.
[2] N. Y. Docs. Rel. to Col. Hist., IX., 755–760, 804.

but were always blocked by opposition from New York. It was not until 1709 that that province was willing to promise its support and that of the Indian allies for a general movement against the French. Sometimes, however, the Schuylers at Albany rendered the New-Englanders substantial service by warning them of impending French and Indian raids. Samuel Penhallow, a contemporary New England writer, notes the timely warning given on the eve of the Deerfield massacre by "Colonel Schuyler who was always a kind and faithful intelligencer." [1]

The history of the American war may be conveniently divided into two periods. The first covers the seven years from 1702 to 1709, and is characterized for the northern colonies chiefly by French and Indian raids on the New England frontier, followed by generally ineffective attempts at reprisal, especially on the part of the Massachusetts government. There was also a large amount of commerce - destroying, in which New England suffered severely from French privateers, especially those from the West Indies and Port Royal. On the sea, however, the New-Englanders were able to give a better account of themselves than on land, and considerable damage was inflicted upon French commerce and fisheries. Meanwhile, South Carolina, in even greater isolation, was

---

[1] Penhallow, *Wars of New England* (ed. of 1859), 24, 35, 43; Schuyler, *Colonial New York*, II., 20, 24; *N. Y. Docs. Rel. to Col. Hist.*, V., 42.

engaged in a serious conflict with the Spaniards of Florida, aided not merely by Indian allies, but also by French forces from the West Indies.

The intervening colonies were less directly involved in the war, but their commerce was exposed to attack. The English government, at considerable expense, provided naval vessels to convoy the fleets that sailed at intervals from Massachusetts or Virginia or Barbadoes, besides guard-ships to patrol the coasts; but these precautions did not always prevent serious loss. Even Pennsylvania, where the Quakers were doing their utmost to keep out of the war, had to feel at times the blows of the enemy. James Logan, Penn's agent in the province, writes repeatedly of the annoyance caused by the "Martinico privateers." In 1708 he observed that after a period of comparative peace, "these coasts begin to be intolerably infested," and that within four days "three vessels of this river" had been sunk and burned, including one "just off our own capes." The next year he noted the plunder of a neighboring town by a French privateer.[1]

In the second period, from 1709 to 1713, the English were more aggressive. Larger enterprises were undertaken, there was more co-operation among the colonies, and there were also considerable reinforcements from England. These larger plans, however,

---

[1] *Penn-Logan Correspondence*, I., 240, 289, 301, II., 123, 275, 348; Chalmers, *Revolt*, I., 354.

were seriously impaired by poor leadership and defective organization, and the results accomplished were relatively small.

Notwithstanding the formal declaration of war, in 1702, there was no serious outbreak on the New England border that year. In 1703, Joseph Dudley, who had recently been appointed governor of Massachusetts and New Hampshire, and thus exercised jurisdiction over practically the whole territory exposed to Indian attacks, held a conference with the Abenaki tribes at Casco, on the Maine frontier. A treaty of peace was then agreed to by the Indians, but within two months, under the influence of the French Jesuits, they reopened the war by a destructive raid which almost wiped out the Maine settlements. In 1704 occurred the most serious disaster of the whole war in New England, the massacre at Deerfield, then the northwestern outpost of settlement in the Connecticut valley. The town was attacked by a force of Indians, accompanied by a few Frenchmen, under the lead of a well-known partisan chief, Hertel de Rouville. Men, women, and children were butchered, and about a hundred prisoners carried off to Canada. The most conspicuous of the prisoners was the Reverend John Williams, pastor of the church, who left a record of the hardships experienced by himself and his associates in captivity. Many of the weaker prisoners died or were murdered by their captors. Of those who finally reached Canada, some were ultimately exchanged

and returned to their homes; but others, especially
the children, yielded to the efforts of the Catholic
missionaries or were so much influenced by their
Indian captors that they were unwilling to be re-
claimed.[1]

Even more characteristic of the border warfare
than this Deerfield expedition were the innumerable frontier raids made by comparatively small
bodies of French and Indians, or of Indians alone.
In this, as in the previous war, the ravages of the
enemy were not confined to Maine, New Hampshire, and the remote Connecticut valley towns.
The Indian war-parties penetrated into the eastern
counties of Massachusetts, even to such towns as
Reading and Sudbury, within a few miles of Boston,
and Haverhill, which suffered one of the most destructive raids of the whole war. Many of these
expeditions were sent out by Governor Vaudreuil,
and he had the efficient co-operation of the French
missionaries. In 1703 the Jesuit Father Rale reported that the Abenakis would take up the hatchet
whenever he pleased; and Vaudreuil noted com-
placently afterwards that the small parties sent out
had not failed "seriously to inconvenience the English." The French government at home ultimately
gave its approval of this savage warfare; in 1707,
Pontchartrain, the French colonial minister, told
Vaudreuil that he did well "to write to the Mission-

[1] Penhallow, *Wars of New England* (ed. of 1859), 16–23;
Drake, *Border Wars of New England*, chaps. xvi., xviii.

aries among the Abenakis to have the war continued against the English."[1]

Against these terrible onslaughts there seemed to be no certain means of defence. The line of exposed settlements was too long to be continuously defended; the precise point of attack could rarely be anticipated; and the communications were slow and uncertain. It was during the winter of 1703–1704, while Massachusetts and New Hampshire had nearly nine hundred men in service, that the disaster occurred at Deerfield. From time to time small retaliatory expeditions were sent out, and, if successful, they returned with Indian scalps, for which the provincial government offered liberal bounties. Penhallow tells of one such party sent up the Connecticut from Northampton in 1704, consisting of Mr. Caleb Lyman (subsequently elder of a church in Boston) and five friendly Indians. After ten days' absence the party returned, having killed eight Indians and taken six scalps. It was estimated, however, that every Indian killed or taken had cost the English at least £1000. To the direct charges of the war must be added the wide-spread destruction of property on land, and the serious damage done to New England fisheries and commerce by the French privateers.[2]

[1] *N. Y. Docs. Rel. to Col. Hist.*, IX. 755–760, 804; Drake, *Border Wars*, passim; Penhallow, *Wars of New England*, passim.
[2] Penhallow, *Wars of New England*, 25, 31–33, 48, 57; Drake, *Border Wars*, passim, esp. 251.

In 1705, Governor Dudley attempted to solve the problem by proposing the neutrality of the colonies, but he refused to accept Vaudreuil's counter proposal that the New-Englanders should be excluded from the fisheries on the Acadian coasts. Under these circumstances the Indian problem could only be solved by striking at the French, who stood behind the savages. For measures of this sort, however, New England was poorly organized: the colonies of Rhode Island and Connecticut were still under independent governments which could not be counted upon for continuous hearty support; and even in Massachusetts there were serious divisions. The governor, Joseph Dudley, though a man of ability, was regarded with great suspicion by many people under his jurisdiction. He was charged with complicity in an illegal trade which was being carried on with the enemy, and which undoubtedly increased unnecessarily their power for offensive measures against the English. These charges were doubtless much exaggerated, but so conservative a man as Samuel Sewall thought the governor not wholly free from blame.[1]

Again, as in the earlier wars, New England suffered seriously from the absence of trained military leaders and a disciplined soldiery, with the result

---

[1] N. Y. Docs. Rel. to Col. Hist., IX., 770–772, 776, 779; Hutchinson, Hist. of Mass. Bay (ed. of 1795), II., 141–148; Drake, Border Wars, 210–215; Mass. Hist., Soc., Collections, 5th series, VI., 65–131*, esp. 111*.

that expeditions prepared with great enthusiasm and with considerable financial sacrifices often resulted in humiliating failures. The first retaliatory expedition on any considerable scale was that of Church in 1704, the last enterprise of that veteran fighter of King Philip's War. After unsuccessful efforts to find forces of French and Indians along the Maine coast, Church sailed to Acadia, ravaged the French settlements on the Bay of Fundy, and took a number of prisoners. The expedition also entered Port Royal harbor, but the fort was not attacked; and the failure to produce more positive results called forth severe criticism both of **Church** and of Governor Dudley.[1]

As the war proceeded, the importance of Acadia as a base for French operations against New England was keenly felt; and in 1707 a new expedition was organized against it, to which Rhode Island, New Hampshire, and Massachusetts contributed, though Connecticut held aloof. Two regiments commanded by Colonel March were sent by sea under convoy of a royal man-of-war and an armed vessel belonging to Massachusetts, and appeared before Port Royal in June, 1707, with some prospect of success. The French governor, Subercase, made a vigorous defence, and March, though an Indian fighter of good reputation and undoubted courage,

---

[1] Penhallow, *Wars of New England*, 28–30; Hutchinson, *Hist. of Mass. Bay* (ed. of 1795), II., 132–135; Drake, *Border Wars*, chap. xx.

proved unequal to his task. He finally lost heart and after some skirmishing abandoned the siege. There was great indignation in Boston at this fiasco, and Dudley sent peremptory orders to the fleet to return to the siege; but the attacking force was now too demoralized, while the French had materially strengthened their position, so that the siege was a second time abandoned.[1]

While New England was waging this comparatively ineffective warfare with the French and Inddians, the South-Carolinians had been making a creditable stand against their enemies. From its beginning the Carolina settlement had been jealously watched by its Spanish neighbors at St. Augustine, who, in 1686 destroyed the Scotch settlement at Port Royal. The colonists were then eager to organize a retaliatory expedition, but were held back by the proprietary government. During the next sixteen years Spain and England were not only nominally at peace, but for a considerable time allies against France.[2] By 1702, however, this restraint upon the rival colonies was removed.

Early in 1702, before the queen's proclamation of war was known in America, the Spaniards organized a force, composed mainly of Indian allies with a few whites, for a land attack upon South Carolina.

[1] Parkman, *Half-Century of Conflict*, I., 120–127; Hutchinson, *Hist. of Mass. Bay* (ed. of 1795), II., 150–156; Penhallow, *Wars of New England*, 50–52.
[2] McCrady, *South Carolina under Proprietary Government*, 216–222.

The English traders, however, were warned by the friendly Creek Indians, and formed from them a strong opposing force, so that the invaders were surprised and routed. The South-Carolinians now determined to take the offensive, and in the autumn of 1702 sent a small fleet with several hundred provincial militia and Indians from Port Royal against St. Augustine. The town was destroyed but there was not enough artillery for a successful siege of the fort, and before the needed supplies could be secured, Governor Moore, who was in command of the expedition, was alarmed by the appearance of two hostile frigates and hastily retreated. The South-Carolinians, like the New-Englanders before Port Royal, had involved themselves in heavy expense with no tangible results.

In the following year a new governor, Sir Nathaniel Johnson, received his commission from the proprietors, and adopted in the main a defensive policy. Nevertheless, Colonel Moore was allowed to undertake a raid into the enemy's territory; and during the winter of 1703–1704 he fought a pitched battle with several hundred Indians under Spanish leaders. The English were completely victorious, and after ravaging the country returned with a large number of prisoners to Charleston.[1]

Two years now passed without any important operations, and the interval was used by Governor

[1] McCrady, *South Carolina under Proprietary Government*, 377–396; Carroll, *Collections*, II., 348–353, 574.

Johnson in guarding against possible invasion by
land or sea. In 1706 a French and Spanish expedition sailed from Havana under a French commander, Monsieur le Feboure, and, after receiving
reinforcements at St. Augustine, appeared before
Charleston, August 24. There was great anxiety
in the town, which was already suffering a severe
epidemic of yellow fever, but the governor faced
the situation with admirable courage and energy.
Militia were promptly brought in from the surrounding country; and when, after three days' delay,
the French commander presented his demand for
surrender, he received a defiant response. The
enemy then landed a part of his force, but one
landing party was defeated with considerable loss.
The Carolinians now assumed the offensive and
sent a small fleet against the invaders, whereupon
the French commander hastily abandoned the attack and sailed away. Almost immediately after
his departure another French man-of-war appeared,
and, apparently in ignorance of the defeat of the
fleet, entered Sewee Bay, a few miles northeast of
Charleston. A small landing party sent out by
the French commander was defeated and the ship
itself was captured by the Charleston fleet. In a
little more than a week the Carolinians had repelled a formidable invading force and taken over
two hundred French and Spanish prisoners.[1]

[1] McCrady, *South Carolina under Proprietary Government*,
396–401.

This historic defence of Charleston was the last important event of the war on the southern frontier. Neither party had been able to hold territory belonging to the other, but the English inflicted more damage than they suffered, and were, on the whole, entitled to the honors of the conflict.

CHAPTER X

ACADIA AND THE PEACE OF UTRECHT

(1709–1713)

AFTER seven years of indecisive conflict, during which the colonists had been left largely to their own resources, the English government began to direct its attention more seriously to the North American situation. The desirability of the conquest of Canada had been repeatedly urged upon the home government, and now had an unusually zealous advocate in the person of Colonel Samuel Vetch, an adventurous Scotchman, who, after some service in the British army, came first to New York, where he married into the Livingston family, and afterwards engaged in trade at Boston. In 1706, Vetch, with a number of other prominent Boston merchants, was convicted of trading with the enemy and fined, though the sentence was annulled by the crown on technical grounds. This incident does not appear to have affected his standing in England, and he had the advantage of considerable local knowledge of Canadian affairs gained during a recent visit.[1]

[1] Order in council of September 24, 1707, in Hutchinson, *Hist. of Mass. Bay* (ed. of 1795), II., 144; Patterson, " Hon. Samuel Vetch," in Nova Scotia Hist. Soc., *Collections*, IV., 1-20.

In March, 1709, a royal circular was issued to the northern governors announcing an expedition against the French in accordance with Vetch's proposals. A fleet was to be sent out from England with five regiments of British regulars, who were to be reinforced by Massachusetts and Rhode Island militia, and then to proceed by sea against Quebec; Montreal was to be attacked by a land force from Albany, consisting of militia from New York, Connecticut, New Jersey, and Pennsylvania, and an auxiliary force of Indians. Vetch was given general supervision of the enterprise, and the colonial governments were required to furnish supplies and fixed quotas of militia.[1]

The plan was received with enthusiasm in New England, where it seemed to offer a permanent solution of the perplexing French and Indian problem. The necessary preparations were therefore pushed forward with vigor.[2] In the middle colonies the problem was less simple. For New York the new enterprise meant a departure from the quasi-neutral position which had hitherto saved the province from border warfare. Nevertheless, the expulsion of the French from Canada was a prize for which it was worth while to take some risks, so that the New York assembly contributed liberally in men and supplies; and, by the help of the Schuylers, some

[1] N. Y. Docs. Rel. to Col. Hist., V., 70–74; Instructions to Vetch in Nova Scotia Hist. Soc., Collections, IV., 64–68.
[2] Parkman, Half-Century of Conflict, I., 131.

of the Iroquois were induced to co-operate. In New Jersey and Pennsylvania the Quaker influence proved a serious obstacle. New Jersey finally made an appropriation of £3000, but Pennsylvania refused to take any part in the enterprise. Nevertheless, a strong force was collected and a commander chosen in the person of Francis Nicholson, who as governor or lieutenant-governor in New York, Virginia, and Maryland, had had an unusually varied experience. His military capacity was never severely tested, but he was zealous and energetic.[1]

After all these preparations the colonists were finally disappointed by the failure of the home government to do its part. The supposedly more urgent demands of the European war led to a change of plan, and the troops formerly intended for Quebec were sent to Portugal. It was now proposed that with the help of English men-of-war then in American waters an attack should be made on Port Royal. The naval officers, however, refused their co-operation, and the year of hard work and heavy outlay ended with no tangible result.[2]

Nevertheless, the leaders in America refused to give up the enterprise. Nicholson and Schuyler went to England to urge vigorous measures upon the government, and the latter took with him a

---

[1] *N. Y. Docs. Rel. to Col. Hist.*, V., 78–81; *Penn-Logan Correspondence*, II., 351.

[2] Parkman, *Half-Century of Conflict*, I., 137–140; Hutchinson, *Hist. of Mass. Bay* (ed. of 1795), II., 160–163.

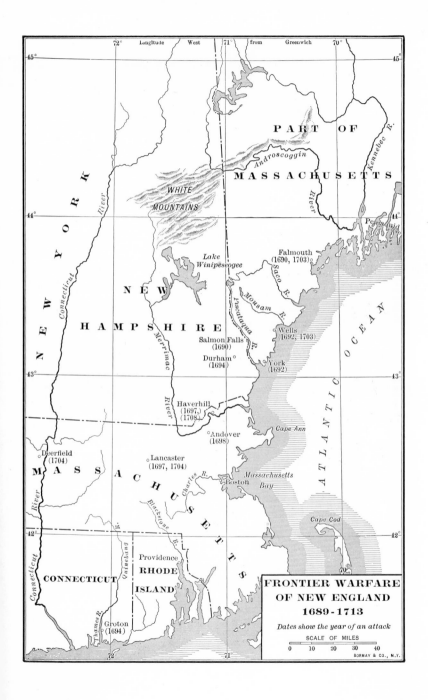

72° Longitude West 71° from Greenwich 70°

45° — 45°

PART OF

Androscoggin

MASSACHUSETTS

Kennebec R.

44° — 44°

WHITE
MOUNTAINS

River

Penaquid

N E W   Y O R K

Connecticut River

Falmouth
(1690, 1703)

Saco R.

Lake
Winipeseogee

N E W

Mousam R.

Piscataqua R.

Wells
(1692, 1703)

H A M P S H I R E

Salmon Falls
(1690)

Durham°
(1694)

York°
(1692)

Merrimac River

43° — 43°

A T L A N T I C   O C E A N

Haverhill
(1697,)
(1708)

°Andover
(1698)

Cape Ann

Deerfield°
(1704)

Lancaster°
(1697, 1704)

M A S S A C H U S E T T S

Charles R.

Boston°

*Massachusetts
Bay*

River

Blackstone R.

42° — 42°

Cape Cod

Connecticut River

Quinebaug R.

Providence°

RHODE

CONNECTICUT   ISLAND

Thames R.

Groton°
(1694)

70°

**FRONTIER WARFARE
OF NEW ENGLAND
1689-1713**

Dates show the year of an attack

SCALE OF MILES

0   10   20   30   40

BORMAY & CO., N.Y.

72° 71°

party of Mohawk sachems who attracted much attention.[1] The more ambitious expedition to Canada was allowed to drop for the present, but one substantial result of these appeals was the Port Royal expedition of 1710, of which Nicholson himself was commander-in-chief, with Vetch as adjutant-general. Four regiments of militia were furnished by New England, and the English government contributed a few men-of-war with a regiment of marines. The French governor at Port Royal was too weak to resist so strong a force, and a week after the arrival of the fleet he was obliged to surrender. Acadia thereupon became the British province of Nova Scotia and Port Royal became Annapolis Royal.[2]

After the capture of Port Royal, Nicholson returned to England to urge once more the larger enterprise against Canada. During the summer of 1710 the ministry of Godolphin and Marlborough, which, though not distinctly partisan, had finally allied itself closely with the Whigs, was overthrown and a new Tory ministry came into office, of which the leading members were Robert Harley, soon after created Earl of Oxford, and Henry St. John, who was also soon raised to the peerage as Viscount Bolingbroke. These men represented the reaction

[1] Schuyler, *Colonial New York*, II., 32-39.
[2] Nicholson, *Journal*, in Nova Scotia Hist. Soc., *Collections*, I., 59-104; Penhallow, *Wars of New England*, 57-62; N. Y. *Docs. Rel. to Col. Hist.*, IX., 853.

against the continental war policy of their predecessors, and they soon set themselves to secure peace with France. On the other hand, the idea of the conquest of Canada appealed strongly to St. John, who wrote of the plan, "It is my favorite project, which I have been driving on ever since I came last into business, what will be an immense and lasting advantage to our country, if it succeeds, and what if it fails, will perhaps be particularly prejudicial to me."[1]

A new campaign was therefore planned. Again, as in 1709, it was proposed to undertake simultaneous movements by sea from Boston against Quebec and by land from Albany against Montreal. The attack on Quebec was to be made by a British fleet carrying seven regiments of regular troops, and an additional force to be raised in New England. The land expedition was to consist of a few regulars, militia from Connecticut and the middle colonies, and Iroquois Indians, all under the command of General Nicholson.

The desire of the government to keep the expedition as secret as possible left the colonists only a scant allowance of time to make their contributions in men and supplies; but they seem, on the whole, to have given cordial and effective support.

---

[1] Stanhope, *England, 1701–1713*, pp. 424–427, 438–441, 469–473; St. John to Hunter, February 6, 1711, quoted in Palfrey, *New England*, IV., 280; cf. Bolingbroke, *Letters and Correspondence*, I., 232, 252.

A conference of governors was held at New London to discuss the necessary arrangements, and even Pennsylvania consented to make a contribution in money.[1] After some discussion the leading Quakers decided that they might "give the Queen money, notwithstanding any use she might put it to, *that* being not our part, but hers."[2] In Boston there was some friction between the royal officers and the citizens, but the general court seems to have done all that could reasonably have been expected. In New York there was another diplomatic contest between Peter Schuyler and the able French agent Joncaire, which resulted in securing the co-operation of eight hundred Iroquois for the attack on Montreal.[3]

Once more the colonists were doomed to disappointment, and the responsibility for the failure must rest mainly with the British naval and military commanders. The admiral of the fleet, Sir Hovenden Walker seems to have been faint-hearted as well as incompetent. The commander of the military forces, the notorious "Jack Hill," a brother of the queen's favorite, Mrs. Masham, had been rapidly promoted in the face of Marlborough's protests and had never shown capacity for important military command.[4] The fleet entered the St.

[1] *N. Y. Docs. Rel. to Col. Hist.*, V., 257–261.

[2] *Penn-Logan Correspondence*, II., 436.

[3] *N. Y. Docs. Rel. to Col. Hist.*, V., 252.

[4] Coxe, *Marlborough*, V., 127; Bolingbroke, *Letters and Correspondence*, I., 94.

Lawrence in August, 1711, but never reached Quebec: through a serious blunder, for which Walker was at least partially responsible, several transports were wrecked in the river with a loss of several hundred soldiers. There still remained a force decidedly superior to any that Vaudreuil could muster at Quebec, but neither Walker nor Hill had any heart for the undertaking, and after taking the advice of a council of war they determined to retreat. The failure of the Quebec movement required the abandonment of the New York enterprise also, greatly to the disgust of its commander.

Few episodes in English colonial history are more humiliating than the failure of this Quebec expedition; and in New England, especially, there was sharp criticism of the management, "some imputing it to cowardice, but most to treachery." An attempt was also made to throw the blame upon the Massachusetts government and people for lack of proper support, but the charge was effectively answered by Dummer, the Massachusetts agent in London, in his *Letter to a Noble Lord.*[1]

Notwithstanding their disappointment, the colonists urged upon the home government a new attempt upon Canada, but the Tory ministers were deep in the negotiations for peace, and in 1712 secured a general suspension of hostilities. After a long and exhausting war both parties were

[1] Penhallow, *Wars of New England*, 70–74; Dummer, *Letter to a Noble Lord.*

ready for concessions, and in 1713 they agreed to the peace of Utrecht. The Spanish succession was settled by a compromise which was reluctantly and after some delay accepted by the Austrians; the establishment of the Bourbon dynasty in Spain and its colonial dependencies was recognized, but the union of the French and Spanish crowns was carefully guarded against. Nevertheless, the tendency of the two related houses to act together proved more than once an important factor in the subsequent history both of Europe and America.[1]

Of great significance for America are the provisions of the peace of Utrecht which mark the advance of England as a maritime power. Her position in the Mediterranean was strengthened by the acquisition of Port Mahon, in Minorca, and the fortress of Gibraltar, captured in 1704. Her interest in the Spanish trade was recognized by the *Asiento* clause, which gave to English merchants for thirty years the exclusive privilege of carrying on the African slave-trade with the Spanish-American colonies. In the West Indies the net result was comparatively small. St. Christopher became a wholly English possession, but the French retained their chief islands, which continued to be important stations for French privateers.[2]

---

[1] Palfrey, *New England*, IV., 285; Treaty with France, Art. vi., in Chalmers, *Collections*, I., 340–386.

[2] Treaty with Spain, Arts. x., xi, xii., *ibid.*, II., 40-107; treaty with France, Art. xii., *ibid.*, I., 340–386.

The North American settlement brought serious disappointment to both parties. Louis XIV. was reluctant to give up Acadia and offered instead various concessions elsewhere; but he was finally forced to yield, although an opening was left for future controversy by the statement that the province was ceded "with its ancient limits." With Acadia, England also established her claim to the Hudson Bay country and Newfoundland, though with certain reservations in the interests of the French fisheries. The old claim that the Iroquois were subjects of the king of England was now formally recognized by the French, though their efforts to bring the confederates under French influence were by no means finally abandoned.[1]

For the New-Englanders the conquest of Canada had seemed one of the desirable and possible results of the war. Dummer, the Massachusetts agent, in his *Letter to a Noble Lord*, insisted that the English colonies could never be at ease while the French remained master of Canada. Writing in 1712, after the failure of Walker's expedition, he urged that Canada as well as Acadia be retained. Doubtless a minister of the type of Pitt, supported by a general like Wolfe, would have anticipated by half a century the English conquest of Canada. A serious defect in the settlement from the English point of view was the retention of Cape Breton Island by

[1] Treaty with France, Arts. x.-xv., in Chalmers, *Collections*, I., 340-386.

the French. The English had proposed a joint occupation of the island, refusing to either party the right to fortify it; but the French rejected this proposal, and in their hands Louisbourg became a formidable base for hostile operations against New England.[1]

The cessation of war between France and England enabled the New-Englanders to come to terms with the eastern Indians. In July, 1713, Governor Dudley held a conference at Portsmouth with representatives of various tribes and a treaty of peace was agreed to. The Indians acknowledged the sovereignty of the queen, promised to respect the rights of the colonists to the territory occupied by them, and to seek redress for future wrongs by peaceful methods. In spite of this solemn treaty another border war broke out a few years later, but for the time being the return of peace encouraged the English to extend their settlements.[2]

The year of the general peace was marked also by the end of a serious Indian disturbance in North Carolina, the so-called Tuscarora war, which required the co-operation of the neighboring colonies and for a time caused some uneasiness so far north as New York. The coming of a new Swiss colony into North Carolina had excited the jealousy of this strong tribe of Indians, and the murder of the provincial surveyor, John Lawson, was followed

---

[1] Bolingbroke, *Letters and Correspondence*, II., 286; Dummer, *Letter to a Noble Lord;* Kingsford, *Canada*, II., 481.

[2] Penhallow, *Wars of New England*, 77–84.

by a general uprising in September, 1711, when some two hundred frontier settlers were massacred. The governments of Virginia and South Carolina were asked for assistance, and South Carolina promptly sent Colonel Barnwell into the neighboring colony. In midwinter of 1712, Barnwell defeated the Tuscaroras in a severe engagement near the Neuse River and compelled them to make peace, but this treaty was soon broken and the war continued. In 1713 another South Carolina force, under the command of Colonel James Moore, son of the man who had led the expedition against St. Augustine, captured the Indian fortress with some eight hundred prisoners. The Tuscaroras were now so demoralized that most of them abandoned the province altogether.[1]

The Five Nations considered themselves bound by kinship to the Tuscaroras, and there was some anxiety in New York lest they might combine forces against the English, especially as the French were then suggesting to the Iroquois doubts as to the sincerity of English friendship. This danger was, however, averted. After their final defeat the Tuscaroras took refuge with the Five Nations, becoming the sixth tribe of the confederacy; and with some hesitation this arrangement was finally accepted by the English governor of New York.[2]

[1] N. C. Col. Records, I., 810 et seq.; McCrady, South Carolina under Proprietary Government, 496–503, 525.

[2] Schuyler, Colonial New York, II., 50–53; N. Y. Docs. Rel. to Col. Hist., V., 343, 387.

For North America as a whole the peace of Utrecht marks, as no previous treaty with France had done, a real advance in the prestige of England. It was true that the French raids had retarded the spread of English settlements and that much damage had been done to New England trade and fisheries. Yet these losses were soon repaired and the net result of French military and diplomatic effort was a serious though not a decisive defeat.

CHAPTER XI

IMPERIAL POLICY AND ADMINISTRATION

(1714-1742)

THE long wars of William and Anne were succeeded by a quarter-century of comparative peace. In spite of Jacobite conspiracies the Act of Settlement was carried out in 1714, and the succession of George I. marked the victory of parliamentary authority over the hereditary rights of the Stuart line. Essentially foreign in their education, tastes, and interests, the first two Georges depended for their administration of English affairs upon the Whig chiefs by whose support the dynasty had been established. Under these conditions the system of party and parliamentary administration was, in course of time, so strongly founded that it finally prevailed even against the aggressively personal policy of George III.

The first years of the Whig domination were occupied with struggles for headship in the party; but they soon ended in the supremacy of Sir Robert Walpole, who became prime-minister in 1721, and held the position until 1742. Though he was then forced to resign by a combination of Tories with dissatisfied Whigs, most of the ministers of the next two decades were men who had been trained in his school. Walpole was a strong though coarse-grained country gentleman and a liberal - minded statesman. He shared the prevailing low standards of public and private morality, and his political power was maintained in part by various forms of parliamentary corruption. His primary policy was to establish securely under Whig auspices the new Protestant succession and to develop the commerce and manufactures of his country. He sought to accomplish these ends by preserving peace abroad, by avoiding extreme measures of any kind which might provoke dangerous antagonism to the existing government, and by some relaxation of commercial restrictions.

Walpole's part in the shaping of British colonial policy has never been thoroughly examined. He has been credited with liberal views and particularly with having opposed a proposal for taxing the colonies. During his administration, parliament enacted some laws in the interest of colonial trade; but, on the other hand, one of the harshest legislative measures of the period, the Molasses Act of 1733, which, if enforced, would have seriously injured the trade of the northern colonies, was strongly supported by his followers and seems to have been distinctly an administration measure. His influence was apparently, in the main, the negative one of discouraging over-aggressive schemes of colonial control.[1]

The system of colonial administration remained essentially unchanged throughout the Walpole era, so that the direct charge of colonial interests was, as before, mainly in the hands of the secretary of state for the southern department and the Board of Trade. Until 1724 no one man held the secretaryship long enough to exert much influence for good or ill upon colonial politics. In that year, however, the southern department was given to the Duke of Newcastle, who retained it during the remainder of Walpole's ministry and for six years longer, in all a period of twenty-four years.

Newcastle was conspicuous even among his contemporaries for his activity in the lower forms of politics, particularly for his prostitution of the patronage to partisan ends. He was also notoriously inefficient. One of his contemporaries said of him that he did "nothing in the same hurry and agitation as if he did everything." According to another *bon-mot* attributed to one of his colleagues, he was always losing " half an hour in the morning, which he is running after the rest of the day without being able to overtake it." He neglected the colonial correspondence, and his chief interest in American affairs, as in home politics, seemed to be the spoils of office. From a politician of this type

[1] *Annual Register*, 1765, p. 25; Cobbett, *Parliamentary History*, VIII., passim; Coxe, *Sir R. Walpole*, I., 163.

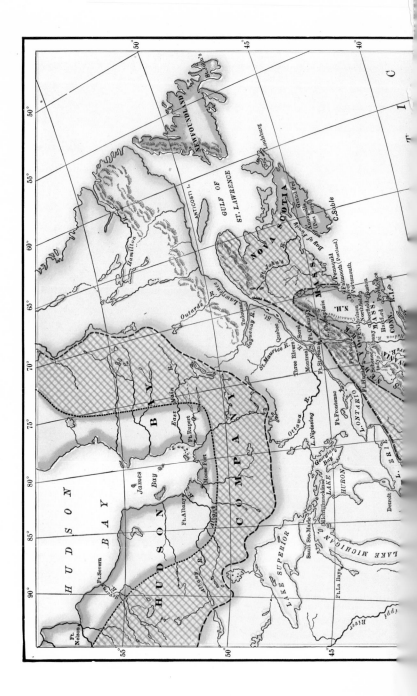

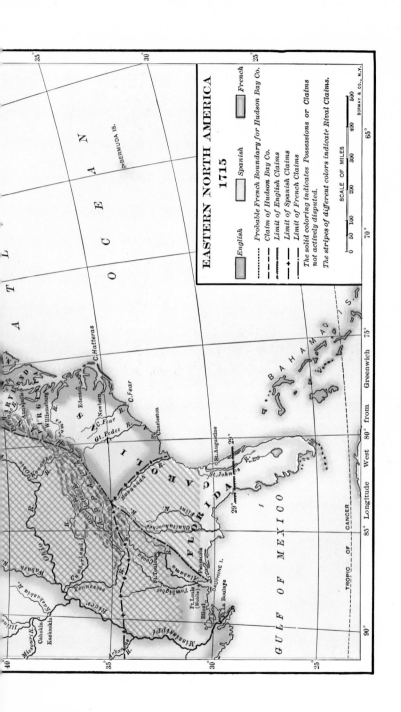

EASTERN NORTH AMERICA
1715

English ▭ Spanish ▭ French ▭

· · · · · · Probable French Boundary for Hudson Bay Co.
– – – – – Claim of Hudson Bay Co.
———— Limit of English Claims
—+—+— Limit of Spanish Claims
—+—+— Limit of French Claims

The solid coloring indicates Possessions or Claims
not actively disputed.
The stripes of different colors indicate Rival Claims.

SCALE OF MILES
0 50 100   200   300   400   500

BORMAY & CO., N.Y.

no constructive policy could reasonably be expected.[1]

The personnel of the Board of Trade was hardly of a kind to supply the deficiencies of the secretary. In 1714 the board was completely changed and a number of comparatively obscure men appointed. During the next thirty years about thirty men in all were appointed and the average tenure was fairly long; four members held office for over twenty years. With one exception, none of the men who saw any considerable service in the board under Walpole could be rated as even a respectable politician of the second class. That exception was Colonel Martin Bladen, a veteran of the War of the Spanish Succession, who entered Parliament as a Whig in 1715, was appointed to the board in 1717, and served continuously until his death in 1746. He was one of the most active and influential members of the board, and he also spoke frequently in the House of Commons, where he steadily supported Walpole. He came to be regarded as an expert on commercial and colonial affairs, and as a member of the Board of Trade was said to have gone by the name of "Trade" while his colleagues were called the "Board."[2]

According to Horace Walpole, the Board of Trade

[1] Horace Walpole, *Memoirs*, I., 162–166, 396; Coxe, *Sir R. Walpole*, I., 192, 327–330; Mahon, *England, 1713–1783*, II., 154.
[2] *N. Y. Docs. Rel. to Col. Hist.*, III., xvi., xvii.; *Dict. of National Biography*, art. Bladen.

in his father's time had become almost a "sine cure"; but the colonial papers of the twenties and thirties indicate that the board held frequent meetings and transacted a considerable amount of business. In the course of a parliamentary debate, General Oglethorpe said of its members that they were "as exact and diligent in all the matters which fall under their province as any board in England," and that it was "one of the most useful boards we have." [1]

The board maintained a fairly regular correspondence with colonial governors, inquired into colonial conditions, and made some elaborate reports and recommendations, notably in 1721 and 1732. Though many of these recommendations were disregarded, others were accepted, and much of the colonial legislation of the period was in accordance with their advice. In their efforts to impose their policies upon the colonial assemblies, they were frequently defeated; but this was due, partly at least, to a division of authority which left them almost no power of final action. Ultimate decisions regarding appointments and other subjects were in the hands of the Privy Council, acting usually on the advice of its own "Committee for Plantation Affairs." An energetic secretary of state acting in full harmony with the members of the board would probably have moulded the colonial policy of the

[1] Horace Walpole, *Memoirs*, I., 396; Cobbett, *Parliamentary History*, VIII., 921.

ministry, but these conditions were never realized
during the Newcastle régime. Generally speaking,
the lack of co-operation between the ministry and
the Board of Trade showed itself not in the adoption by the former of a positive programme at variance with that of the board, but in failure to act
upon its recommendations.[1]

Other administrative boards continued to take a
considerable part in questions of colonial policy.
Thus the admiralty was interested in fostering the
production of naval stores in America, and one of
its leading members, Sir Charles Wager, was regarded as an expert in American affairs. Horace
Walpole the elder, a brother of Sir Robert, and a
diplomatist of some reputation, held the profitable
office of auditor-general of the colonial revenues.
He took part in the parliamentary proceedings of
1731-1733 which ended in the passage of the Molasses Act, and in 1735 he urged upon his brother a
closer attention to colonial affairs.[2]

Horace Walpole particularly commended "one
Coram, the honestest, the most disinterested, and
the most knowing person about the plantations I
ever talked with." Coram, after many years residence in Massachusetts, finally settled in London.
Having a special interest in colonial trade and ship-

[1] N. Y. Docs. Rel. to Col. Hist., V., VI., passim; N. C. Col.
Records, III., IV., passim; cf. Egerton, Short Hist. of Col.
Policy, 140.

[2] Coxe, Sir R. Walpole, III., 243; Cobbett, Parliamentary
History, VIII., 992-1002.

ping, he advocated the bounty on naval stores in
1704; but he also favored the policy of restricting
colonial manufactures. He was one of the Georgia
trustees, and was also interested in the settlement
of Nova Scotia. Doubtless, Coram was only one
among a number of more obscure personages who
contributed each his small share to the shaping of
British official opinion.[1]

A fair test of a colonial administration is its exercise of the appointing power. Newcastle kept the
patronage largely in his own hands, and numerous
letters among the colonial papers show that their
writers looked to him as the dispenser of desirable
offices. Even before his time the Board of Trade
complained of not being consulted with regard to
appointments. Sinecure positions continued to be
a serious evil in colonial administration; during the
first half of the eighteenth century the important
government of Virginia was generally held by a
non-resident governor, while the actual work of
administration was performed by a lieutenant-governor. The commercial conception of public patronage may be illustrated by the case of Lord Delaware,
who, having been appointed governor of New York
in 1737, was asked three years later to resign in
favor of Lieutenant-Governor Clarke, and was promised one thousand guineas, to be paid when the new
appointment had actually been made. A new gov-

[1] *Dict. of National Biography*, art. Coram; *N. J. Docs. Rel. to
Col. Hist.*, V., 308–314.

ernor was appointed, but Clarke's application was
unsuccessful.[1]

Not all appointments, however, were unfit. There
were bad governors like Cosby in New York, but
he was probably no worse than Lord Cornbury, his
predecessor, in Queen Anne's reign. The Newcastle régime must, on the other hand, be credited
with such good appointments as those of Morris in
New Jersey and Shirley in Massachusetts. Though
disposed to stand for the royal prerogative, both
these governors were men of public spirit. Nor
was the home government wholly irresponsible in
the making of removals. In Massachusetts, it
showed its sensitiveness to local sentiment on the
death of one governor who had made himself obnoxious to the colonists, by appointing as his successor the agent who had been sent to act against
him. Probably the home government was not
always reasonably firm in its support of men whose
unpopularity arose largely from their vigorous assertion of imperial authority.

A governor once appointed was supposed to be
controlled by his instructions. During the Newcastle period there was no marked change in the
general instructions issued to the governor on his
appointment, though there were a few additions.
Some governors were criticised for failing to make
regular reports to the secretary of state and the

[1] Chalmers, *Revolt*, II., 35; *N. C. Col. Records*, III., passim,
esp. 80; *N. Y. Docs. Rel. to Col. Hist.* VI., 163.

Board of Trade; but in other instances a voluminous correspondence was kept up, enough to give the
home government a lively picture of provincial conditions, especially on the political side, though the
board seems not always to have had full confidence
in the accuracy of the returns.   The adverse criticism which the board passed upon colonial officials
was sometimes reciprocated.   In October, 1736, a
North Carolina governor wrote that he had had no
communication from the board since the previous
December, and, with the exception of a short note
then, nothing for over a year.   A similar complaint
was made by Governor Clinton, of New York, a few
years later.[1]

Even in this era of "salutary neglect," colonial
legislation was scrutinized with some care, though
there was no such wholesale disallowance of provincial statutes as had taken place during the reigns of
William and Anne.   This may have been due partly
to lack of energy in the Board of Trade, but it is
explained partly also by the fact that the assemblies had adjusted themselves to a sort of *modus
vivendi* in which some demands of the crown were
acquiesced in and others avoided by indirect methods.   Governors also were now more definitely instructed with regard to legislation.   In the new
royal government of North Carolina, out of the first
two hundred and seventy-one acts approved by the

[1] *N. C. Col. Records*, III., IV., passim, esp. IV., 173, 242;
N. Y. Docs. Rel. to Col. Hist., V., VI., passim, esp. VI., 270.

governors, only eight were disallowed by the crown, and even in Massachusetts the percentage of royal vetoes was small. In Massachusetts the charter provision that acts not disallowed within three years after presentation to the crown should remain laws until repealed by the provincial assembly, was avoided by postponing presentation. It was a common practice of the Board of Trade to order colonial acts "to lie by probationary," awaiting examination by legal counsel or objections from any other quarter. Some acts which were not disallowed were adversely criticised by the board or its legal counsel, and sometimes the governor was cautioned against the passage of similar acts in the future.[1]

The colonies frequently gave offence by their tariff legislation. Discriminating duties were laid in favor of colonial shipping as against that of Great Britain, and duties on slaves and on goods imported from England were also frequently complained of. Governors were forbidden to pass acts of this kind without at least a clause suspending execution until approved by the crown; and several such acts were disallowed Again, the home government forbade the passage of private acts without the suspending clause, and for several years the Massachusetts general court gave up such legislation altogether.[2]

[1] Raper, *North Carolina*, 45, 49, 56; Massachusetts Bay, *Acts and Resolves*, II., passim, esp. 31, 66, 790.

[2] *N. Y. Docs. Rel. to Col. Hist.*, V., 706; Massachusetts Bay. *Acts and Resolves*, II., 69, 128; *N. C. Col. Records,* III., 95, Chalmers, *Revolt*, II., 72–75.

A striking instance of the use of a royal veto to check a strong popular demand was the disallowance of a New York act providing for triennial assemblies. After two long assemblies, lasting ten and nine years respectively, it was felt that more frequent elections were necessary to secure genuine representation. The movement was resisted by Governor Cosby, but in 1737 the triennial act was approved by his successor, Lieutenant-Governor Clarke. An elaborate argument was made in its favor, laying stress upon the practice of annual elections in New England and Pennsylvania; but the Board of Trade, accepting the advice of its special counsel, Mr. Fane, recommended the disallowance of the act and an order in council was issued accordingly.[1]

The home government could not always impose its wishes upon the colonial assemblies. Royal instructions did not prevent temporary grants to governors or extravagant issues of paper money. As a solution of this problem, and also in order to control the legislation of the chartered colonies which was not subject to veto, the House of Lords proposed that all colonial laws should be sent to the Board of Trade, and that except in case of urgency none should take effect until approved by the king in council. This drastic measure, however, was not adopted.[2]

[1] *Doc. Hist. of N. Y.*, IV., 243 et seq.
[2] *Talcott Papers*, I., 296–298.

Generally speaking, the Whig ministries accepted the mercantilist colonial theories, and governors were carefully instructed to enforce the navigation acts. Colonial enterprises were jealously watched, and the board continued its efforts to check colonial manufactures by encouraging the production of naval stores. Most English statesmen regarded the southern colonies, and more particularly the sugar islands, as deserving special attention and favor, because their trade was more clearly advantageous to the mother-country. In case of conflict, the interests of the northern colonies were likely to be sacrificed to those of the West Indies.

These views were embodied in a considerable number of acts of Parliament dealing with American affairs. The most vital phase of English foreign relations was the antagonism with Spain, arising from the efforts of enterprising English merchants to secure for themselves more of the Spanish-American trade than they could fairly claim under existing treaties. This subject was almost constantly discussed in Parliament, and a more aggressive policy was urged upon the ministry, until in 1739 it was reluctantly forced into war with Spain. These conditions, of course, made it easier for colonial officials to gain the attention of Parliament.[1]

[1] Mahon, *England, 1713–1783*, I.–III., passim; Coxe, *Sir R. Walpole*, passim; Cobbett, *Parliamentary History*, VII., VIII., passim.

In 1721 a recommendation of the Board of
Trade in favor of encouraging the production of
naval stores was indorsed in the king's speech to
Parliament and a new bounty act was passed.
Other acts of this year placed furs and copper on
the list of enumerated articles, but, on the other
hand, removed all export duties on British manufactures, with a few exceptions.   In 1727 Parliament
established the right of the Pennsylvanians to import their salt directly from Europe, as the New-Englanders were already allowed to do, and a few years
later the same privilege was secured to New York.[1]

With the year 1730 begins a period of considerable parliamentary activity in colonial affairs.
Readiness to stimulate desirable lines of trade was
shown by allowing the planters, first of South Carolina and then of Georgia, to send their rice, one of
the enumerated articles, directly to European countries south of Cape Finisterre.   A few years later a
similar concession was made to the sugar planters
of the West Indies.   Generally speaking, however,
the spirit of British legislation during the next two
decades was restrictive.   In 1732 Parliament prohibited the intercolonial trade in hats, and otherwise
restricted their manufacture in America.   A similar
policy with regard to iron manufactures had already
been urged, but it was not carried out until the

---

[1] *N. Y. Docs. Rel. to Col. Hist.*, V., 628; Cobbett, *Parliamentary History*, VII., 913–916; 8 George I., chaps. xii., xv., xviii.;
13 George I., chap. v.; 3 George II., chap. xii.

act of 1750 prohibiting the manufacture of that metal beyond the stage of pig or bar iron.[1]

The most important commercial regulation of this period was the Molasses Act, which, after two years of discussion in Parliament, became law in 1733. Its chief importance consists not in its actual economic effects, but in the light which it throws on colonial policy, and in the constitutional questions which were raised while the bill was under discussion. This act, imposing prohibitory duties on molasses, sugar, and rum imported into the continental colonies from the West Indian colonies of other powers than England, was intended to revive the declining trade of the British West Indian planters by compelling the continental colonies to buy of them instead of encouraging their French and Dutch competitors. Its enforcement would have crippled the commerce of the northern colonies, and its passage in the face of their protests shows clearly the relative importance of the West Indies from the official point of view. Sir John Barnard, one of Walpole's leading antagonists in the House of Commons, and General Oglethorpe, both argued ably but unsuccessfully against this sacrifice of continental interests to those of the islands.[2]

Three other acts may be mentioned as marking

[1] 3 George II., chap. xxviii.; 8 George II., chap. xix.; 12 George II., chap. xxx.; see below, chap. xvii.
[2] 6 George II., chap. xiii.; Cobbett, *Parliamentary History*, VIII., 856–1200, passim., 1261–1266; see Howard, *Preliminaries of the Revolution* (*Am. Nation*, VIII.), chap. vi.

some real advance in imperial control. In 1732 Parliament determined to intervene in the judicial administration of the colonies for the protection of British merchants who had complained of legal obstacles in the collection of debts due them in America. It was provided that debts due to residents in Great Britain or to the crown might be proved by testimony taken in England, and that colonial real estate should be "chargeable with all just debts" as "real estates are by the law of England." In 1741 the Land Bank of Massachusetts was summarily dealt with by applying to the colonies the provisions of a previous statute dealing with similar speculative companies. Finally, in 1751, Parliament undertook to check the paper-money craze in New England by prohibiting the issue of legal-tender bills. The act which destroyed the Land Bank was retroactive and therefore peculiarly arbitrary. Mr. Andrew McF. Davis, the leading authority on this subject, has accepted as "probably true" the opinion of John Adams that this act was more influential than the Stamp Act in the development of opposition to the supremacy of Parliament among the people of Massachusetts. Franklin also thought that the hostility of the home government to colonial currency experiments was a large factor in the growth of colonial discontent.[1]

[1] 5 George II., chap. vii.; 14 George II., chap. xxxvii.; Davis, *Currency and Banking in Mass. Bay*, II., chaps. vii.–xii.; Franklin, *Works* (Bigelow's ed.) III., 418.

Some of the more aggressive officials of the Georgian period continued to cherish projects of direct
royal government in all of the colonies, and the
union of all under one general governor to whom
the governors of particular colonies should be subordinate. Little, however, was accomplished in the
realization of these ideals.

At the beginning of this period one backward
step was taken. Maryland, which had been ad-
ministered since 1692 by royal governors, was in
1715 re-established as a proprietary province. The
Catholicism of the proprietor had been one of the
reasons urged for the institution of royal government, and now the succession of a Protestant heir
was considered to justify the restoration of full
proprietary rights. The negotiations for the surrender of Pennsylvania had also, as has already
been observed, come to nothing. Thus the two
proprietorships which had been most seriously
threatened during the early years of William III.
survived to the close of the colonial era.[1]

One decided advantage was gained, however, by
the abolition of proprietary government in the
Carolinas, largely on the initiative of the colonists
themselves. Both of the Carolina governments had
long been under fire for lax administration of the
navigation laws and for various other irregularities.
The intolerance of the high-church party, supported

[1] Steiner, in Am. Hist. Assoc., *Annual Report*, 1899, I., 231
et seq.

by the proprietors, helped to bring on a civil war in North Carolina, while in the southern province it provoked an appeal by the colonists to the crown. In the latter case the prestige of the proprietors was weakened by the queen's intervention on behalf of the colonists, and the annulling of the charter was seriously considered.[1]

The exposed position of these frontier colonies also showed the need of a stronger government. This need was illustrated by the struggles of South Carolina with the French and Spaniards, and of North Carolina with the Tuscarora Indians; and it was still further emphasized two years after the peace of Utrecht by the Yemassee war. The Yemassee Indians, who were settled in the southern part of South Carolina, were led, partly by unfriendly treatment at the hands of English traders and partly by the instigation of the Spaniards, to take up arms against the province. The invasion was finally repelled by the colonists themselves, with some help from Virginia and North Carolina; but several hundred settlers were massacred, and the proprietors gave no substantial protection. Exasperated by the negligence of the proprie ors, the colonists in 1716 presented through their agent a memorial asking the intervention of the crown.

Soon afterwards the proprietors gave great offence to the colonists by vetoing a number of popular laws which had been enacted by the assembly.

[1] See above, p. 60

The most important was one changing the method
of election for the members of the assembly, so
that instead of being chosen altogether at Charleston they should be elected by the voters in the
various districts of the province. This veto seemed
to be intended to secure the continued domination
of a little group of politicians in Charleston, and led
finally to armed resistance. In 1719 the colonists
assembled in arms and called upon their governor,
Robert Johnson, to renounce the proprietors and
assume the government in the name of the crown.
This Johnson loyally refused to do. He was, therefore, set aside and Moore elected governor in his
place, with the understanding that he was to hold
office for the king.[1]

The home government accepted the results of
this revolution by appointing Francis Nicholson as
the governor of South Carolina, and the attorney-
general was ordered to proceed against the charter.
No such legal steps were actually taken, however,
and the royal government of South Carolina remained for ten years on a purely provisional basis.
The proprietors tried at first to recover their control of the government; failing in this attempt, they
began negotiations for the surrender of their proprietary rights as a whole. In 1729 these negotiations were consummated by an act of Parliament,
and royal governments were then permanently es-

[1] *Proceedings of the People of South Carolina*, in Carroll, *Collections*, II., 141–192; *N. C. Col. Records*, II., 224–234.

tablished in both provinces. Three years after this event the crown granted a charter for the part of this territory lying between the Savannah and Altamaha rivers to the Georgia trustees. The government of the new province was delegated for twenty years to a private corporation, but it was then to revert to the crown.[1]

From time to time the general plan of abolishing all the chartered governments was revived. In 1715 a bill for the "better regulation of Charter and Proprietary Governments" passed the first and second readings in the House of Commons; and in 1721 the Board of Trade urged that all proprietary governments be abolished. To meet attacks of this kind, Jeremiah Dummer, agent in England for the colony of Massachusetts, wrote his famous *Defence of the New England Charters*, addressing it to Newcastle's immediate predecessor, Lord Carteret. He defended the colonists effectively against the common charges brought against them, such as lack of zeal in imperial defence, arbitrary government, violation of the navigation acts, and the enactment of laws at variance with those of Great Britain. He asserted strongly the loyalty of the colonists to the mother-country, denied any tendency towards independence, and insisted that the prosperity of the mother-country was bound up with that of the colonies. He held that the pros-

[1] McCrady, *South Carolina under Proprietary Government*, chaps. xxiii.–xxx.; 2 George, II., chap. xxxiv.

perity of the latter was founded on the liberal provisions of the early charters, which could not,
therefore, be withdrawn without serious injury to imperial interests. The power of Parliament to resume
the charters was not denied; but, he said, "the question here is not about *power* but *right; and shall not
the supreme legislature of all the nation do right ?*"

During the next quarter-century schemes for the
reorganization of the colonial governments were
frequently proposed; in 1723 Rhode Island and
Connecticut were asked to submit to union with
the royal province of New Hampshire; and in 1744
Governor Clinton of New York referred to a printed
proposal which he had seen for a general governor
over all the continental colonies.[1]

In the same letter Governor Clinton referred to
a closely related proposal for colonial taxation.
The possibility of taxation by Parliament for the
support of colonial administration was discussed at
intervals throughout the eighteenth century. In
an essay submitted by Bladen to Lord Townshend
in 1726, a stamp duty was suggested as a means by
which Parliament might raise a revenue in the
colonies, and this was the particular form of tax
referred to by Clinton in 1744. Clinton declared
the colonists were "quite strangers to any duty,
but such as they raise themselves," and that the

[1] Dummer, *Defence of the New England Charters;* Kellogg, *Am.
Colonial Charter*, in Am. Hist. Assoc., *Report*, 1903, I., 308 et
seq.; *N. Y. Docs. Rel. to Col. Hist.*, V., 627, VI., 268.

proposed tax "might prove a dangerous consequence to His Majesty's interests."[1]

The most important parliamentary discussion of taxation and representation took place in the debate on the Molasses Act in 1733, with special reference to a Rhode Island petition against the bill. Sir William Yonge, in arguing against receiving the petition, objected to a clause declaring the bill "prejudicial to their charter," "as if this House had not a power to tax them, or to make any laws for the regulating of the affairs of their colony." Another speaker was sure that "they can have no such charter" which "debars this House from taxing them as well as any other subject of this nation." Sir John Barnard, speaking for the petitioners, argued that the colonists had a special claim to be heard by petition, because "the people of every part of Great Britain have a representative in this House who is to take care of their particular interest, as well as of the general interest of the nation . . . but the people who are the petitioners . . . have no particular representatives in this House; and, therefore, they have no other way of applying or of offering their reasons to this, but in the way of being heard at the bar of the House by their agent here in England." As against this view of Barnard, however, another member, Mr. Conduit, set forth the orthodox theory of virtual representation,

[1] *N. C. Col. Records*, II., 635; Bassett, *Writings of William Byrd*, 365; Chalmers, *Revolt*, II., 138.

that as the colonies were "all a part of the people
of Great Britain they are generally represented in
this House as well as the rest of the people are." [1]

In the *Annual Register* in 1765, for which Ed-
mund Burke was then writing, the statement is
made that a scheme for taxing the colonies was
proposed to Walpole and rejected by him, with the
remark that he would leave that "to some of my
successors who may have more courage than I
have." In his opinion, the royal exchequer would
gain more indirectly by the development of colonial
commerce, which would be "taxing them more
agreeably to their own constitution and to ours." [2]

It has been customary to speak of this period of
British colonial policy as one of "salutary neglect,"
but this, like some other attractive generalizations,
cannot be accepted without many qualifications.
Though the trade laws were less vigorously enforced
than they were in later years, and though the proposal of taxation by Parliament was never carried
out, the colonists were by no means left to themselves. Popular legislation was repeatedly defeated
by the royal veto, and Parliament exerted its authority over the colonies even in the face of strong
resistance. Sometimes, as in the suppression of the
Massachusetts Land Bank, these assertions of parliamentary authority left a smouldering fire of discontent to trouble the statesmen of a later time.

[1] Cobbett, *Parliamentary History*, VIII., 1261–1266.
[2] *Annual Register*, 1765, p. 25.

It is not easy to determine with precision what in this period were the theories and feelings of the colonists regarding the authority of the home government. If the views of aggressive imperialists had been carried out, if Parliament had remodelled the colonial governments and levied a stamp tax, radical theories like those of Samuel Adams and Thomas Jefferson would probably have come earlier to light. There were, indeed, royal officials under George II., as under Queen Anne, who thought the colonial assemblies were moving clearly towards independence. Attorney-General Bradley of New York set forth this theory at length in 1729, pointing out the difficulty of suppressing a revolt if the colonists were once united; and Dummer thought it necessary to discuss the question in his *Defence of the New England Charters.*[1]

Nevertheless, the colonists generally were loyal to the king and did not question the supremacy of Parliament. Dummer, in his argument against legislative resumption of the charters, insisted that the colonists were unreservedly loyal and would accept a decision by Parliament as final, even if it abolished their chartered privileges. He admitted that "the legislative power is absolute and unaccountable, and King, Lords, and Commons may do what they please." Doubtless, as Clinton intimated, there was an underlying assumption that

[1] *N. Y. Docs. Rel. to Col. Hist.*, V., 901; cf. Anderson, *Church of England in the Cols.*, III., 351.

taxation by Parliament would be a violation of
colonial rights, but the colonists had not yet been
obliged to define with precision their theories of
constitutional limitations.[1]

[1] Dummer, *Defence of the New England Charters;* cf. Egerton,
Short Hist. of Col. Policy, 143; Hutchinson, *Hist. of Mass. Bay*
(ed. of 1795), II., 319.

CHAPTER XII

PROVINCIAL POLITICS

(1714–1740)

IN spite of the prevalence of similar political ideas among the colonies, there was much of mutual jealousy and antagonism due in part to boundary controversies. In 1702 none of the colonies had its boundaries accurately marked; and in every case except that of New Jersey the disputed lands were of considerable importance for the future development of the colony. Massachusetts had boundary disputes with Rhode Island and Connecticut on the south, and New York on the west; while she could not agree with New Hampshire either regarding the northern limits of the old Bay Colony or the western boundary of Maine. The disputes with New York and New Hampshire were important because of the large area involved; and the comparatively small strips at issue with Rhode Island and Connecticut related to settled townships. Connecticut had also a dispute with Rhode Island on the east and an unsurveyed line on the west which was still to cause some trouble with New York.[1]

New York had a comparatively small controversy to adjust with New Jersey and a more important one with Pennsylvania as to the whole northern line of Penn's charter. The latter issue did not, however, become serious during the first half of the century because of the slow movement of settlers into that territory. On the south, Penn and his heirs had a much more difficult question to settle. The Baltimores continued to claim the "lower counties" on the Delaware, and the southern line of Pennsylvania was still undetermined when in the second quarter of the eighteenth century immigrants began to enter the disputed territory. Of all the boundary controversies of the period, this was the most persistent and acrimonious. In the south there were similar boundary disputes which embittered the relations of the two Carolinas with each other and those of North Carolina with Virginia.

Before the middle of the eighteenth century marked progress was made towards the settlement of these disputes. The interior lines of New England were substantially determined, though Massachusetts and New York had not yet come to terms regarding the territory between the Hudson and the Connecticut. In 1750 the Pennsylvania-

[1] Palfrey, *New England*, IV., 356–364, 554–559, 586; *N. Y. Docs. Rel. to Col. Hist.*, VI., 125, 143, 454, 510.

Maryland controversy was passed upon by the lord chancellor in England, though there was still some wrangling about details. A few years earlier, the North Carolina lines were drawn for some distance westward from the coast by agreement with her neighbors to the north and south.[1]

Trade jealousies were another source of friction. Discriminating duties in favor of home shipping were common and sometimes provoked retaliation, as in 1721, when New Hampshire retaliated against a Massachusetts law imposing double duties and light-house fees upon the inhabitants of the former province. There were similar incidents in the middle and southern colonies, and a serious instance of hostile feeling awakened by commercial regulations occurred between Virginia and North Carolina. The latter colony, being poorly supplied with ports, was accustomed to ship tobacco through Virginia; but this practice was prohibited by the Virginia assembly in acts of 1725 and 1726, on the ground that North Carolina tobacco was of an inferior quality. North Carolina complained to the Board of Trade, which recommended the disallowance of both acts.[2]

There was also a considerable intercolonial rivalry in the Indian trade, notably between Virginia and South Carolina and between the latter colony and

[1] Shepherd, *Proprietary Government in Pa.*, chap. vii.; *N. C. Col. Records*, II., viii., 205, IV., viii.

[2] Weeden, *Econ. and Soc. Hist. of New England*, II., 593; Hill, "Colonial Tariffs," in *Quarterly Journal of Economics*, VII., 78; *N. C. Col. Records*, II., 683, III., 196, 210.

Georgia. In both instances serious ill-feeling developed.[1]

Some intercolonial disputes were settled by amicable agreement; but often the intervention of the home government was necessary, and the final award left bad feeling behind on the part of one or both the parties. The difficulty of maintaining cordial relations between neighboring colonies is well illustrated by the experience of two pairs of provinces united for a time by the assignment of a single governor to both governments. New Hampshire and Massachusetts were combined under one governor over forty years, until 1741; when, partly because of the bad feeling between the two provinces, generated by the boundary dispute, this personal union was abandoned and New Hampshire received a separate government. For over thirty years the crown commissioned the same person as governor of New York and New Jersey; but in this case, as in the other, the weaker colony felt that its interests were being sacrificed to those of the stronger, and the practice was given up in 1738. The southern colonies were no more friendly neighbors during much of this period. William Byrd, one of the Virginia commissioners in the boundary dispute, repeatedly expressed his contempt for the North Carolina people; and in 1730 the South Carolina agents in London characterized the same province

---

[1] Smith, *South Carolina*, 212 et seq.; *N. C. Col. Records*, II., 251 et seq.

as the "receptacle of all the vagabouns & runaways of the main land of America, for which reason and for their entertaining Pirates they are justly contemned by their neighbors." [1]

Notwithstanding these unpleasant facts of intercolonial jealousy and strife, the most significant thing in the life of the colonies is the growing similarity of their political usages and aspirations. Leaving the two elective governments out of account, the fundamental fact of American politics in this as in the earlier period was the antagonism between the appointed governor and the elected assembly, between the organized colonists and the agent of external authority. The underlying constitutional issues remained essentially as they were at the close of the seventeenth century, but they sometimes presented themselves in different aspects; and among the colonists themselves there appeared new lines of party cleavage.

Numerous controversies arose regarding the composition and organization of the assembly, in which the lower house sought to secure as much freedom as possible from executive control. Thus in North Carolina the lower house refused for many years to admit members elected from districts which had been created by the governor without the sanction of the assembly. Nevertheless, in this, as in a similar controversy in New Hampshire, the repre-

[1] *N. C. Col. Records*, II., 394–396; Bassett, *Writings of William Byrd*, passim.

sentatives were finally beaten. The attempts to limit the governor's freedom in summoning and dissolving assemblies also continued. Acts providing for triennial elections were passed during this period in South Carolina, New Hampshire, New Jersey, and New York; but the New Jersey and New York acts were disallowed by the crown. The Board of Trade regarded such acts as interfering with the legitimate prerogatives of the crown, and the governor's point of view was probably stated accurately by Governor Montgomerie of New Jersey, when he said that his predecessors "could not have carried on the publick business so quietly and Successfully as they did, if they had been obliged to call a new Assembly every three years." [1]

One of the most important questions of legislative privilege during this period was whether the house of representatives had the right to choose its own speaker independently of the governor. In most of the colonies, as in the mother-country, the presentation of the speaker to the governor was a mere formality; but in Massachusetts and New Hampshire the governors sometimes rejected candidates chosen by the house. The most important contest took place in Massachusetts in 1720, when Governor Shute vetoed the choice of the opposition leader as speaker of the house, on the ground that the charter gave him a negative upon all acts of

[1] Raper, *North Carolina*, 89–92; Greene, *Provincial Governor*, 147, 155–157.

the general court. The home government finally
issued, in 1725, an "explanatory charter" which
decided the point in the governor's favor.[1]

By the beginning of the Hanoverian period the
practice of making temporary grants to the governors had been adopted by several of the colonies;
but the home government was by no means ready
to yield. The ideal of the board was a salary fixed
by the crown, and governors were instructed to in-
sist upon permanent settlements. The most interesting contests of this period took place in Massachusetts and New York.

In Massachusetts the crisis came during the administration of Governor Burnet in 1728. The
governor argued strongly for a permanent civil list
as necessary to his freedom of action in legislative
matters. He supported this argument by referring
to the practice of the mother-country, and claimed
also that temporary grants had been used to extort
legislation in opposition to the governor's judgment. The position of the house was summed up
in a resolution declaring that, after a salary had
once been settled, the governor with his uncertain
tenure would have little interest in serving the welfare of the people. In this instance the governor
held to his instructions and died at his post, refusing to the end the liberal grants which the as-

[1] Hutchinson, *Hist. of Mass. Bay*, II., 211–214, 226, 241;
Poore, *Charters and Constitutions*, I., 954; *N. H. Provincial
Papers*, IV., 485–488.

sembly was willing to give if he would only consent to give up the principle of a permanent establishment. The Privy Council in 1729, after the
Massachusetts agents had argued the assembly's
case, commended Burnet and reiterated the demand
for a permanent settlement of the governor's salary;
but under Burnet's successors, Belcher and Shirley,
the home government practically gave up the fight.
A permanent settlement was still urged, but if that
could not be had, temporary grants might be accepted.

In New York the practice for several years after
Queen Anne's War was to grant the salary list for
periods of five or three years; but the house finally
resolved to grant revenue for one year only, and
the home government was obliged to submit. At
the beginning of the last French war the board
practically acknowledged its defeat, as it had already done in Massachusetts, by instructing the
governor not to press the matter. The same issue
arose in South Carolina during the first years of
the royal government, and the outcome was the
same.[1]

The result of these controversies was that in South
Carolina as well as in New England and the middle colonies the provincial assemblies had in their
hands an effective offset to the administrative control exercised by the home government. A con-

---

[1] Greene, *Provincial Governor*, 168–173; Smith, *South Carolina*, 75–77.

temporary statement regarding the proprietary province of Pennsylvania may be taken as applicable to several of the royal governments: "Every proprietary Governor has two Masters: one who gives him his Commission and one who gives him his Pay." [1]

The powers thus gained, the assemblies were not slow to use for purposes which the royalists regarded as subversive of the constitution; and in these radical measures New England continued to exercise a strong influence, which was naturally felt most strongly in the neighboring provinces of New York and New Jersey, where it attracted the attention of the royal governors. Cosby, of New York, said in 1732 that the "example and spirit of the Boston people begins to spread amongst these colonys in a most prodigious maner"; and a few years later Governor Morris, of New Jersey, wrote of the fondness of his assembly for the example of "their neighbours in Pennsylvania & New England." It is noteworthy that the New York assembly, in defending the triennial act of 1737, urged that their people ought not to be deprived of a privilege enjoyed by their neighbors. Even in the Carolinas the prevalence of "commonwealth maxims" was attributed to New England influence. [2]

The most common encroachments of the provin-

---

[1] *Historical Review of the Const. and Govt. of Pa.* (1759), 72.
[2] Chalmers, *Revolt*, II., 99; *Morris Papers*, 162; *N. J. Docs. Rel. to Col. Hist.*, V., 321; S. C. Hist. Soc., *Collections*, I., 283.

cial assemblies were in the field of finance. In several colonies the assemblies attempted, with more or less success, either to authorize payments of money without the governor's warrant, required by his instructions; or to make the warrant a mere formality by requiring a particular vote of the representatives in each instance. The assemblies also generally refused to allow the council to amend money bills, a policy which had appeared much earlier and was unsuccessfully resisted by the Board of Trade. In the first years of the royal government in South Carolina the issue was raised there. The governor's instructions explicitly gave the council equal rights with the house; but the assembly denied that the king could limit their privileges in this way, and insisted upon their right to all the privileges of the House of Commons. The dispute went on for over twenty years and the house finally carried its point. In 1740 the Board of Trade made a stand in favor of the New Jersey council, but here again it was defeated. By the middle of the eighteenth century the exclusive control in the lower house of money bills was almost everywhere established.[1]

Provincial treasurers were generally appointed by the assemblies during the quarter-century following the English revolution; but there was some con-

[1] *N. Y. Docs. Rel. to Col. Hist.*, **VI.**, 614; Greene, *Provincial Governor*, 122, 180; Raper, *North Carolina*, 197; Smith, *South Carolina*, 289 et seq.

troversy as to whether the appointment should be controlled by the lower house alone or whether it should follow the regular process of legislation by governor, council, and assembly. Usually the control rested practically if not formally with the lower house. Sometimes, as in Virginia and North Carolina, the close relation between the House and the treasurer was shown by combining that office with the speakership in a way which suggests the position of the English chancellor of the exchequer in the House of Commons.

Other executive officers were frequently appointed by the assemblies during the eighteenth century. When, about the middle of the century, Governor Glen of South Carolina declared that the executive power was largely in the hands of commissioners appointed by the assembly, he made a statement which, with some allowance for exaggeration, might have been made with regard to several of the provincial governments. In 1751 the Board of Trade made a long statement about New York, in which they rehearsed the "fatal measures, by which the legal prerogative of the Crown (which alone can keep this or any Province dependent on the Mother Country) has been reduced" and "the most essencial powers of Goverm[t] violently wrested out of the hands of the Governor."[1]

While governor and assembly were thus strug-

---

[1] Greene, *Provincial Governor*, 183-195; *N. Y. Docs. Rel. to Col. Hist.*, VI., 614 et seq.

gling for control of the provincial administration, other important issues were raised, involving the rights of individuals and the extent to which they shared in the legal privileges of English subjects. The general principle was stated during this period in two important legal opinions. The first, delivered by Richard West, special counsel to the Board of Trade, in 1720, declared that the common law of England was the common law of the plantations. "Let an Englishman," he said, "go where he will, he carries as much of law and liberty with him as the nature of things will bear." The second opinion was delivered by Attorney-General Yorke in 1729, and dealt with the more difficult question of the statute law, which had been for many years an important political issue in Maryland. With special reference to that colony, Yorke asserted that general statutes enacted by Parliament since the settlement of the province, and not expressly applied to that colony or to the colonies in general, were not applicable there, unless they had either been declared so by act of assembly or "received there by long uninterrupted usage or practice," which might imply the tacit consent of the proprietor and the colonists.

The Maryland assembly asserted, however, that general statutes passed by Parliament, and not specifically restricted, were the common privilege of English subjects whether in England or America. The proprietor denied this proposition; and though the matter was frequently discussed and the assembly gained a partial victory, it was never precisely settled.[1]

As a part of their inheritance in the common law, the American colonists enjoyed the familiar safeguards of property and personal liberty, and were accustomed to trial by jury both in civil and criminal cases. The habeas-corpus act of 1679 was not applicable to the colonies, and their acts extending its provisions to themselves were sometimes disallowed; but the privilege of the writ was generally secured in practice under the common law. Certain other personal rights now regarded as a matter of course were not then generally conceded. One of these was religious liberty; for, notwithstanding the substantial progress of the previous century, Catholics and Jews were still deprived of equal rights, and many men were compelled to support religious establishments of which they disapproved. So also the right of free criticism of public men and measures was not enjoyed as of course by the American of the provincial era, but was the outcome of serious conflicts with arbitrary power.[2]

Shortly before the revolution of 1688 a clause had been commonly inserted in the governor's instructions providing that no book should be printed and no printing-press set up without the governor's

---

[1] Chalmers, *Opinions*, 206; Mereness, *Maryland*, 257-278; see below, p. 221.

[2] Carpenter, "The Habeas Corpus" in *Am. Hist. Review*, VIII., 18-27.

leave. This clause was retained during the reigns of William and Anne, and for a time in some of the colonies the censorship was actually enforced. In 1721, Governor Shute of Massachusetts asked for penal legislation against the authors of seditious papers, but the house of representatives refused, and resolved instead that " to suffer no books to be printed without a license from the governor will be attended with innumerable inconveniences and danger." In the instructions to later governors the censorship clause was omitted.[1]

Yet the withdrawal of the governor's censorship by no means perfectly secured the free expression of public opinion, which was still much restricted by prosecutions for criminal libel, in which the rights of defendants were not always thoroughly guarded. Representative assemblies also were at times guilty of arbitrary procedure in this respect.[2]

Fortunately for the American people, the principle of a free press found an able defender in 1735, when John Peter Zenger, publisher of the *Weekly Journal* in New York, was tried for publishing false and malicious libels against Governor Cosby. Cosby had removed the chief-justice, Lewis Morris, for deciding against him in a suit about his salary, and the libels consisted in sharp criticisms of the governor's conduct in the columns of Zenger's *Journal*. The case was tried before the new chief-justice, De

[1] Greene, *Provincial Governor*, 127.
[2] Cf. above, p. 88.

Lancey, who had a natural bias against the prisoner. According to De Lancey's theory the jury had to decide only on the fact of publication, simply accepting the decision of the court as to the libellous character of the statements made. This would of course have secured Zenger's conviction.

The defendant's friends had, however, secured the services of an able counsellor in the person of Andrew Hamilton, a well-known lawyer and politician of Pennsylvania. Hamilton insisted that the jury must decide whether the publication was really a false and malicious libel, and argued strongly for public criticism as the only safeguard of free government. By this appeal he won the jury, who acquitted Zenger and thus established a new barrier against arbitrary power.[1]

These constitutional controversies between the colonists and their governors were complicated by other disputes, especially on economic issues. In the royal and proprietary governments the land question was in some form or other an almost constant source of friction, the governors finding it difficult to secure the proper collection of quit-rents. In the proprietary provinces the colonists struggled to secure public control of land administration.

Paper-money issues constituted another prolific source of party conflicts in which the governors and the administration parties sometimes stood out

[1] Rutherfurd, *John Peter Zenger*.

against the popular demand, but often yielded to the
pressure of colonial opinion, especially when they
needed financial support.   Even in the elective governments this became a disturbing political issue.
In 1731, Governor Joseph Jenckes of Rhode Island
carried his opposition to paper-money issues to the
point of indorsing his dissent upon a bill which had
been passed by both houses of the assembly.   The
charter, however, made no reference to an executive
veto, and the legal advisers of the home government decided against the governor, holding that
the assembly might make any law not actually in
conflict with the laws of England.   At the next
election Jenckes lost his office.[1]

No definite and permanent organization of political parties can be traced in the provincial era, and
the lines of party cleavage varied at different times
and in different colonies.   In Massachusetts there
was a tendency to party division between social
classes, especially during the period in which currency problems were under discussion.   A radical party, recruited largely from the farmers and
small traders, was opposed by the conservative "men
of estates and the principal merchants," who held
out against the paper-money radicals and became
later the basis of a distinctly royalist party.   There
was a similar division of parties in Rhode Island.[2]

---

[1] *R. I. Col. Records*, IV., 456–461.
[2] Hutchinson, *Hist. of Mass. Bay*, (ed. of 1795), II., 188, 200,
315, 354; Bates, *R. I. and the Formation of the Union*, 36.

In New York, party contests assumed a more distinctly factional character. The suffrage was closely limited, and politics during the first half of the eighteenth century was largely a contest between a few influential families, such as the Livingstons and the De Lanceys, who built up their influence by means of marriage alliances and other social ties. This aristocratic type of family politics continued until after the War of Independence; but the constitutional controversies between the governor and the assembly were preparing the way for more clearly defined parties based on political principles rather than on personal allegiance.[1]

In Pennsylvania the Quakers formed a compact political body which until the middle of the eighteenth century controlled the provincial assembly, with the help of the conservative Germans. By that time the Penn family had joined the established church and the Quakers were usually in opposition. On the proprietary side there were usually the Anglicans, a small but relatively influential party, and the Presbyterians. During the last French war this proprietary party favored vigorous measures of defence. The comparative conservatism of the dominant Quaker party may be illustrated by the more moderate paper-money issues of Pennsylvania as compared with New England.[2]

[1] Becker, " Nominations in Colonial New York," in *Am. Hist. Review*, VI., 260–275.
[2] Sharpless, *Quaker Experiment in Government*, I., chap. iv.

In the tobacco colonies, especially in Maryland, the divergent interests of the large and small planters led to important political disputes as to the regulation of the tobacco trade. Gradually the poorer and less educated people began to find political leaders in the lawyer class. In Virginia a prominent feature of politics during the first half of the eighteenth century was the great power exercised by a small group of aristocratic families who were strongly represented in the council and were able to make quite uncomfortable any governor whose policy interfered with the interests of their class. In South Carolina there was a strong group of Charleston merchants which, until about 1760, formed the backbone of the government party, opposing the paper-money legislation desired by the planters and taking a generally conservative position on public questions. It was largely this class which dominated the council, while the planters controlled the lower house.[1]

[1] Mereness, *Maryland*, pt. i., chaps. iv., v.; Bassett, *Writings of William Byrd*, Introd.; Spotswood, *Official Letters*, passim; Smith, *South Carolina*, 234, 330.

CHAPTER XIII

PROVINCIAL LEADERS

(1714–1740)

THE politics of thirteen small communities united to each other only by their common dependence on the mother-country hardly offered an adequate field for the larger kind of statesmanship. The governor's position gave him, of course, a certain opportunity for leadership, but he was mainly confined within the limits of his particular province. Still more distinctly was this true of the popular leaders. Nevertheless, a few efficient governors showed in their restricted field some of the elements of true statesmanship; and among the colonists there were some aggressive and intelligent champions of the popular will.

Probably none of the provincial governors had on the whole so interesting a personality or gave so much evidence of political foresight as Alexander Spotswood, who, with the title of lieutenant-governor, was the actual head of the Virginia administration from 1710 to 1722. Spotswood was a Scotchman by descent, but was born in Tangier, where his father was stationed as an army surgeon.

Like several other royal governors of the time, he had had an important military experience, having held the rank of colonel under Marlborough in the Blenheim campaign; yet when he began his career in Virginia he was not quite thirty-five.

From the beginning of his service as governor, Spotswood showed remarkable energy, public spirit, and breadth of interest. He was an active patron of William and Mary College, concerned himself seriously with the supply of ministers for the Virginia parishes, and corresponded with the bishop of London about the best method of improving the general position of the clergy.

Spotswood was also deeply interested in the economic development of his province. Much of the credit for breaking up piracy belongs to him. He also saw the value of the iron-mines, and may be regarded as the founder of the iron industry in Virginia. In its interest he secured from the assembly liberal legislation for the encouragement of German settlers, and tried also to enlist the aid of the home government. His largeness of view was perhaps most clearly shown in the emphasis which he laid upon western exploration. He believed that the French plan of connecting Canada with the Mississippi might be thwarted by pushing the English settlements westward along the line of the James River. A few months after his arrival he sent out an exploring company to the mountains, and in 1716 he personally led an expedition over

the Blue Ridge. Two years later he urged upon
the English government the desirability of an establishment on Lake Erie.

With all his strong qualities Spotswood was unfortunate in his relations with his associates in the
provincial government. He found a local aristocracy strongly intrenched in the council and accustomed to political control. His plans for a reform
of the land administration were contrary to their
interests and prejudices, and he asserted his prerogative as governor in ways which seemed to encroach upon their constitutional privileges. He
also antagonized James Blair, the commissary of
the bishop of London. These difficulties were partially overcome, but he was soon after removed
from office.

He then retired to his country place at Germanna,
on the Rapidan, where he engaged, on a considerable
scale, in the manufacture of iron. Here he was
visited in later years by his former antagonist in
the council, William Byrd, who wrote a charming
account of the Spotswood establishment. His public career was not, however, completely closed.
As governor he already had done what he could
towards the development of the colonial postal
system under the act of 1710; and in 1730 he
became deputy postmaster - general for America.
Finally, on the outbreak of the Spanish war, he
received the rank of major-general, and at the age
of sixty-four was actively engaged in the work of

gathering the colonial forces for an expedition
against Carthagena, when his long and varied life
was suddenly ended in 1740. His career, taken as
a whole, is an admirable example of a royal official
identifying himself with American life and sincerely
devoted to the solution of its problems.[1]

Two years before Spotswood's retirement from
the Virginia governorship, William Burnet began a
short but eventful service in America as governor
of New York. Burnet was not so strong nor so
picturesque a personality as Spotswood; but the
two men were alike in watchful care for English
interests in the continental rivalry with France, in
zealous assertion of their prerogatives against rival
elements in the government, and in the unfortunate
antagonisms which marred their official service.
William Burnet was a son of Bishop Gilbert Burnet,
the famous counsellor of William and Mary and a
leading personage in church and state. The son had
a university education at Cambridge, supplemented
by study abroad, and during his residence in America was recognized as a gentleman of refined and
scholarly tastes. Before his appointment as governor
he had been in the customs service and had suffered
from some unfortunate speculations. In 1720 he
succeeded Robert Hunter as governor of New York
and held that office until 1728, when his difficulties

---

[1] Spotswood, *Official Letters*, passim, esp. I., Introd., 4–13, 18–
42, 163 et seq., II., 70, 295 et seq., 305 et seq.; Bassett, *Writings
of William Byrd*, Introd., 355 et seq.

with the opposing faction became so serious that he was transferred to the government of Massachusetts, which he held until his death in the following year.

Burnet's American career is chiefly notable for two things: his far-sighted policy for the promotion of English influence in the region of the Great Lakes and among the western Indians; and his constitutional conflict with the Massachusetts assembly on the salary issue. Before coming to New York, Burnet had conferred with his predecessor, Hunter, and acquired some knowledge of American conditions. On his arrival he accepted as one of his expert advisers on provincial policy the famous Cadwallader Colden, best known for his *History of the Five Indian Nations;* and in accordance with Colden's views he adopted two important measures of policy. One was the establishment of a British trading - post and fort at Oswego on Lake Ontario. In 1726 he secured a small appropriation from the assembly for this purpose, but was obliged to supplement this amount by advances from his own purse, for which he was never fully repaid. Burnet hoped that this would prove the foundation of an important English trade with the western Indians, an expectation which seemed to be justified by the attitude of the French, who regarded the new post as a serious menace to their interests and demanded, though without success, that it should be given up.

Burnet also sought to check the trade between Albany and Canada, on the ground that it supplied the French with European goods which they used in the Indian trade. Thus, Burnet argued, the merchants were playing directly into the hands of their French rivals. He secured the passage of several acts of assembly prohibiting or restricting this trade, but the opposition at Albany was so strong as to prevent strict enforcement; and several of these provincial measures were disallowed by the crown.

The salary dispute in Massachusetts has already been considered.[1] In this episode, as in his measures relating to Oswego, Burnet showed remarkable steadiness in the face of opposition, and commendable readiness to make financial sacrifices in support of what seemed to him a sound public policy. It may, however, be open to question whether more tact and judgment in dealing with men might not have given him greater success in administration.[2]

Burnet's place in the governorship of Massachusetts and New Hampshire was taken by Jonathan Belcher, who served for about eleven years. Unlike Spotswood and Burnet, Belcher was a provincial by birth and early training, coming from a mercantile family in Boston and graduating from Harvard College. He had, however, seen some-

[1] See above, p. 196.
[2] *N. Y. Docs. Rel. to Col. Hist.*, V., passim; Smith, *New York* (ed. of 1792), 167 et seq.

thing of the outside world, not only in England but
in continental Europe, and on his return he took an
important place among the merchants and politicians of Boston.   His correspondence shows the frequent use of religious phrases after the Puritan
manner, with some suggestion of sanctimoniousness.

For many years Belcher was known as a "prerogative" man; but during Burnet's controversy
with the assembly on the salary question he identified himself with the opposition, and was presently
sent to England as provincial agent to secure a
modification of the governor's instructions.   The
home government refused to yield; but soon afterwards Burnet died and Belcher was sent as his
successor, apparently on the theory that he would
be more successful in bringing the assembly to
terms.

As governor, Belcher had the reputation of being
showy in his manner of life, unusually masterful in
his dealings with the council, and much inclined to
use his power of appointment and removal for personal and political purposes.   Though at first popular with both the previously existing parties, he
drifted into controversies which aroused bitter antagonism.   On the salary question his instructions
were drastic enough; but, on the failure of all attempts at compromise, he finally secured the consent of the Board of Trade to the practical surrender
which has already been recorded.[1]   On some im-

[1] See above, p. 197.

portant issues, however, Belcher held his ground,
and during his administration the house was obliged
to give up the practice of issuing money from the
treasury by simple resolutions. He also held out
firmly against new issues of paper money in Massachusetts.

Near the end of his term, Belcher earned his
chief title to fame by his fight against the Land
Bank party, which then controlled the house of
representatives. All persons prominently identified with the bank he marked out for political
ostracism, rejecting, in 1740, the speaker chosen
by the house, and thirteen councillors, besides re-
moving a number of administrative officers. In
the fight for sound money, Belcher had the support of the mercantile interests; but by this time
there was a formidable combination of dissatisfied
elements. The assembly of New Hampshire was
convinced that he had not dealt fairly with that
province in its recent boundary controversy with
Massachusetts, and charged him with having been
influenced by a considerable grant of money made to
him by the Massachusetts assembly while the controversy was pending. Various political devices
were used against him; and in 1741 he was removed
in favor of William Shirley, who was to become so
prominent a figure in the last two wars with the
French.

Belcher's removal from his New England governments did not close permanently his political career,

for he was afterwards appointed governor of New Jersey, where he helped to found Princeton College. In New England he left an unfortunate impression of indirect dealing, insincerity, and self-seeking.[1]

Sir William Keith, the proprietary governor of Pennsylvania (1717–1724), may be taken as a good example of the demagogue in the governor's office. Keith was a Scotchman who had previously served as surveyor-general of customs for the king. Throughout his administration he was notoriously negligent in the observance of his instructions— a serious matter for the proprietors, under the Pennsylvania constitution, which left legislation wholly in the hands of the governor and the representatives. Efforts were made to check him by stringent instructions, requiring him to approve no bill without the consent of a majority of the council. Keith then appealed openly to the people against the proprietary instructions, but this was more than the proprietors would tolerate and he was soon removed.

After his removal Keith entered the assembly and attempted the rôle of opposition leader, apparently with the purpose of breaking down the proprietary government. He subsequently returned to England, where he was consulted by the Board of Trade as an expert on colonial questions. Keith's lack of trustworthiness in private as well as public

[1] Hutchinson, *Hist. of Mass. Bay* (ed. of 1795), II., 318, 323, 329, 331 et seq.; *Belcher Papers* (Mass. Hist. Soc., *Collections*, V., VI.).

relations has been recorded for all time by Franklin in his *Autobiography;* but Franklin, from the point of view of a popular leader, thought that Keith had in the main given good service as governor, especially in the passage of desirable legislation.[1]

The elective governors of Rhode Island and Connecticut were officers of a wholly different type; for they were themselves of the people, chosen representatives of their neighbors. Their authority was closely limited by the charters, and in theory they were little more than the first among the councillors. Yet as spokesmen for the people in negotiations with the neighboring colonies and with the home government they had important parts to play.

During the first half of the eighteenth century these little republics showed remarkable steadiness in their treatment of their political leaders. Governor Cranston, of Rhode Island, was elected year after year for twenty-eight years; and from 1707 to 1741 Connecticut had only two governors, both of whom died in office. One of these Connecticut governors was Joseph Talcott, whose tenure of office covered the seventeen years from 1724 to 1741; and his career is of interest not because it showed any remarkable statesmanship, but because it is that of a characteristic republican leader.

[1] Shepherd, *Proprietary Government in Pa.*, passim; Proud, *Pennsylvania*, II., 178 et seq.; Franklin, *Works* (Bigelow's ed.), I., 76, 83–87; *N. J. Docs. Rel. to Col. Hist.*, V., 245.

Talcott belonged to one of the old and prominent families of Connecticut, but he had little education of an academic kind. Before becoming governor, however, he served a varied apprenticeship in public employments; first, in the town of Hartford as selectman or townsman, then successively as representative in the assembly, assistant, and deputy-governor. Besides his legislative and executive responsibilities he held various judicial positions extending from that of justice of the peace to judge of the superior court. He performed his share of military service in defending the colony against the Indians, and was also active in the Hartford church. Talcott may therefore be regarded as a typical public servant.

The period of his governorship brought many perplexing problems, some of which involved the essential principles of the Connecticut constitution. During the early years he was engaged in somewhat vexatious correspondence with New York and Rhode Island regarding boundary disputes, but these were settled during his term of office. More serious and perplexing were his relations with the home government. In 1728 came the news that in the case of Winthrop vs. Lechmere, carried on appeal from the colonial courts, the Privy Council had declared invalid the Connecticut law distributing the property of intestates among the heirs.[1] The enforcement of such a decision would have caused

[1] Thayer, *Cases in Constitutional Law*, I., 34–40.

great confusion in the colony, and during the remainder of his life a large part of Talcott's correspondence with the Connecticut agents was made up of arguments in favor of maintaining the long-established local usage.   The final issue did not appear until after Talcott's death, when the Privy Council by its decision in the new case of Clarke *vs.* Toucey, in 1745, practically abandoned the position taken in Winthrop *vs.* Lechmere.

These negotiations were peculiarly difficult because all communications with the English government served to direct attention to the somewhat exceptional and anomalous position of Connecticut under the charter.   It was noted that her laws were not subject to disallowance like those of most colonies, and that there were not the necessary securities for an exact enforcement of the navigation acts. From time to time there was talk of radical parliamentary action, and of a remodelling of the charter, which at the best would place Connecticut on a footing somewhat like that of Massachusetts.   In dealing with these threatening proposals, Talcott showed himself diplomatic as well as firm, making minor concessions when necessary, but holding fast in essentials and constantly defending his people from the charges of insubordination and disloyalty.[1]

The constitutional controversies of the provincial

[1] *Talcott Papers* (Conn. Hist. Soc., *Collections*, IV., V.), esp. I., chaps. xvii.–xxviii., 53, 64, 89, 114, 217–229, II., 75–97; cf. Andrews in *Yale Review*, III., 261–294.

governments brought out a few men of real capacity for parliamentary leadership. In the south two such leaders may be mentioned, Charles Pinckney, of South Carolina, and Daniel Dulany the elder, of Maryland. Pinckney was a native South-Carolinian who had been educated in England. On his return he soon took a prominent place as a lawyer, and in 1732 became attorney-general of the province. He held that position, however, only for a short time, and presently became a member of the "Commons House of Assembly," serving as speaker from 1736 to 1740. Though a man of considerable wealth, he identified himself with the house in its struggle with the council for exclusive control of money bills. Before he became speaker he draughted some important resolutions on this subject which were adopted by the house and which claimed for the latter in this respect all the powers of the English Commons. The resolutions were strongly worded throughout and ended with this notable paragraph:

"Resolved, That after the Estimate is closed and added to any Tax Bill, that no additions can or ought to be made thereto, by any other Estate or Power whatsoever, but by and in the Commons House of Assembly."

Pinckney showed himself a man of unusually liberal views by claiming equal rights for Protestant dissenters and entering his protest on the journals against a bill to impose upon them as members of the assembly an objectionable form of oath. He belonged to the second generation of a strong South Carolina family, several of whom played important parts in the later struggle for independence and nationality.[1]

Dulany was active in the Maryland assembly at nearly the same time. Beginning his career in America as a poor Irish immigrant, he became a considerable landholder and founded an important Maryland family. Like Pinckney, he had a high reputation as a lawyer, being considered in his day the best lawyer in the province.

The chief constitutional question with which Dulany concerned himself was that of the applicability of English statutes in Maryland. Dulany, though holding the office of attorney-general, was also a member of the lower house and accepted the popular theory that the colonists were entitled to all the benefits of English statutes. In 1724 he led the house in demanding that judges should swear to do justice "according to the laws, statutes, and reasonable customs of England and the acts of assembly and usage of this province of Maryland."

The proprietors stubbornly resisted this view, and prolonged parliamentary struggles ensued with a series of able state papers from the lower house, usually draughted by Dulany, who was chairman of the

[1] McCrady, *South Carolina under Royal Government*, 173–175, 279; Smith, *South Carolina*, 116, 296 et seq., 412, 415.

committee on laws. He also wrote a pamphlet in defence of the assembly's position, entitled " The Right of the Inhabitants of Maryland to the Benefit of the English Laws," which doubtless helped to raise the public excitement to the point described by Governor Ogle in 1731, when he wrote that the country was "as hot as possible about the English statutes and the judge's oath." The controversy ended in a compromise which, though not determining the question with precision, was nevertheless regarded as a victory for the lower house. Yet Dulany objected when Bishop Gibson's commissary undertook to apply the same principle to ecclesiastical law and custom.

Dulany subsequently became a councillor and one of the governor's supporters, though he showed his moderation by helping to bring about a reduction of officers' fees. Like Pinckney, he had a distinguished son, Daniel Dulany the younger, who took a prominent part on the colonial side in the great Stamp-Act debate of 1765.[1]

Pinckney and Dulany, though parliamentary leaders of the popular party, allied themselves at one time or another with the administration and held important appointments. The middle colonies produced a similar personage in Lewis Morris,

[1] Mereness, *Maryland*, 114–116, 122, 180, 270, 275, 449; Sioussat, *Economics and Politics in Maryland*, and *English Statutes in Maryland* (*Johns Hopkins University Studies*, XXI., Nos. 6, 7, 11, 12).

of New York and New Jersey, a severe critic of
arbitrary government during Governor Cosby's administration, but a man of aristocratic tempera-
ment, who afterwards became a royal governor himself and was involved in the usual constitutional
controversies with his assembly.

One of the most representative leaders of provincial democracy was Andrew Hamilton, of Pennsylvania, who is notable also because of the intercolonial range of his influence. Hamilton's public
career began in the Maryland assembly, and in
1715 a committee of which he was a member framed
a code for that province which "remained the law,
with little change," during the rest of the colonial
era. Already, however, Hamilton had an important practice in Pennsylvania, and in 1717 he became attorney-general of that province. A few
years later he entered the assembly, was for several
years its speaker, and in 1739 made a valedictory
speech in which he congratulated the province on
its comparatively democratic forms of government,
with officers generally elected by the people or their
representatives, and an assembly which sat upon
its own adjournments "when we please and as long
as we think necessary."

The most memorable incident of his life took place
in another province when, in the trial already mentioned, he argued before Chief-Justice De Lancey, of
New York, the case of John Peter Zenger. That
speech is significant not merely as an incident in

the history of the struggle for freedom of the press, but also as a recognition of political principles held in common by Americans of the provincial era.[1]

In Massachusetts the most important radical leaders of the early eighteenth century were the two Elisha Cookes, father and son, whose careers taken together cover about half a century of provincial politics. The importance of the elder Cooke as an opposition leader has already been noted, and his son was equally conspicuous in the constitutional controversies of the early Georgian period. In 1718 the younger Cooke defended in the house of representatives the right of the colonists to cut pine-trees on their own estates, notwithstanding the prohibition of the royal surveyor of the woods. The house supported him, and in 1720 showed its defiant spirit by electing him as speaker. Governor Shute met the challenge by vetoing the election, and the quarrel which followed prevented the transaction of business during that session. The next house chose another speaker; but Cooke retained his leadership, and the governor, though afterwards sustained in principle by the explanatory charter of 1725, was forced to leave the province.

During Burnet's administration Cooke pursued his father's policy of insisting upon temporary grants; and though under Belcher, to whom he was

[1] Steiner, in Am. Hist. Assoc., *Annual Report*, 1899, pp. 251, 260; Proud, *Pennsylvania*, II., 217.

more friendly, he was willing to make some concessions, he refused to yield the essential principle at issue. The historian Hutchinson, who was just beginning his public career as Cooke's drew to a close, said that he had "the character of a fair and open enemy," and remarked on his unusual success during the earlier part of his career in "keeping the people steady in applause of his measures." [1]

During the second quarter of the eighteenth century a few men were rising into prominence who were to play still larger parts in the revolutionary era. In Massachusetts, Thomas Hutchinson, as a representative from Boston in the general court, was already a leader in the fight for sound money against the Land Bank and paper-money faction, and was urging, without effect at first, but with final success, the redemption of the currency in specie. Then, as in later years, he showed his readiness to resist a strong popular movement which seemed to him mistaken. [2]

Franklin also had begun his long and varied career of public service. Born in Boston, he had while still a boy assisted his brother in publishing the *New England Courant*, and thus seen something of party politics in Massachusetts. His stay in England from 1724 to 1726 gave him a broader

---

[1] Hutchinson, *Hist. of Mass. Bay*, II., 200, 211, 293, 335, 351.
[2] Davis, *Currency and Banking in Mass. Bay*, II., 168–189; Hutchinson, *Hist. of Mass. Bay*, II., 352 et seq.

knowledge of the world than most of his contemporaries, and before he was twenty he had made the acquaintance of some of the most prominent men of his time both in England and America.   In 1729, at the age of twenty-three, he took charge of the *Pennsylvania Gazette*, which soon became the principal paper of the province; and three years later came the first issue of *Poor Richard's Almanac*. During these early years he showed that combination of business shrewdness with public spirit which was to distinguish him through life.   Before 1740 he had been appointed postmaster at Philadelphia, and had set on foot a number of important public enterprises in the city, including its fire company and its public library.

From the beginning he took a keen interest in provincial politics.   In support of the paper-money policy he published in 1729 his *Modest Inquiry into the Nature and Necessity of a Paper Currency*, which, though not in accord with modern economic views, was above the average level of contemporary publications on that subject.   In 1736 he began his long service as clerk of the assembly, and soon became a recognized leader of the popular party.   In 1748 one of the proprietors characterized his "doctrine that obedience to governors is no more due than protection to the people" as "not fit to be in the heads of the unthinking multitude," adding, "He is a dangerous man, and I should be glad if he inhabited another country, as I believe him of a

very uneasy spirit. However, as he is a sort of
tribune of the people, he must be treated with regard." [1]

[1] Franklin, *Works* (Bigelow's ed.), I., passim, esp. 53–57, 146–
149, 153, 167–205; Penn, *Letter-Book*, quoted in Shepherd, *Proprietary Government in Pa.*, 222

CHAPTER XIV

IMMIGRATION AND EXPANSION

(1690–1740)

DURING the fifty years after Penn began his colony only two new English provinces were permanently organized in North America; these were Nova Scotia, conquered from the French in 1710, and Georgia, which was carved out of South Carolina in 1732. Placed on the northern and southern frontiers of the British dominions, these two colonies had a considerable political importance; but in point of population both remained insignificant throughout the provincial era. The story of colonial expansion during this period is, therefore, chiefly concerned with the development of the older colonies.

Between 1690 and 1740 the population of the continental colonies increased from something over two hundred thousand to about one million. There was substantial growth in every colony, but the most decided increase came in the middle group. By about the middle of the eighteenth century Pennsylvania outstripped all the older colonies ex-

cept Virginia and Massachusetts, and in white population she was nearly equal to Virginia.[1]

The important natural increase of population was
reinforced in most colonies by a large immigration,
partly from England but more largely from Scotland, Ireland, and the continent of Europe. Comparatively few of these non-English settlers came
to New England, though there were some French
Huguenots and Scotch-Irish. With something of
the old exclusive spirit, the later Puritans scrutinized jealously immigrants of alien faith and race,
and thus, to the close of the colonial era, New
England remained distinctly Puritan and English.[2]

In New York the conditions seemed more favorable for growth by immigration. Its population
at the beginning of the eighteenth century was
more distinctly cosmopolitan than that of any
other colony. The majority of its people were of
Dutch descent, though in New York City the
Dutch language and the Dutch church lost ground
during the next half-century, and the young people came to "speak principally English and go only
to the English church." In other counties, like
Albany, the Dutch language predominated, and it
was difficult to find men sufficiently acquainted
with English to serve as jurors. A community so
varied in its racial and religious elements was ap-

[1] Dexter, *Estimates of Population in the American Colonies.*
[2] Belknap, *New Hampshire*, II., 30, 71; Proper, *Colonial Immigration Laws*, 22–34.

parently well adapted to attract the foreign immigrant.[1]

This opportunity was lost, however, largely because of the mistaken policy of the provincial authorities. The land legislation of New York was less liberal than that of other colonies, particularly Pennsylvania. The unfortunate experience of some Palatinate Germans who settled in New York during Queen Anne's reign discouraged others of that nationality from coming to New York, and placed the province at a serious disadvantage in the competition with her neighbors to the south.[2]

During the eighteenth century Pennsylvania was especially attractive to non-English immigrants from Europe. She offered land and citizenship on easy terms, and she adhered more consistently than any other colony to the principles of religious freedom. The result was a volume of immigration which profoundly influenced the subsequent history of the colony and the state.

The first to come in considerable numbers were the Germans. Some of this nationality were among the earliest settlers of Pennsylvania, but their numbers were then comparatively small. The Germans first became important during the second decade of the eighteenth century, partly because of peculiar conditions in the mother-country, partly

[1] Kalm, *Travels*, in Pinkerton, *Voyages*, XIII., 463, 586; Valentine, *Hist. of City of New York*, 299.
[2] Proper, *Colonial Immigration Laws*, 38–44.

PART OF
NORTH AMERICA
SIMPLIFIED FROM
POPPLE'S MAP
1733

BURMAY & CO., N.Y.

through the action of the British government, and
partly because of the liberal policy of the proprietary
government.

The treaties of Westphalia in 1648 failed to secure either the domestic or the international peace
of the disintegrating German empire, and thousands
of people belonging to various Protestant sects were
led to seek refuge from persecution under a foreign
flag. The great international wars of Louis XIV.'s
reign also left their mark upon the unfortunate border regions of western Germany, especially in the
Palatinate, which suffered severely from the French
armies.

To these persecuted Protestants the government
of Queen Anne and her successors offered protection
and religious freedom under the English flag, and
the result was an immense immigration to England
and her colonies. For their benefit Parliament
enacted its first general naturalization law, which,
though repealed three years later, gave to large
numbers of them the rights of English subjects.
A few Palatines were sent to Ireland, but the great
majority found their way to America. In 1709
the Board of Trade sent a considerable colony of
them to New York, where they were expected to
devote their energies largely to the production of
naval stores. They were dissatisfied, however,
with the plans made for them, and after some
serious disagreements with the provincial government, a considerable number of them left New

York for Pennsylvania. Others came directly from Europe, and about the same time a considerable body of Swiss Mennonites came into the colony.[1]

About 1727 the German and Swiss immigration began to assume large proportions, sometimes amounting to several thousand new arrivals in a single year. These immigrants included adherents of various Protestant sects: the Lutherans, the German Reformed, the Mennonites, the Dunkards, and finally the Moravians, perhaps the most attractive representatives of eighteenth-century Pietism.

This strong infusion of alien influences was looked upon with some misgiving, and Penn's secretary, Logan, suggested the danger of the province being transformed into a German colony. It was pointed out that the new-comers frequently squatted on their lands without making regular purchases from the proprietary agents, and that "being ignorant of our language and laws, and settling in a body together," they formed "a distinct people from his Majesty's subjects." A German newspaper was founded at Germantown as early as 1739, and in 1743 another was issued in Philadelphia. In time the Germans became an important factor in colonial politics, uniting with the Quakers to form a conservative peace party in opposition to those

---

[1] Proper, *Colonial Immigration Laws*, 14, 40; Carpenter, in *Am. Hist. Review*, IX., 293; Kuhns, *German and Swiss Settlements of Colonial Pennsylvania*, chaps. i.–iii.; *N. Y. Docs. Rel. to Col. Hist.*, V., passim.

who were trying to establish an efficient military system.

Some efforts were made to check the tide of immigration, or at least to regulate it. In 1727 the Pennsylvania council ordered masters of vessels to furnish lists of their passengers, and immigrants were required to declare their allegiance to the king and the proprietor. In 1729 a duty was imposed on the importation of foreigners and Irish servants. The act was repealed almost immediately, but the feeling which prompted the measure evidently persisted. The proprietary governors, however, usually desired to encourage immigration, and in 1755 a bill restricting it was defeated by the governor's veto.[1]

More aggressive politically than the Germans were the Scotch-Irish Presbyterians. This immigration first assumed importance a few years after the close of Queen Anne's War, but it developed rapidly during the next two decades. The Scotch-Irish, like the Germans, were not regarded with unmixed satisfaction. During the early years they received liberal terms and were encouraged to form barrier settlements on the frontier. Logan found them as little disposed to pay for their land as some of the Germans had been; they were quoted as arguing that it was "against the laws of God and

[1] Shepherd, *Proprietary Government in Pa.*, 545; Watson, *Annals of Philadelphia* (ed. of 1857), II., 254–259, 398; Proper, *Colonial Immigration Laws*, 46–54; [Burke], *European Settlements*, II., 201.

nature that so much land should be idle while so many Christians wanted it to labour on, and to raise their bread." They were also criticised for their tendency to embroil themselves with the Indians, and this aggressive and warlike spirit made them particularly objectionable to the Quakers, who tried to restrict their political influence by refusing them proportionate representation in the assembly.[1]

Many Germans and Scotch-Irish also found their way into New Jersey. One important German settlement in that colony was that of New Brunswick, which by 1750 had two German churches. The strength of the Scotch-Irish element in that colony may be seen in the rapid extension of the Presbyterian church.[2]

This immigration impressed more strongly than ever upon the middle colonies that complexity in race and religion which had been characteristic of them from the first. Nowhere did this complexity find clearer expression than in the colonial churches. In New York City in the middle of the eighteenth century there were English, Dutch, French, German, and Jewish places of worship, besides a Presbyterian church which was affiliated with the established church of Scotland. Of twelve churches in Philadelphia, noted by Kalm during his stay there in 1749, at least seven represented non-Eng-

[1] *Logan MSS.*, quoted in Watson, *Annals of Philadelphia*, II., 259; Shepherd, *Proprietary Government in Pa.*, 546.
[2] Kalm, in Pinkerton, *Voyages*, XIII., 448–450.

lish elements in the life of the colony, including
Swedish and German Lutherans, German Calvinists,
a Moravian church where services were conducted
both in English and German, and the "great house"
of the Roman Catholics. Outside of Philadelphia
there were several German communities, made up
almost if not quite exclusively of members of a single
religious body, as in the case of the German Baptists
at Ephrata and the Moravians at Bethlehem.[1]

During the eighteenth century, the southern colonies also sought to encourage immigration, sometimes making religious concessions for this purpose.
The French Huguenot immigration, which began
some years before the revolution of 1689, continued
for several years afterwards, and in Virginia and
South Carolina these settlers were numerous enough
to form several churches. In spite of their Calvinistic traditions they maintained, as a rule, friendly
relations with the established Anglican church, and
often united with it. Other Protestant settlers in
South Carolina were not so friendly to these refugees,
but the early antagonism gradually passed away.[2]

Aside from the French Huguenots, the non-
English immigration into the south was comparatively unimportant until the second quarter of the
eighteenth century. Then the Scotch-Irish and the

---

[1] Kalm, in Pinkerton, *Voyages*, XIII., 388, 457, 584; cf. Sachse,
German Sectarians of Pennsylvania, passim.

[2] *Cal. of State Pap., Col.*, 1693-1696, p. 85; McCrady, *South
Carolina under Proprietary Government*, 180, 181, 233, 239, 304,
319, 323, 339, 374, 391, 404.

Germans began to appear in force in the up-country of Virginia and especially in the Great Valley. In order to develop these settlements on the frontier, the royal government was willing to concede religious toleration. Under the leadership of their pioneer ministers, the Great Valley became, as it is to-day, a stronghold of Scotch-Irish Presbyterians, standing out in marked contrast, sometimes in sharp antagonism, with the Anglican influence of the tide-water.[1]

In South Carolina the overthrow of the proprietary government was followed by vigorous efforts to stimulate immigration. A favorite plan at this period was that of laying out new townships and offering them to communities or groups of settlers. In this way the Scotch-Irish settlement of Williamsburg was formed, with a special guarantee of freedom of worship. Other similar communities were founded by Swiss, German, and Welsh settlers. Here, as in Pennsylvania, the new-comers tended to form on the frontiers communities with sympathies and interests quite different from those of the seaboard. It was not, however, until the period of the last French war that the great Scotch-Irish immigration into the Carolinas took place; and not until then did the mutual jealousy and antagonism of tide-water and back-country become a really important factor in their provincial politics.[2]

A large proportion of the early American immi-

[1] McIlwaine, in *Johns Hopkins University Studies*, XII., No. iv.
[2] McCrady, *South Carolina under Royal Government*, chap. viii.

grants belonged to the servant class. The best of them were the "redemptioners," who sold their services for fixed terms of years in return for their passage money. Both in Pennsylvania and Maryland these white servants formed an important part of the industrial system; and many of them became, after their term of service, prosperous land-owners and useful citizens.

A much less desirable kind of servants were the convicts. Under a parliamentary statute of 1717 certain classes of criminals might at the discretion of the court be transported to the colonies for a term of not less than seven years.[1] It has been estimated that some fifty thousand convicts were shipped from Great Britain and Ireland during the remainder of the colonial period. Maryland has the distinction of receiving more of them than any other single colony, and the convicts there formed the larger portion of the servant class. Several of the colonies attempted to check this introduction of servants, especially that of the Irish Catholics and the convicts. Such restrictive measures were, however, discouraged by the home government and frequently disallowed.[2]

No other form of immigration during this period had so serious a meaning for the future of the

[1] 4 George I., chap. xi.
[2] Kalm, in Pinkerton, *Travels*, XIII., 500; Geiser, *Redemptioners and Indented Servants in Pennsylvania* ; McCormac, *White Servitude in Maryland* (*Johns Hopkins University Studies*, XXII., Nos. iii., iv.).

American people as that of the negro slaves. At the close of the seventeenth century the slaves constituted only a small minority of the population in all of the colonies except South Carolina. During the next fifty years this condition was radically changed through the development of the African slave-trade. The Royal African Company, which was chartered in 1672, carried on an increasing trade with monopoly privileges until, in 1698, Parliament admitted private merchants to a share in it. In 1713 the Asiento contract with Spain gave England a larger interest in this branch of commerce, which had the special favor of the crown. Between 1698 and 1707 some twenty-five thousand slaves were probably brought annually from Africa to America, and the number was increased after the Asiento privilege had been secured. The proportion which went to the continental colonies also increased. By the middle of the eighteenth century, there were about three hundred thousand slaves in British North America, so that they had increased at least twice as rapidly as the white population.[1]

This negro population was very unequally distributed. On the western shore of Narragansett Bay there was a small slave-holding aristocracy which had an important influence in the social and political life of Rhode Island; but in New England, generally, the negro population was insignificant. Of the

[1] Du Bois, *Suppression of the Slave-Trade*, chap. i.

middle colonies, New York had the largest proportion of slaves, from one-sixth to one-seventh of the total population. There was even then a decided transition in this respect on passing southward from Pennsylvania into Maryland, where perhaps one-fourth of the people were slaves. In Virginia the proportion was probably about two-fifths, and in some Virginia counties, as well as in South Carolina, the negroes outnumbered the whites.[1]

As the slaves increased, their legal status was more carefully defined by legislation, and they were more sharply differentiated from the white servants. Stringent laws were enacted to prevent the intermixture of the races; and a Virginia statute classed negroes, for certain purposes, as real estate. The power of the master over his slave, though not absolute, was very great, especially in the south; in Virginia, for instance, manslaughter, as distinguished from wilful murder, was not punishable if committed by a master upon his slave. The testimony of a negro could not be accepted as evidence except against those of his own race, and special courts were provided for the trial of his more serious offences, "without the solemnitie of a jury." [2]

[1] Du Bois, *Suppression of the Slave-Trade*, chaps. ii.–iv., esp. statistics in notes; *Doc. Hist. of N. Y.*, I., 695; Channing, *Narragansett Planters*, and Ballagh, *Slavery in Virginia (Johns Hopkins University Studies*, IV., No. iii. and extra vol.).

[2] Hening, *Statutes*, III., 86, 102, 333, 447 et seq., IV., 133; cf. Channing, *Narragansett Planters;* Ballagh, *Slavery in Virginia;* Steiner, *Slavery in Connecticut (Johns Hopkins University Studies*, IV., No. iii., XI., Nos. ix., x., and extra vol.)

Opinions differed then, as now, regarding the actual grievances of the negro. Burnaby, who visited Virginia in 1759, thought slaves were very harshly treated; while Byrd, a somewhat fair-minded slave-owner, thought they were not worked so hard as the poorer people in other countries, and that cruelty was exceptional. The house-servants of the wealthy planters were doubtless well treated and even trained to a certain kind of refinement and dignity of manner. The conditions of the half-savage field-laborers were quite different, and the constant dread of slave insurrections showed how largely the servile relation depended upon the superior force and discipline of the dominant whites.[1]

In the north, the most familiar examples of real or imaginary slave insurrections are the so-called "negro plots" of 1712 and 1741 in New York, in both of which the danger was grossly exaggerated. Both of these "plots" were followed by severe measures of repression; and in the panic of 1741, on rather doubtful evidence, fourteen negroes were burned at the stake and eighteen were hanged. In the southern colonies the large negro population made the danger much more real, and the proximity of hostile Spaniards and Indians was an additional source of embarrassment in South Carolina. The most important actual outbreak took place in South Caro-

[1] Pinkerton, *Voyages*, XIII., 714, 750; Bassett, *Writings of William Byrd*, xxxv.; Jones, *Present State of Virginia* (ed. of 1865), 37.

lina in 1739; but the prevalent feeling is shown
by the elaborate patrol system of the province.[1]

The evils of the system were recognized even in
the south. William Byrd expressed his sympathy
with the efforts of the Georgia trustees to prohibit
slavery in their new colony, emphasizing the danger
of insurrections and the depressing influence of
slave-labor upon the whites. The southern colonies
tried to protect themselves from an excessive slave
population by a number of acts imposing prohibitory or retaliatory duties; but these acts were frequently disallowed by the crown.[2]

Some efforts were made to instruct and Christianize the slaves. Eliza Lucas, of South Carolina,
who afterwards married Chief-Justice Pinckney,
mentions "a parcel of little Negroes whom I have
undertaken to teach to read";[3] and considerable
efforts were also made to Christianize the negroes.
The theory that baptism might work emancipation
caused some anxiety at first; but it was expressly
denied by provincial statutes and in a formal declaration by the bishop of London. Both in the
northern and the southern colonies negroes became
members of churches, though their inferior status

---

[1] *N. Y. Docs. Rel. to Col. Hist.*, V., 341, VI., 195 et seq.; Valentine, *Hist. of City of New York*, 268–276; McCrady, *South
Carolina under Royal Government*, 183–187.

[2] Du Bois, *Suppression of the Slave-Trade*, chap. ii.; *Am.
Hist. Review*. I., 88.

[3] *Journal and Letters of Eliza Lucas*, 16.

was marked by their being confined to a special corner or gallery.[1]

The ethical aspect of slavery was rarely considered. Though comparatively few slaves were held in New England, this was largely the result of economic considerations, and some of the most prominent and respected merchants of Boston and Newport were deeply involved in the slave-trade. Here and there, however, the moral objection found expression.

In 1688 the Germantown Quakers protested against slave - holding by Friends as contrary to the golden rule and a scandal to the society; and during the next half - century there were similar protests. Nevertheless, many of the Quakers continued to hold slaves, and no positive action was taken against slavery by the " Yearly Meeting " of the society until 1758. Perhaps the finest expression of antislavery feeling during this period was Judge Sewall's *Selling of Joseph*. Without neglecting the economic argument against slavery, he lays the emphasis upon religious and ethical considerations: " These Ethiopians, as black as they are; seeing they are the Sons and Daughters of the First Adam, the Brethren and Sisters of the Last Adam and the Offspring of God; They ought to be treated with a Respect agreeable." [2]

---

[1] Hening, *Statutes*, III., 460; McCrady, *South Carolina under Royal Government*, chap. iii.

[2] Moore, *Slavery in Mass.*, 74–77; Sharpless, *Quaker Experiment in Government* (ed. of 1902), I., 31; Sewall, *Diary*, II., 16–20.

As late as 1750 the south had scarcely any real urban centres. In Maryland the seat of government, Annapolis, was hardly more than a village; and Baltimore had hardly a hundred inhabitants. In Virginia, Williamsburg had been made the capital and had some public buildings which attracted attention, but its permanent inhabitants were few. Richmond was not laid out as a town until about the close of this period. Norfolk, at the entrance of Chesapeake Bay, was described by William Byrd in 1728 as having "most the ayr of a Town of any in Virginia." The principal places of North Carolina were mere country villages. South Carolina, alone of all the southern colonies, had a real urban centre in Charleston, which, more than any other town in America, concentrated in itself the economic, social, and political activity of the colony to which it belonged.[1]

In the middle colonies two important centres of population grew up at Philadelphia and New York. Philadelphia, in the first sixty years of its history, developed into a town of about thirteen thousand people and was still growing rapidly when Kalm visited it a few years later. Only a few miles away was the thriving settlement of Germantown with its one street, "near two English miles long," and its four churches, two English and two German. The growth of New York was less rapid; in 1703

---

[1] Winsor, *Narr. and Crit. Hist.*, V., 261–268; [Burke], *European Settlements*, II., 212, 233; Burnaby, in Pinkerton, *Voyages*, XIII., 707; Bassett, *Writings of William Byrd*, 28.

it had about five thousand inhabitants, white and black; in 1741 the number had increased to about twelve thousand, and during this decade it stood next to Boston and Philadelphia. There were no other large towns in the middle colonies; but New York, New Jersey, and Pennsylvania each had a few other substantial places. Parts of this middle region were so well occupied with Europeans, that according to a contemporary witness, "few parts of Europe are more populous."[1]

In New England, town life had, of course, been relatively important from the first; and during the first half of the eighteenth century Boston held its place as the most considerable centre of population and trade on the continent, though the number of its inhabitants probably did not much exceed twenty thousand. Second in importance among the New England towns was Newport, which grew very rapidly after the peace of Utrecht. Along the coast from New Hampshire to New York were such considerable port towns as Portsmouth, Salem, New London, and New Haven. In New England even more than in the middle colonies the prosperity of the large towns rested upon what was, according to the standards of that day, a fairly compact surrounding population.[2]

[1] Watson, *Annals of Philadelphia*, II., 404; Kalm, in Pinkerton, *Voyages*, XIII., 395, 406, 449; Valentine, *Hist. of City of New York*, 217 and App.
[2] Weeden, *Econ. and Soc. Hist. of New England*, II., 583; Winsor, *Memorial Hist. of Boston* II.. 496, 510, 529.

More important, on the whole, than the formation of a few urban centres was the gradual recession of the frontier. The rapidity of this movement varied greatly at different points along the seaboard, but the final result was a surprise to European observers. One traveller remarked that in most places one might travel "about a hundred and twenty English miles from the seashore before you reach the first habitations of the Indians"; or spend half a year in the seaboard towns without seeing an Indian.[1]

On the extreme north the frontier still extended to the coast. Only a few years after the peace of Utrecht another Indian outbreak, inspired by the Jesuit Rale and known as Lovewell's war (1722–1725), checked the advance of settlement north and east. In 1743 the town of Brunswick, in Maine, was one of a little group of exposed frontier settlements and military posts extending only a short distance beyond the Kennebec. In New Hampshire there was a movement of settlers up the Merrimac valley to Concord, and settlements were also formed on the east bank of the Connecticut River. The first English occupation beyond the river, in what is now Vermont, was Fort Dummer, built in 1724, near the present site of Brattleboro. Farther south, the Massachusetts pioneers moved forward after Queen Anne's War across the Connecticut valley into the Berkshire region, first occupied about

---

[1] Kalm, in Pinkerton, *Voyages*, XIII., 449.

1725; and the line of settlement was soon carried close to the present western boundary of the state.[1]

In New York, the movement into the interior was comparatively slow. In 1740, as in 1690, the population of the province was confined almost wholly to Long Island and to narrow lines of settlement on both banks of the Hudson between New York City and Albany. A few weak German settlements were formed in the Mohawk valley; and on Lake Ontario there was the isolated post of Oswego.

The rapidly growing population of Pennsylvania made possible a more substantial advance. By 1744 there were considerable settlements of Germans and Scotch-Irish in the Susquehanna valley, including the substantial town of Lancaster. On the upper Schuylkill, Reading had developed by 1752 to a place of one hundred and thirty dwellings; and in 1740 the Moravians advanced the frontier towards the north by the founding of Bethlehem in the Lehigh valley.[2]

More interesting still was the westward movement in the southern colonies. At the close of the seventeenth century the estate of William Byrd the elder, at the falls of the James, on the present site of Richmond, occupied an isolated frontier

[1] Winsor, *Narr. and Crit. Hist.*, V., 127, 181–188; Holland, *Western Massachusetts*, I., chap. x.; Williamson, *Maine*, II., 214.

[2] Watson, *Annals of Philadelphia*, II., 147–150; Kuhn, *German and Swiss Settlements in Colonial Pennsylvania*, passim.

position and was exposed to Indian attacks. Within the next fifty years, and especially during the latter half of that period, population moved west and up the great rivers, the York, the Rappahannock, and the James, to the eastern slopes of the Blue Ridge. Finally, the southward course of the Scotch-Irish and Germans from Pennsylvania into the Great Valley beyond the Blue Ridge brought a population which required the organization of new county governments. In 1738 the counties of Augusta and Frederick were organized, both in the territory west of the Blue Ridge.[1]

In the Carolinas there was a similar development though somewhat later in time. When the first royal governor of North Carolina, Burrington, began his administration in 1731 almost the whole population was to be found close to the coast below the falls of the rivers, from the Roanoke southward to the Cape Fear. Twenty years later Governor Johnston, reporting on the rapid increase of population, especially from Pennsylvania, said that thousands had already come in; they were settling mainly in the west and had nearly reached the mountains. In South Carolina also the back settlements had been only slightly extended before 1730; but during the next decade settlements of Scotch-Irish, Germans, Swiss, and Welsh were made in the middle region between the tide-water and

[1] Bassett, *Writings of William Byrd*, p. xxix.; Hening, *Statutes*, V., 78.

the up-country. Finally, in the fifties, the main stream of Scotch-Irish immigration made its way into the up-country.[1]

[1] McCrady, *South Carolina under Royal Government*, chap. viii.; *N. C. Col. Records*, III., chap. xii., IV., 1073.

CHAPTER XV

FOUNDING OF GEORGIA

(1732-1754)

WHILE the older colonies were developing by the help of immigrants from Europe, occasional projects appeared for the organization of new provinces. In 1690 a proposed charter to a new colonizing company was submitted to the attorney-general. It provided for a colony in North America, lying between the thirty-fourth and the forty-sixth degrees of latitude, bounded on the east by the western boundaries of New York, Pennsylvania, New Jersey, Maryland, and Virginia, and on the west by the Pacific. The attorney-general offered no objection, but the plan was never carried out. Soon after the conquest of Acadia another new province was planned between Nova Scotia and Maine, but this project also was dropped.[1]

One of the reasons most frequently urged for new settlements was the formation of a barrier against rival colonizing powers; and the need of such a barrier colony was especially felt on the ex-

---

[1] *Cal. of State Pap., Col.*, 1689-1692, p. 761; Hutchinson, *Hist. of Mass. Bay*, II., 203.

posed frontier of South Carolina. Here, in the wilderness now occupied by the states of Georgia and Alabama, the traders and soldiers of England, France, and Spain were competing for the Indian trade and for ultinate political control. Within the present limits of Georgia there had been almost no permanent occupation by white men before the year 1733, but explorers, during the latter part of the seventeenth century, brought reports of Spaniards working mines in the mountainous regions of upper Georgia. The French, too, with their headquarters on Mobile Bay, were reaching out to secure a monopoly of the Indian trade.

To this region the English had already asserted their title by the charter of 1665, which extended the nominal jurisdiction of the Carolina proprietors to the twenty-ninth parallel, several miles south of St. Augustine. This extreme claim was never enforced; but early in the eighteenth century the South Carolina government began to push forward its posts into and beyond the valley of the Savannah. In 1716 Fort Moore was established on the Savannah opposite the present site of Augusta, Georgia. In 1721 Fort King George was established on the Altamaha and garrisoned by a few British regulars. This fort was abandoned in 1727, but another had already been built on the western bank of the Savannah, which was maintained until 1735.[1]

---

[1] Charter in Carroll, *Hist. Collections of S. C.*, II., 39; Smith, *South Carolina*, 208.

In 1730 a vigorous effort was made to counter-
act the French influence among the Indians of the
hill country by sending Sir Alexander Cuming on a
dangerous but successful mission to the Cherokees,
which resulted in their acknowledging the English
supremacy and promising the monopoly of their
trade.[1] Thus when, two years later, the British
government renewed its claims to the disputed region by granting a considerable part of it to the
Georgia trustees, the step was a natural development from the policy of the previous decade.

In the final settlement of Georgia this idea of a
barrier colony was combined with a distinctly phil-
anthropic motive. The new province should serve
as a barrier against foreign attacks and a safeguard of English interests in America; but it was
also to be a refuge for the unfortunate. Both of
these motives are explicitly stated in the charter
of the colony and both are admirably illustrated in
the personality and the public career of its founder.

James Edward Oglethorpe was born in 1689,
and had therefore reached middle life before his
American career began. After a short military
service in the English and Austrian armies, he entered the House of Commons in 1722, and, in spite
of his prolonged absences in America, he retained
his membership for over thirty years. He soon became a conspicuous member and showed the breadth
of his public interests by speeches on a variety of

[1] Winsor, *Mississippi Basin*, 183; Jones, *Georgia*, I., 76–80.

subjects. He agreed with Walpole's critics in demanding a more aggressive assertion of English interests against the Spaniards, and he objected to a treaty with the emperor, because it failed to secure the Protestants of Germany against religious persecution; he also showed his appreciation of the colonial point of view by opposing the molasses act of 1733. The words attributed to him on this occasion deserved to be remembered: "Our colonies are all a part of our own dominions; the people in every one of them are our own people, and we ought to show an equal respect to all." [1]

The most attractive aspect of Oglethorpe's parliamentary career is his disinterested service in behalf of poor debtors. Not only were honest debtors then generally subjected to the humiliation of arrest and imprisonment, but they were frequently placed at the mercy of jailers who had purchased their appointments and regarded them as investments. Oglethorpe became interested in the reform of this system, and in 1729 he secured from the Commons the appointment of a committee of inquiry. As chairman of this committee he made a series of reports to the house, bringing to light many instances of extreme cruelty and extortion.

Oglethorpe was now convinced of the existence of a large class of honest but unfortunate people who might under the more favorable conditions of

[1] Wright, *Oglethorpe*, chaps. i.–iii.; Cobbett, *Parliamentary History*, VIII., 920.

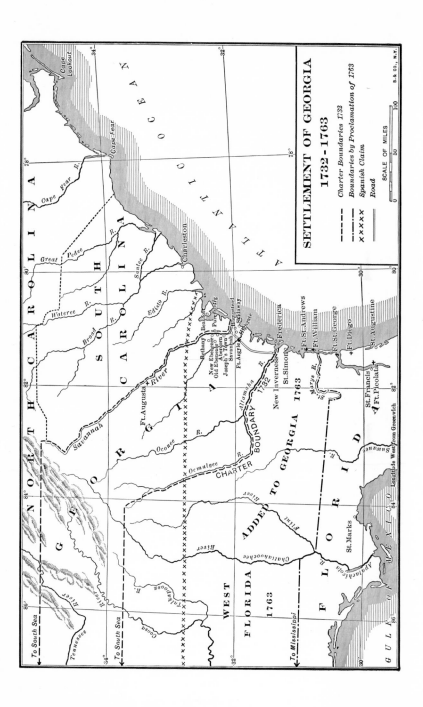

SETTLEMENT OF GEORGIA
1732-1763

Charter Boundaries 1732 — · — · —
Boundaries by Proclamation of 1763 — · · —
Spanish Claim × × × × ×
Road

SCALE OF MILES
0   50   100

B. & Co., N.Y.

a new country, and with a little assistance at the start, be enabled ultimately to stand on their own feet. Public interest had been awakened by the recent investigations, and almost at the same time the surrender of the Carolina charter left the field clear for the founding of a new colony on the southern frontier.

Many prominent noblemen and clergymen agreed to support the enterprise; and in June, 1732, they received a royal charter incorporating them as "the Trustees for establishing the colony of Georgia in America." The objects of the colony were declared to be two: first, the relief of the king's "poor subjects" who in the New World might "not only gain a comfortable subsistence for themselves and families, but also strengthen our colonies and increase the trade, navigation, and wealth" of the kingdom; secondly, the protection of the frontier against the attacks of the savages.[1]

The territory of the new colony was defined as that lying between the Savannah and Altamaha rivers and extending from their head-waters westward to the "south seas." An undivided eighth part of this territory was still the property of Lord Carteret, one of the Carolina proprietors who had refused to yield his share in the original Carolina grant. The trustees, however, promptly secured the surrender of Carteret's claim.

[1] Charter, in Poore, *Charters and Constitutions*, I.; *Some Account of the Designs of the Trustees* (*Am. Colonial Tracts*, I., No. ii.).

This charter was a return to the principle of proprietary government. The soil of the colony and the government of its people were intrusted to a private corporation which was to exercise authority over the colonists without reference to any representative assembly. It differs from the older charters, however, in two important respects. In the first place, the enterprise was purely disinterested: members of the corporation were expressly prohibited from receiving any profits from membership or the holding of office, and all the lands of the colony, with any contributions which might be received, were to be held in trust. In the second place, the reserved rights of the crown were more strongly asserted than in any previous proprietary charter. The corporation was required to present annual reports of receipts and expenditures, and all its legislation was to be submitted to the crown for approval. Every new governor had to be approved by the crown and was required to take the oaths and offer the financial securities usually required of royal governors. Even this modified proprietary government was to be temporary, for after twenty-one years Georgia was to become a royal province.

The charter provisions, taken together with the early legislation of the trustees, bring out clearly the benevolent paternalism of the founders. The corporation was authorized to transport foreigners who were willing to become subjects of the crown, and religious liberty was promised to all except "papists." A number of the regulations show the desire of the trustees to protect the moral and economic welfare of the colonists even, if necessary, against themselves. Thus, though the charter allowed one person to hold land up to five hundred acres, the maximum grant was made only to those who transported at least ten persons to the colony. These grants were entailed so that they could not be alienated or divided, and according to the original regulations estates could only pass to male heirs, reverting in the absence of such heirs to the trustees. The purpose of these rules was to protect the settlers against their own improvidence, to prevent the formation of excessively large estates, and to build up a considerable soldier-farmer class.

A logical part of this plan for developing a class of small landed proprietors was the prohibition of slavery. In South Carolina the system of large plantations worked by savage negro slaves had exposed the small white population to serious dangers from slave insurrections. The large number of fugitive slaves protected by the Spaniards and sometimes enlisted in their military service was also a serious annoyance. These dangers the trustees wished to avoid in their new colony; in close contact with the slave-holding plantation system of South Carolina they hoped to establish a new community founded on the opposite principle of free labor. The trustees also imposed important restrictions on trade: no rum was to be imported into the colony, and no trade could be carried on with the Indians without a license.[1]

The trustees now set themselves to secure desirable immigrants. They were ready to help the unfortunate, but they did not wish to fill up the colony with recruits from the vicious and degenerate classes. Besides, the funds of the trustees were insufficient to enable them to send over all who wished to take advantage of this opportunity. Hence, a careful sifting process became necessary. By the autumn of 1732, however, about one hundred men, women, and children had been gathered, including men of various occupations: carpenters, bricklayers, and farmers are among those mentioned. Oglethorpe offered to assume the conduct of the colony, and was accordingly appointed its first governor. After a voyage of nearly two months the colonists arrived at Charleston in January, 1733.[2]

South Carolina was strongly interested in the formation of this new barrier colony, and Oglethorpe and his charges were cordially received. Temporary quarters were provided for the settlers in the frontier port of Beaufort, and both the government and the people showed every disposition to help in putting the new colony on its feet.

In the mean time, Oglethorpe had to undertake

[1] *Account Showing the Progress of Georgia* (*Am. Colonial Tracts,* I., No. v.).
[2] *Ibid.;* Jones, *Georgia,* I., chaps. vi., vii.

the delicate and important task of reaching a satisfactory understanding with the Indians. The eastern part of the new province was mainly occupied by various Creek tribes. With the help of an Indian woman who had married a white trader, Oglethorpe entered into negotiations with the chief of one of these tribes, and secured from him a grant of land near the mouth of the Savannah. With the help of the same chief, a convention of the lower Creek Indians was subsequently held and a treaty of alliance was entered into. The Indians surrendered a tract of land near the coast between the Savannah and the Altamaha, and agreed to have no communication with the French and the Spaniards. These arrangements, subsequently agreed to by the Indians of the back country, were formally ratified by the common council of the trustees, and proved effective in protecting the colony from Indian attacks during the critical period of its early history.[1]

Before these negotiations were completed, Oglethorpe had brought his colonists to the tract ceded by Tomochichi and laid the foundations of the present city of Savannah. By the summer of 1733, the town had been laid out and lands allotted to individual settlers, in regular assignments including a town lot, a garden, and a farm—in all, fifty acres. For the first ten years the land was to be held rent free; but after that an annual rent of two shillings was to be paid. During the early stages of the

[1] Text of treaty in Jones, *Georgia*, I., 141–144.

settlement the inhabitants were dependent upon the common stock; they were governed by Oglethorpe in paternalistic fashion, and for many years the colony had only the most rudimentary political organization.[1]

In 1734 an important new element was introduced by the coming of the Protestant Germans from Salzburg. These Germans were subjects of the Catholic archbishop of Salzburg, who had been driven by his persecution to seek refuge in various other states and countries, including Prussia and England. In December, 1733, the trustees agreed to transport a considerable number of them to Georgia. They were to receive their passage and allowances for tools, provisions, and seed, and were to have in the province all the rights and privileges of Englishmen. Under the direction of a German nobleman, the Baron von Reck, and of their Lutheran ministers, a company of them came to Georgia in 1734. The chief settlement of the Salzburgers was at Ebenezer, a little north of Savannah on a small tributary of the Savannah River. They soon, however, removed to a new site a few miles away; both the old and the new Ebenezer have long disappeared from the map of the state. The original company was subsequently reinforced by others of the same nationality, most of whom settled in the region between Savannah and Ebenezer.

[1] Jones, *Georgia*, I., 155 et seq.; *Account Showing the Progress of Georgia*, 44–46.

In 1735 a Moravian settlement was begun, but the unwillingness of these people to perform military service made them unpopular and they soon found a more congenial home in Pennsylvania.

By 1741 it was estimated by the secretary of the trustees that at least twelve hundred German Protestants had arrived in the colony. The Germans maintained a distinct community life, whose most striking characteristics as recorded by contemporary observers were the industry of the people, the strong influence of their clerical leaders, and the primitive simplicity of their civil organization. They had for some time no regular court of justice, and their disputes were settled by the ministers in concert with three or four of "the most prudent Elders."

A more aggressive group of colonists came from the Highlands of Scotland. About one hundred and eighty people were sent out in 1735 and formed their first settlement on the north bank of the Altamaha, a few miles above its mouth; the district was named Darien and the first town New Inverness. A fort was constructed here and the colony was afterwards strengthened by new arrivals from Scotland; for the Highlanders, unlike most of the Germans, took an important part in the defence of the frontier.[1]

From the beginning, military and defensive con-

[1] Jones, *Georgia*, I., chaps. xi.–xiv.; Stevens, *Georgia*, I., 85–139.

siderations exerted a strong influence on the policy
of the trustees.   Georgia, more nearly than any
of the other North American provinces, approxi-
mates the Roman conception of a military colony
planted for the defence of the empire.   Nowhere
does this policy appear more clearly than in the
post of Frederica, at the extreme limit of the charter grant, on St. Simon's Island at the mouth of the
Altamaha.   Beginning in 1736 as a military post,
the town and its approaches were laid out with
definite reference to defence against the Spaniards.
Its people were largely engaged in supplying the
soldiers, and when, at the close of the war, the
troops were withdrawn the town rapidly declined.[1]

A more substantial and permanent settlement was
developing on the northern frontier at Augusta.
Here on the Savannah River a fort was established
in 1735, and a town laid out which soon became an
important centre for the Indian trade, especially
with the Cherokees.   Besides these principal towns,
there were a number of small villages or private
plantations in the low country adjoining Savannah
and extending southward along the coast towards
the Ogeechee.   These settlements suffered from un-
healthy situations and some of them soon disappeared.[2]

---

[1] Jones, *Dead Towns of Ga.* (Ga. Hist. Soc., *Collections*, IV.),
No. ii.

[2] *Ibid.*, esp. Nos. iii., vii.; *A State of the Province of Georgia*
(*Am. Colonial Tracts*, I., No. ii.).

From the outset the young colony was obliged to guard against attack by the Spaniards at St. Augustine, who regarded the Georgians, like the Virginians and Carolinians before them, as mere intruders. The charter grants of Carolina and Georgia constituted a direct defiance of Spanish pretensions; but the challenge was brought closer home when Oglethorpe, not content with his colony at Frederica, established a series of small military posts extending from the Altamaha to the St. John's River, well within the limits of the present state of Florida.

The Walpole ministry strongly desired to avoid war, and in 1736 an English agent was sent to St. Augustine to settle the dispute; conferences were also held by Oglethorpe with some of the Spanish officers. No final agreement could be reached, however, and with threatening language the Spanish agents asserted their claim to all the coast so far north as St. Helena Sound, only a few miles below Charleston.

It was now necessary to make thorough preparation for defence, and Oglethorpe returned to England for this purpose in the winter of 1736–1737. The Spanish government demanded his recall; but in answer to a petition from the trustees, he was authorized to raise a regiment of troops for Georgia, of which he himself was colonel. Some additional regulars were sent directly from Gibraltar, and Oglethorpe was also made commander-in-chief of all the royal forces in South Carolina. He returned to Georgia in 1738 with instructions to maintain a cautious defensive attitude until actually attacked. Then he might adopt any necessary measures whether defensive or offensive.

One of the most essential conditions of success in the conflict with the Spaniards was the good-will of the Indians. This was now endangered, partly by the misconduct of English traders and partly by the intrigues of the Spaniards. To guard against this danger, Oglethorpe undertook, in 1739, a long and dangerous journey into the back country to Coweta, the principal town of the Creek Indians, where he secured a renewal of their alliance with the English.[1]

Soon after this mission word came to Georgia of the formal declaration of war between England and Spain, brought on chiefly by the increasing friction between English merchants and Spanish customs officials. On the Georgia frontier the chief interest of the war lies in two leading operations, the English attack on St. Augustine and the successful defence of St. Simon's Island against the Spaniards.

In 1740 St. Augustine was believed to be weakened by the want of provisions and by the sending of a part of its naval force to Havana. Oglethorpe proposed to take this opportunity for an offensive

---

[1] Wright, *Oglethorpe*, chaps. viii.–xii.; Oglethorpe's letters in Ga. Hist. Soc., *Collections*, III., 28–43, 55, 81; Stevens, *Georgia*, I., 145–159.

movement, and it was agreed that with the help
of the South-Carolinians, the Indians, and some
vessels of the royal navy, St. Augustine was to be
attacked by sea and land. The land forces were
to cut off Spanish supplies from the interior and the
fleet was to prevent relief by reinforcements from
the West Indies. The combined forces arrived at
St. Augustine and began a siege; but they failed to
work effectively together and the result was a
humiliating failure.[1]

In the following year Oglethorpe reported that
the Spaniards had been strongly reinforced and
were planning an invasion of South Carolina and
Georgia. Appeals were made to the home government and to South Carolina, but with little effect.
Finally, in 1742, the blow fell. A formidable invading expedition was organized, consisting of some
four or five thousand men with a considerable fleet,
and a landing was effected at the southern end of
St. Simon's Island. Oglethorpe had only a few hundred men for the defence of Frederica, but the
character of the road which the Spaniards were
obliged to take was such that they could be attacked in detail and in disadvantageous positions.
These opportunities were effectively used and the
attacking army was defeated and demoralized. Over-
estimating the opposing force, the Spaniards withdrew
from the island and the invasion was abandoned.

[1] Jones, *Georgia*, I., chap. xxi.; McCrady, *South Carolina under
Royal Government*, chaps. xi., xii.

In 1743, Oglethorpe led a retaliatory expedition into the immediate vicinity of St. Augustine, but before the end of that year he returned to England and there were no subsequent military operations of any importance on the Georgia frontier. Though the offensive movements of the English failed to accomplish any positive result, the significant fact of the war was that they had held their ground and could not be dislodged.[1]

The early years of the colony were also troubled by internal dissensions, many of which were petty enough. One small affair has gained a certain historical interest because of the subsequent career of one of the persons involved. In 1736 the brothers John and Charles Wesley came to Georgia, John as minister of the Anglican church in Savannah and Charles as Oglethorpe's private secretary. Both the brothers showed at this stage in their careers some lack of tact in their criticism of their neighbors. John Wesley was very popular at the outset, but his aggressive churchmanship soon gave offence; and his attempt to discipline a young woman whom he had himself courted before her marriage provoked so much feeling that he was indicted on a series of petty charges. The case was never brought to trial; but Wesley was convinced that his usefulness in the colony was ended, and shortly afterwards

---

[1] Jones, *Georgia*, I., chap. xxii.; Ga. Hist. Soc., *Collections*, III., :17-155; *Gentleman's Magazine*, XII., 694-696.

sailed for England after a stay of less than two years in Georgia.[1]

Almost from the beginning there was a considerable element in the colony antagonistic to Oglethorpe, and, indeed, to the general policy of the trustees. Some of the opposition leaders were forced out of the colony; and, taking refuge in South Carolina, they published a vehement criticism of the Georgia government, charging Oglethorpe with arbitrary conduct and emphasizing his failure in the campaign against St. Augustine. Great stress was laid on the misconduct of the "storekeeper" who had been left in charge of colonial affairs during one of Oglethorpe's visits to England, though the trustees had already dismissed the offender from their service. The chief point of historical interest in this partisan statement is the claim that the growth of the colony had been checked by certain principles of economic policy which the trustees regarded as essential; the writers especially emphasize the prohibition of slavery and the restrictions imposed on the alienation of land.

In 1738 over one hundred of the freeholders signed at Savannah a petition to the trustees asserting that unless these restrictions were removed they could not compete successfully with their neighbors to the north. They urged, therefore, that lands should henceforth be granted in fee-sim-

[1] Tailfer, *True and Historical Narrative* (*Am. Colonial Tracts.* I., No. iv.), 32–39; Jones, *Georgia*, I., chap. xviii.

ple and that the introduction of negroes "with proper limitations" should be permitted. The Scotch settlers in Darien and the Salzburgers were equally convinced that slavery would be injurious to their interests, and sent in counter - petitions. The trustees rejected the Savannah petition, though they relaxed somewhat the restrictions on the alienation of land. In 1742 the opposition party sent an agent to London, who tried by petition to secure a parliamentary declaration against the policy of the trustees; but the House of Commons voted down a resolution in favor of slavery in Georgia, and the petitioner was reprimanded by the speaker for his "false, scandalous, and malicious charges" against the trustees.[1]

Nevertheless, the agitation against the policy of the trustees continued. The production of silk and wine, which had been intended to serve as the chief staples of the colony, failed to develop on any considerable scale, and it was believed that, in the production of rice, white labor could not compete with that of negro slaves. It was found difficult also to hold in the colony enough white laborers.

Among those who urged the legalization of slavery were James Habersham, an influential merchant; and the famous missionary, Whitefield, who had founded

---

[1] Tailfer, *True and Historical Narrative; Account (Am. Colonial Tracts*, I., Nos. iv., v.); Samuel Quincy's letter, in Hart, *Contemporaries*, II., 116; *Journals of the House of Commons* (ed. of 1803), XXIV., 192, 216, 221, 288.

an orphan house in Georgia and believed that its
success had been impaired by the want of negro
slaves. In this state of public feeling the prohibition of slavery gradually became ineffective and in
1749 it was finally repealed, though as a pre-
caution against slave insurrections the proportion
of negroes to white servants was limited. The
other restrictive regulations were also abandoned.
In accordance with a vote of the House of Commons the trustees repealed the act prohibiting the
importation of rum, and in 1750 the restrictions
on the tenure and alienation of land were removed.
After the removal of these restrictions Georgia
developed much more rapidly, and a considerable
movement of planters from South Carolina began
into the so-called Midway District between the Ogeechee and South Newport rivers. These planters
brought their slaves with them in such large numbers that a contemporary writer estimated the
negroes brought into the colony during the years
1751 and 1752 at nearly a thousand. Thus the low
country of Georgia began, in spite of the theories
of the trustees, to reproduce in its essential features
the social system of South Carolina.[1]

The political experience of Georgia was in many
respects unlike that of any other English colony.
No provision was made in the charter for a representative legislature and none was established un-

[1] Jones, *Georgia*, I., chaps. xxv., xxvi., xxx.; Stevens, *Georgia*,
II , 262–318.

der the proprietary government. An assembly which met in 1751 was not authorized to make laws, but only "to propose, debate, and represent to the Trustees."

The superior legislative authority was vested in the trustees, but a large discretion was left to their agents in the colony. At first, Oglethorpe had an indefinite paternalistic authority over the whole province, but a local government was soon organized at Savannah; and in 1741, while Oglethorpe was making Frederica his military headquarters, the colony was divided into two counties, one including the territory extending from the Savannah to a little beyond the Ogeechee, and the other covering all the territory to the southward. Oglethorpe retained direct control of Frederica, but the government of the northern county was intrusted to William Stephens, the former secretary of the trustees, with four assistants. In 1743, on Oglethorpe's final departure for England, the authority of President Stephens and his assistants was extended over the whole province. This arrangement continued until the surrender of the charter and the final institution of the royal government in 1754. After that date the government of Georgia was substantially that of the typical royal province, with its governor and council appointed by the king and its assembly chosen by the people.[1]

[1] *Account Showing the Progress of Georgia*, 45; Stevens, *Georgia*, I., 216–261, 372, 381–384.

In caring for the religious interests of their province the trustees showed in the main a broad and tolerant spirit. Men of all religious faiths, except that of the Roman Catholic church, were allowed freedom of worship. The population of the colony included Anglicans, Presbyterians, Moravians, Lutherans, Anabaptists, and Jews, the latter sect being sufficiently numerous to rent a room in Savannah for their public worship. Among the most conspicuous and influential men in the colony were the Lutheran ministers, such as Martin Bolzius, who served the religious interests of the German population. With all this variety the Anglican church had the advantage of special official recognition: several of the trustees were well-known Anglican clergymen; with the first company of colonists they sent out an Episcopal chaplain; and with the help of the Venerable Society they maintained a succession of ministers for the church of Savannah, including such distinguished men as John Wesley and George Whitefield.

At the beginning of the revolutionary era Georgia still remained much the smallest and weakest of the thirteen colonies. As late as 1760 it had a population of about ten thousand people, of whom over three thousand were negroes. Its historical significance lies mainly in its advanced position on the Anglo-Spanish frontier.[1]

[1] Jones, *Georgia*, I., 440–449, 541; Stevens, *Georgia*, I., 319–370.

CHAPTER XVI

PROVINCIAL INDUSTRY
(1690–1740)

THE growth of population just described implies a corresponding development of economic activity, partly on lines already indicated and partly in new directions.[1] In the south the most important characteristic of the period is the gradual rounding out and crystallizing of the plantation system. In Virginia during the seventeenth century the tendency to form large estates, favored by the physiographical conditions and the almost exclusive cultivation of tobacco, was somewhat restrained by the rule limiting grants to fifty acres for each person actually imported. These headrights gradually became more valuable, till, in 1699, the council fixed a definite purchase price for land in sterling money. Very large grants now became common: Governor Spotswood signed on one occasion several grants of ten, twenty, and forty thousand acres, including an aggregate of over eighty-six thousand for himself. Theoretically, grants were

[1] Cf. Andrews, *Colonial Self-Government* (*Am. Nation*, V.), chaps. xviii., xix.

conditioned upon occupation and improvement, but the land administration was in the hands of the governor and council, or even sometimes of the councillors alone, who, being themselves large landowners, were lax in enforcing rules which operated against the interests of their class. An extreme illustration is furnished by the record of William Byrd, of Westover, the most famous Virginian planter of the early eighteenth century. Byrd inherited from his father an estate of some twenty-six thousand acres, added to it at various times by fresh grants, one of which amounted to over one hundred thousand acres, and "owned when he died no less than 179,440 acres of the best land in Virginia." [1]

Similar laxity in other parts of the south resulted in a similar absorption of landed estates in comparatively few hands; the tendency was least marked in North Carolina and most so in South Carolina. The Carolina proprietors had begun by granting some large tracts, or baronies; but they afterwards tried to keep grants within more moderate limits; and, under the royal government, efforts were made to resume lands which had been improperly taken out in the first instance or never actually occupied. The best lands of South Carolina were monopolized by a few landholders and speculators; and after the overthrow of the proprietary government their claims were confirmed by a

[1] Bassett, *Writings of William Byrd*, Introd.

statute of 1731 which, though strongly opposed by
the royal surveyor-general, finally escaped disallowance. By 1732 it was estimated that there
were not "one thousand acres within one hundred
miles of Charleston or within twenty miles of a
river or navigable creek which were not already
taken possession of." Many estates so formed were
held together by the system of entails, which in Virginia during the early years of the eighteenth century became even stricter than that of the mother-
country. Land and slaves became the dominant
passion of the planter, who could rarely be induced
"to sell or even lease the smallest portion of his
lands."[1]

As the land system developed, the growing import trade in slaves furnished the kind of cheap
labor desired for the great estates, and, especially
in Virginia and South Carolina, gradually superseded the system of white service in the fields. In
Maryland, however, white service continued to be
important.[2] Notwithstanding all efforts towards di-
versification, Virginia and Maryland continued during this period to devote themselves almost wholly
to tobacco. For the marketing of this product the
planter was dependent upon the London merchants,
who sent out their ships, not to a few trading ports
in the colony, but up the rivers to the individual

[1] Smith, *South Carolina*, 28–70, esp. 41; Ballagh, *Land System in the South* (Am. Hist. Assoc., *Report*, 1897), 117; Hening,
Statutes, III., 320.   [2] See above, p. 237.

plantations, though the large planters sometimes acted as agents for their neighbors. The attempts to establish towns at which tobacco might be collected for export, especially by the small planters, were almost wholly unsuccessful. The planters complained of exorbitant freight rates, and, indeed, of difficulty in securing regular transportation on any terms. The small planters suffered most; but even the larger planters with their regular correspondents in London sometimes failed to secure sufficient shipping.

The London merchant was the planter's agent in the purchase of goods as well as in the sale of tobacco, and the natural result was a large development of the credit system. The long delays in exchange between America and England often left the planter in considerable uncertainty as to the exact extent of his balance. Thus a Virginia planter wrote to his agent in 1695, pressing him to send his account at once, "for not knowing how my account stands, I dare not send for goods though my wants are very great and pressing." This system certainly did not promote sound business methods, and many of the larger land-owners were, like Byrd himself, heavily in debt to their English agents.[1]

It was essential to the prosperity of the tobacco colonies that their products should maintain a good

[1] Bassett, *Writings of William Byrd*, xxxv.–xxxix.; Bassett, *Virginia Planter and London Merchant* (Am. Hist. Assoc., *Report*, 1901, I.), 553–575.

standard of quality, and this need was a frequent subject of provincial legislation. In this respect Maryland was less fortunate than Virginia, and her trade was seriously depressed in consequence. Bills for the inspection of tobacco, with a view to enhancing its price, were strongly urged by the small planters, who were relatively strong in the lower house; but the insistence of the latter on reducing the fees of public officers, regularly paid in tobacco, prevented the passage of such a measure by the office-holders in the council, until 1747, when a satisfactory compromise was reached and efficient inspection secured.[1]

No one product in the Carolinas had quite the same position in provincial life which tobacco had in Virginia, although in South Carolina rice soon became the chief article of export, and competed with great success in the markets of southern Europe. This promising trade was checked in 1705 by an English statute which added rice to the list of enumerated articles; but in 1730 the restriction was removed as to ports south of Cape Finisterre, and the trade revived, though not on the scale which had been hoped for. Indigo, later second to rice as a staple export, was not produced in considerable quantities until near the middle of the eighteenth century. Both the Carolinas produced considerable quantities of lumber, of naval stores, including pitch and tar, and of provisions; but North

[1] Mereness, *Maryland*, 106–118.

Carolina had no one important staple, and her aggregate production for export was comparatively small. The most striking economic difference between South Carolina trade and that of the tobacco colonies was its concentration in the one important port of Charleston; but there was no such development in North Carolina.[1]

The engrossing of estates by a few large owners and the increasing use of slave-labor checked the development of an independent small-farmer class and discouraged immigration. In North Carolina, however, where land could be had on easier terms, and where governmental authority was comparatively lax, the population was quite different from that of tide-water Virginia or South Carolina, and the large planter did not have the same overshadowing importance as in the two neighboring colonies At the other extreme of the social scale stood the shiftless farmers whom William Byrd described so effectively in his *History of the Dividing Line*, who kept "so many Sabbaths every week, that their disregard of the Seventh Day has no manner of cruelty in it, either to Servants or Cattle"; they loitered "away their lives, like Solomon's Sluggard, with their Arms across, and at the Winding up of the Year scarcely have Bread to Eat." Yet some allowance must be made for the prejudices of a Vir-

[1] McCrady, *South Carolina under Royal Government*, 109, 262–265; *N. Y. Docs. Rel. to Col. Hist.*, V., 609; Anderson, *Origin of Commerce*, III., 200, 224, 229; *N. C. Col. Records*, III., xv.

ginia planter; and undoubtedly there stood between these two extremes a substantial though less picturesque class of small farmers.[1]

In the second quarter of the century the Scotch-Irish and German immigration was just beginning to complicate the social structure of the planter colonies by bringing in a class of settlers who cultivated comparatively small farms on the frontiers, without slaves for the most part, and produced wheat instead of tobacco or rice. They were still, however, of minor importance in southern life.

The industrial life of the northern colonies was developing on lines clearly divergent from that of the south. There is nothing comparable to the great plantation systems of Virginia and South Carolina, except among some exceptional communities like the Narragansett and Hudson River farmers. In New York the English governors after the revolution of 1689 continued the practice of lavish grants begun under the Dutch régime; but these grants failed to develop to any large extent a real plantation system, for the number of slaves imported was comparatively small. On the other hand, few immigrants cared to become tenants on the great estates. The chief effect of this unwise administration was, therefore, to divert immigration to other provinces. Generally speaking, therefore, the middle colonies as well as those of New England continued to be occupied by comparatively small hold-

[1] Bassett, *Writings of William Byrd*, chap. xii., 61, 76.

ings, not isolated economic units like the Virginia plantations, but grouped together in more or less compact communities.[1]

The labor system of the north shows a similar divergence from southern conditions. Negroes were few, and though white servants were numerous in Pennsylvania, even they did not form a permanently servile class. Aristocratic usages and traditions existed, but the general trend of economic development was towards a democratic society. The greater variety of northern industry appeared the moment one passed from the Chesapeake colonies into Pennsylvania. In 1700, Robert Quarry reported that the Pennsylvanians as the result of their industry had made "bread, flower and Beer a drugg in all the Markets in the West Indies." In later years beef, pork, and lumber appear as important articles of export. The agricultural products of New York and New Jersey were in the main similar to those of Pennsylvania. In a word, the middle colonies were the great producers of provisions.[2]

The colonists still depended mainly upon England for their clothing and other manufactures, though their early experiments in this field were important enough to arouse the jealousy of the mother-country. In these enterprises the southern colonies were ob-

---

[1] *N. Y. Docs. Rel to Col. Hist.*, V., 368–371; cf. Ballagh, *Land System in the South* (Am. Hist. Assoc. *Report*, 1897), 110–113; Shepherd, *Proprietary Government in Pa.*, 45 et seq.

[2] *N. Y. Docs. Rel. to Col. Hist.*, V., 601–604, 686; Ames, *Pa. and the English Govt.*

served to be far less active and successful than those
of the north. The Board of Trade declared in 1732
that there were "more trades carried on and manufactures set up in the provinces on the continent of
America to the northward of Virginia, prejudicial
to the trade and manufactures of Great Britain,
particularly in New England, than in any other of
the British colonies." [1]

The colonial woollen industry which Parliament
had attempted to check by the act of 1698 continued to be an object of special interest and suspicion to the Board of Trade.   During Queen Anne's
War and the consequent interruption of trade, there
was apparently a considerable development of the
industry, especially in New England.   In 1708 a
zealous royal official in New England made the extreme assertion with regard to the country people
that "not one in forty but wears his own carding,
spinning, etc."; and soon afterwards Governor Dudley reported that "the people here clothe themselves with their own wool, though they would be
glad to buy English wool if they could afford it."
Later reports, however, indicate no considerable development beyond the production of the coarser
grades for domestic use, which went on more or less
in all the colonies.   There were also some manufactures of linen, as among the Germans of Pennsylvania and the Scotch-Irish of New Hampshire.

One detail of clothing acquired during this period

[1] Anderson, *Origin of Commerce*, III., 194.

an unusual historic importance. In 1721 the Board
of Trade noted in its report on New England that
"some hatters have lately set up their trade in the
principal Towns." The industry also appeared in
New York, presently came to the knowledge of the
London Company of Feltmakers, and finally called
forth an act of Parliament in 1732 prohibiting the
export of hats from one colony to another, requiring for makers of hats an apprenticeship of seven
years, and forbidding any master to employ more
than two apprentices.[1]

One other class of industrial experiments excited
the interest and jealousy of the mother-country.
These were the small beginnings of the American
iron industry, which was carried on in several of
the continental colonies during the early years of
the eighteenth century. Iron was then mined in
New England, Pennsylvania, Maryland, and Virginia, and all of these colonies began the rudimentary
forms of iron manufacture in charcoal furnaces. In
the Board of Trade reports for 1721 the iron works
of New England are referred to as furnishing small
quantities for common use, but English iron was
said to have a better reputation and to be more
generally used. In 1732 the Massachusetts colonists were said by one official to make "all sorts of
iron-work for shipping"; but the governor, while

---

[1] N. Y. Docs. Rel. to Col. Hist., V., 63, 591-630, 938; N. C.
Col. Records, III., xv.; Palfrey, New England, IV., 326, 399;
5 George II., chap. xxii.; N. J. Docs. Rel. to Col. Hist., V., 306.

admitting that the local iron-works afforded the
people iron for some common necessaries, asserted
that British iron was wholly used for the shipping
and that the colonial product could not supply one-
twentieth of the local demand. William Byrd, about
the same time, describes several iron-works in Virginia in which the former Governor Spotswood,
among others, was interested. During the next
decade New England sent insignificant quantities
of pig-iron to England; but Pennsylvania, and especially the Chesapeake colonies, exported more
largely.[1]

There was a considerable sentiment in England
in favor of developing the iron resources of the
colonies; but the more finished products were objectionable as likely to come into competition with
those of the mother-country. In 1719 it was proposed in Parliament to prohibit the manufacture
of iron wares or even of bar-iron. About twenty
years later there was a lively agitation in favor of
encouraging the importation of partially worked
iron from the colonies on the ground that it would
stimulate the more finished manufactures of the
mother-country and would also free English merchants from their dependence on Sweden and Rus-
sia. The discussion did not take shape in legisla-

---

[1] Weeden, *Econ. and Soc. Hist. of New England*, I., 396, II.,
497–500; *N. Y. Docs. Rel. to Col. Hist.*, V., 598; Anderson,
Origin of Commerce, III., 192; Bassett, *Writings of William Byrd*,
342–361.

tion until 1750, when an act was passed allowing the free importation into England of colonial pig-iron, and, at the port of London, of bar-iron, but prohibiting American manufacture beyond that stage. Probably the colonial industry was not sufficiently advanced to suffer seriously from this statutory prohibition; but it doubtless caused some irritation.[1]

Two kinds of colonial manufacture which were thoroughly established and carried far beyond provincial limits were the building of ships and the distilling of rum, and the chief seat of both was New England. New-Englanders had been ship-builders almost from the first; but the industry assumed much larger proportions during the first half of the eighteenth century. The small craft of the seventeenth century were gradually replaced by larger ones, though even in 1780 a ship of five hundred tons was considered unusually large. New England ship-building was not confined to a few leading ports but spread to nearly all the coast and river towns; and Pennsylvania also developed a considerable ship-building industry. Both Pennsylvania and New England built ships not merely for their own use, but for sale abroad, in the West Indies and in Europe; hence English jealousies were again aroused, and the ship-carpenters of the Thames

[1] Anderson, *Origin of Commerce*, III., 88, 167, 170, 217; Weeden, *Econ. and Soc. Hist. of New England*, II., 683; 23 George II., chap. xxix.

complained of the New England competition. Richard West, the legal adviser of the Board of Trade, reported that though their grievance might be well founded, "they might as well complain of ship-building at Bristol, because the acts of navigation recognized colonial ships as English built." The Board of Trade apparently sympathized with the ship-masters, but nothing was done.[1]

During the same period the manufacture of rum first assumed large proportions. The chief seats of this industry were Massachusetts and Rhode Island, especially Newport, and it was made from West Indian molasses. It was not only consumed at home, but was regarded as indispensable for the fishing fleets, the Indian trade, and the African slave-trade.[2]

[1] Weeden, *Econ. and Soc. Hist. of New England*, I., 366–369, II., 573–576; Chalmers, *Revolt*, II., 33; *N. Y. Docs. Rel. to Col. Hist.*, V., 604; cf. Andrews, *Colonial Self-Government* (*Am. Nation*, V.), chap. xix.

[2] Weeden, *Econ. and Soc. Hist. of New England*, II., 459, 501–503; Anderson, *Origin of Commerce*, III., 180–182.

CHAPTER XVII

PROVINCIAL COMMERCE
(1690–1740)

IN the commerce of the provincial era the Indian fur trade continued to play an important part. In New York, peltry was one of the chief articles of export; and Cadwallader Colden, the historian of the Iroquois confederacy, said that in this trade New York was the only English colony that could successfully compete with the French. Reference has already been made to Burnet's establishment at Oswego and his efforts to break up the trade between Albany and Montreal. It was found impossible to stop the trade altogether, and a new measure was therefore adopted which aimed to discourage it by imposing higher duties than on the direct trade with the western Indians.[1]

A considerable Indian trade was also developed on the frontiers, from Pennsylvania southward. The founder of the Byrd family in Virginia was interested in the trade carried on by pack-horse caravans with the Catawbas, Creeks, and Cherokees of

[1] *N. Y. Docs. Rel. to Col. Hist.*, V., 687, 726–733, 745 et seq., 781, 818, 820, 824; see above, p. 212.

the southwest. During the eighteenth century
there was often sharp rivalry between individual
colonies for the control of this trade. The Virginians, gradually losing ground before the Carolinians, complained of unfair regulations imposed by
South Carolina, which afterwards had similar complaints to make of Georgia. In the south as well
as in the north the international rivalry between
French and English was also active. The Board of
Trade complained that the trade which ought to
be a source of strength to the English interest
was tainted with so many abuses that it often provoked the hostility of the Indians. They therefore urged new regulations for Indian affairs. No
general measures were adopted, however, for many
years.[1]

Except for the Indian trade, American commerce,
whether intercolonial or international, was mainly
carried on by sea, and in sea-going commerce New
England easily took the lead. The abundance of
good harbors on her coasts, the rich resources offered by the northern coast and deep-sea fisheries,
and the ready supply of lumber for ship-building had
all combined to make the New-Englanders a sea-
going people.

The prosperity of New England commerce was
closely related to the development of the fisheries.

[1] Bassett, *Writings of William Byrd*, chaps. xvii.–xix.; Smith,
South Carolina, 212–219; *N. Y. Docs. Rel. to Col. Hist.*, V., 611,
626, 627.

During the early French wars this interest suffered severely, and it was not until the second quarter of the eighteenth century that the New-Englanders fairly established themselves in the northern fisheries. Then the industry developed rapidly all along the north shore, and in 1741 the single port of Gloucester had seventy vessels engaged. The cod-fisheries were the most important; but there was also an interesting development in whaling, from the early catch of drift-whales and the small-boat fisheries near the coast, to the deep-sea whaling which reached its prime by the middle of the eighteenth century and carried New England seamen on perilous voyages to the most remote regions of the Atlantic.[1]

The fisheries of New England may fairly be described as the foundation of her international trade; for fish was, on the whole, her steadiest article of export. The better grades were shipped to the Catholic countries of southern Europe and the produce of the trade was expended sometimes in the illegal importation of European products; but in the main, probably in English manufactures or in wine from the Azores or the Canaries, a permissible article of direct import under the navigation acts. Other important exports for this transatlantic trade were lumber and naval stores, though New England herself gradually came to depend for naval stores upon

[1] Weeden, *Econ. and Soc. Hist. of New England*, I., 430–447, II., 595–598.

the Carolinas. Frequently the voyage to Europe resulted in the sale of the ship itself.

Probably no branch of New England commerce has had a more direct and evident influence upon her history than the trade with the West Indies. Here again the fisheries furnished a large part of the material for export, especially the "refuse fish" then thought good enough for the West Indian slaves. With fish went lumber, horses, provisions, and some British manufactures. From the West Indies the New-Englanders took in return various tropical products, including sugar, and especially large quantities of molasses for the distilleries of Massachusetts and Rhode Island. This commerce was closely connected with the rapid development of the African slave-trade; for, as has been seen, New England rum was sent to the Guinea coast for slaves, and these in turn found their best market in the plantation colonies, especially in the West Indies. Newport especially profited largely by this trade.[1]

Philadelphia, the chief commercial port of the middle colonies, followed to a limited extent the lines of New England commerce, though her exports were somewhat different. Grain formed an important article of export from the middle colonies to the West Indies, the Azores, and even

---

[1] Weeden, *Econ. and Soc. Hist. of New England*, I., 353 et seq., 371–373, II., chaps. xii., xiv.; *N. Y. Docs. Rel. to Col. Hist.*, V., 595, 597.

to southern Europe. Beef, pork, and lumber were
also exported, and, as in the case of the New-
Englanders, the ship itself was sometimes sold.
Return voyages brought clothing and other manufactures from England; sugar, molasses, and other
tropical products—often Spanish money from the
West Indies. So large a share of the latter, however, was paid for European goods that little remained in the colonies. New York's trade was
similar to that of Philadelphia, though her export
of peltry was more important and her ship-building
less so. One other branch of trade in which the
northern colonies were engaged was that of bringing logwood from Central America to be re-exported
to European markets.[1]

There are no accurate statistics as to the trade
of the continental colonies, but some figures furnished by the Board of Trade in 1721 will illustrate
the general situation. The annual exports from
England to the continental colonies were then
valued at about £430,000, of which a little over
two-thirds were British goods and the rest foreign
articles re-exported. Woollen goods constituted
roughly one-half of the whole value of British articles exported. Next in importance stood wrought
iron and nails. The imports from the continental
colonies were valued, roughly, at £300,000, and of
this amount about one-half was tobacco. Next in

[1] *N. Y. Docs. Rel. to Col. Hist.*, V., 601, 685; Anderson, *Origin
of Commerce*, III., 171.

order came naval stores, rice, and peltry. More than three-fourths of the total English imports from the continental colonies came from Virginia, Maryland, and the Carolinas, and a much larger amount (more than two-thirds of all the imports from the American colonies) came from the British sugar islands of the West Indies. Of the English export trade a much larger proportion went to the sugar islands than to either the northern or the southern group of continental colonies. In the aggregate trade of England with the continental colonies she exported more largely than she imported, this condition being due to the northern colonies, which sent no great staples directly to England and paid for their English manufactures indirectly through their ship-building and carrying trade and their commerce with the West Indies and southern Europe.

These figures show the greater value of England's direct trade with the West Indies as compared with that carried on with the northern colonies; and the same fact is emphasized by the statistics of shipping. The tonnage to the British West Indies was more than twice as large as that to New England, New York, and Pennsylvania combined, and somewhat larger than the aggregate for the Chesapeake colonies and the Carolinas. These facts explain the emphasis given by British colonial administrators to West Indian interests. It is to be remembered also that the trade of the northern colonies, especially that of New England, was carried on largely

in their own shipping, while that of the south and
the West Indies was in the hands of British merchants.[1]

Even from the mercantilist point of view there
were decided advantages in the trade between the
northern colonies and the West Indies; it supplied
the sugar islands with provisions and lumber on
cheaper terms than would otherwise have been possible, and it enabled the New-Englanders and Pennsylvanians to buy more freely of English manufactures.   After 1713, however, the British West
Indian planters grew jealous of the trade between
their continental countrymen and the French and
Dutch islands.   The French relaxed their old restrictions, and their sugar production developed
rapidly until it began to displace the British product in European markets.   The New - Englanders
also found that they could buy their sugar and molasses more cheaply from the French and Dutch.
In 1721 the Board of Trade called attention to this
undesirable form of New England enterprise, and
in 1731 the sugar-planters and the merchants trading to the West Indies petitioned Parliament for
relief.   In the latter year a bill for this purpose
passed the House of Commons but was dropped in
the House of Lords.

During the next two years the question was much
debated, but the final outcome was the molasses
act of 1733, imposing prohibitory duties on foreign

---

[1] *N. Y. Docs. Rel. to Col. Hist.*, V., 613–619.

sugar, molasses, and rum imported into the English colonies.[1] The friends of the bill emphasized the value of the sugar colonies as a market for English manufactures and for African slaves and the large amount of shipping employed in the trade. They asserted also that the trade of the continental colonies was chiefly responsible for the too successful competition of the foreign sugar islands in Europe. The northern colonies claimed that the British West Indies could not meet the whole American demand in addition to that of the mother-country, dwelt on the importance of their own shipping interests and of the rum industry, and insisted that the unfortunate condition of the British sugar plantations was largely due to improvidence and mismanagement. Finally, they argued that it was the trade with the French islands which enabled them to pay for British manufactures. The act was passed, but it involved so serious a disturbance of the natural course of trade that it was systematically violated.[2]

Of great importance, but extremely difficult to estimate even approximately, was the intercolonial coasting trade. Thus the middle colonies sent bread-stuffs to New England as well as to South Carolina. A large part of the coasting trade was carried on in New England vessels, which supplied

[1] 6 George II., chap. xiii.

[2] N. Y. Docs. Rel. to Col. Hist., V., 597; Anderson, Origin of Commerce, III., 140, 171, 177–182; Beer, Commercial Policy of England, chap. vi. For later effects, see Howard, Preliminaries of the Revolution (Am. Nation, VIII.), chap. iii.

the southerners not only with their own domestic
commodities but with the proceeds of the European and West Indian trades, North Carolina in
particular being largely dependent upon them for
contact with the outside world.[1]

The intercolonial wars gave rise directly or
indirectly to several abnormal forms of colonial
enterprise. On the border-line between war and
commerce, technically legal yet tending always to
degenerate into distinctly criminal courses, was privateering. The privateer had a regular commission
from his government to prey upon the enemy's
commerce, thus enabling him to combine patriot-
ism with private advantage. The peace of Utrecht
closed for a time the opportunity for legitimate
privateering, but it developed again on a large
scale upon the outbreak of war with Spain in 1739.
Rhode Island merchants were conspicuous for their
investments in this form of business.[2]

In time of peace the more reckless privateersmen were easily drawn into piracy. Just before
and after the revolution of 1689 piracy was very
common, and in many of the colonial seaports was
looked upon somewhat indulgently by the local
merchants, who were glad to have the pirate's
money without inquiring too closely as to its source.

[1] Weeden, *Econ. and Soc. Hist. of New England*, II., 589–592;
N. Y. Docs. Rel. to Col. Hist., V., 686; *N. C. Col. Records*, III.,
xv.–xvii.

[2] Weeden, *Econ. and Soc. Hist. of New England*, I., 337 et seq.,
II., 598 et seq.

Much was said about the laxity of the proprietary governors in this respect, but one of the most notorious offenders was the royal governor Fletcher, of New York. To remedy this crying evil the British piracy act of 1699 was passed, and in the succeeding years pirates were severely dealt with in several of the colonies. The best-known piratical adventurer of this period was Captain William Kidd, who, under the auspices of Lord Bellomont, governor of New York, and the great Lord Chancellor Somers, set out to capture pirates, but ended by turning pirate, or half pirate, himself, and thus brought scandal on his distinguished patrons. He was finally arrested by order of Bellomont, sent to England for trial, and executed there, upon somewhat inadequate evidence, for the crimes of piracy and murder. In 1704 some pirates were executed in Boston, affording a grewsome entertainment to Samuel Sewall and his fellow-citizens.[1]

The climax of American piracy was reached at the close of the War of the Spanish Succession, when the forces of the pirates were swelled by accessions from former privateersmen. Their chief haunts during this period were the Bahamas, which had for a time fallen into a state of anarchy; and the convenient inlets and rivers of North Carolina.

---

[1] *Dict. of National Biography*, art. Kidd; Cobbett, *Parliamentary History*, V., 1276; *N. Y. Docs. Rel. to Col. Hist.*, IV., 275, 454, 470, 551, 583, 815; Weeden, *Econ. and Soc. Hist. of New England*, I., 340 et seq., 423, II., 559–565; Sewall, *Diary*, II., 108–110.

Two of these maritime desperadoes who stand out above their fellows are Teach, or Thatch, sometimes known as Blackbeard, and Steve Bonnet, formerly a respectable inhabitant of Barbadoes. The leading proprietary officials of North Carolina were strongly suspected of complicity with the pirates, and finally, after a succession of outrages all along the coast, the neighboring governments were forced to act. In 1718, Governor Spotswood, of Virginia, sent an expedition into North Carolina, which in a pitched battle killed Thatch and some of his accomplices. In the same year the South Carolina government sent a similar expedition to the Cape Fear River, where after another desperate encounter Bonnet and his crew were captured. Bonnet himself and most of his followers were soon after tried and executed. Before the year ended, another engagement off Charleston resulted in the capture and execution of several other desperadoes. These and other vigorous measures soon made piracy a more exceptional feature of maritime life.[1]

The extent of the colonial trade carried on in violation of the navigation acts has been and still is a matter of controversy. Some provisions of these acts were undoubtedly well observed, as, for instance, the rule limiting trade with the colonies to English (including colonial-built) vessels. It is also generally agreed that the molasses act, which

---

[1] Hughson, *Carolina Pirates* (*Johns Hopkins University Studies,* XII., Nos. 5-7).

attempted to break up colonial trade with the foreign sugar colonies, was systematically violated.
Probably the export of enumerated articles was in
the main confined to England, as the law provided,
though there was said to be some illicit exportation
of Virginia and North Carolina tobacco from the ill-
guarded coasts of the latter colony, with the convenient aid of New England traders. The greatest
doubt exists as to the enforcement of the clause requiring that all European goods should be imported
by way of England. During the two decades following the revolution of 1689 the colonists were
charged with carrying on a large amount of this
illegal import trade; but something must undoubtedly be allowed for the zealous efforts of royal
agents to discredit the chartered governments, and
something, perhaps, for friction in the inauguration
of a new system.

After the peace of Utrecht there appear from
time to time references to illegal imports from
Europe. Thus Thomas Amory, of Boston, wrote to
one of his correspondents in 1721, "If you have a
Captain you can confide in, you will find it easy to
import all kinds of goods from the Streights, France,
and Spain, although prohibited." The famous
Peter Faneuil was also involved in the illicit trade
in European goods, and disposed to resent any excessive strictness on the part of admiralty judges.
A fair general conclusion would seem to be that
though there was much illegal trading, the volume

of this illicit trade, with the exception of that carried on with the West Indies in defiance of the
molasses act, was not relatively large, and that the
eighteenth - century colonists drew the great bulk
of their European goods from English ports.[1]

One of the most perplexing of colonial problems
was that of securing an adequate medium of exchange.   At the close of the seventeenth century
the chief metallic money of the colonists was the
Spanish silver piece-of-eight. This Spanish silver
was not only limited in quantity, but it was subject
to a confusing variety of ratings in the different
colonies, and the efforts of the home government
to regulate it were not successful. Nearly all the
colonies during this century depended largely upon
various systems of barter or payment in kind.
Thus Virginia had her tobacco currency and Massachusetts her "country pay," or payment in commodities at certain fixed values. In North Carolina this primitive barter system continued until
the middle of the eighteenth century.[2]

The want of a satisfactory circulating medium
was aggravated by the financial difficulties of the
colonial governments. In the colonies as in England the wars with France subjected the financial

[1] Ashley, *Surveys Historic and Economic*, 336–360; Beer,
Commercial Policy of England, esp. 134–143; Weeden, *Econ. and
Soc. Hist. of New England*, II., 556–558, 611 et seq.; *N. C. Col.
Records*, III., xvi.

[2] Bullock, *Monetary Hist. of the U.S.*, chaps. ii., iii.; see above,
p. 39.

resources of the state to an unusual strain, which they could hardly meet by the immediate imposition of taxes. From one or the other of these motives, or both of them together, paper money was issued by all of the colonies.

The first bills were issued by Massachusetts to meet the expenses of Phips's disastrous expedition against Quebec in 1690. Though declared "in value equal to money," they depreciated rapidly; but during the next twenty years the issues were kept within moderate limits, and the notes were brought for a considerable time to par with coin. The first serious tendency to inflation appeared near the close of Queen Anne's War. The volume of bills was then swelled by numerous emissions, while credit was also impaired by postponing the taxes necessary for their redemption.

All the New England colonies were led to the same course by financial necessities and the real or supposed need of a circulating medium. Efforts to check the depreciation by legal-tender legislation and other forcing measures all failed. New issues were made to replace the old; but the "new tenor" bills only added new rates of depreciation, bringing great hardships not only to the creditor class, but to all recipients of fixed incomes. In 1749 Massachusetts was able to restore her currency to a specie basis; but her neighbors continued to suffer from a depreciated currency, Rhode Island having a particularly bad record in this respect.

During Queen Anne's War, and as a direct result of the financial burdens imposed by the French and Indian wars, paper currencies were issued by New York and both the Carolinas. They were largely increased afterwards, with the same results of extreme depreciation, which could not be effectively checked by legal tender and forcing clauses. Virginia was much more conservative during this period, issuing no bills until 1755. Maryland and the middle colonies, except New York, were comparatively prudent also, though the Pennsylvanians were thoroughly convinced of the desirability of paper money, and their most eminent citizen, Benjamin Franklin, early distinguished himself in its defence.[1]

One of the worst phases of the paper-money movement was the "bank," a natural product of a time when the nature and limitations of credit were not clearly understood, a period marked by such disastrous experiments as the French "Mississippi Scheme " and the "South Sea Bubble," in which many prominent English politicians were involved. A colonial "bank" has been described as "simply a batch of paper money " lent out either by the government or by a private company. In either case there was little or no specie value behind the

[1] Bullock, *Monetary Hist. of the U. S.*, 29–59, 125–156, 207–245; Weeden, *Econ. and Soc. Hist. of New England*, I., 319–330; 379–387, II., 473–486; Smith, *South Carolina*, 229–275; Dewey, *Financial Hist. of the U. S.*, chap. i.

notes, and usually very poor security for the payment either of the principal or of the interest pledged. Such "banks" were undertaken by colonial governments in New England and elsewhere, often with disastrous results. The best-known of these schemes was the Massachusetts "Land Bank" of 1740, a private institution which, however, became a conspicuous factor in provincial politics. Only an insignificant part of the stock of this bank was subscribed in cash, and for the rest commodities of various kinds might be accepted. The bank then issued notes which added perceptibly to the confusion of currency in the province, until Parliament put a stop to its operations.[1]

Throughout the eighteenth century the British government showed its hostility to paper-money issues and tried to check them in various ways, especially by instructions to the governors. These instructions were, however, frequently evaded or disobeyed; for governors could be brought to terms by the assemblies refusing to vote salaries or withholding money for urgent public needs. The colonists themselves were divided on the question, as, for instance, in South Carolina, where there was a sharp contest between the planters who wished a paper currency and the merchants who opposed it. In a similar division in Massachusetts the con-

[1] Bullock, *Monetary Hist. of the U. S.*, 29–32; Davis, *Currency and Banking in Mass. Bay*, esp. pt. ii., chaps. v.–ix.; 14 George II., chap. xxxvii.

servative business interests finally secured the withdrawal of the paper altogether. Parliament also
interested itself in the question, and, after some
previous inquiries and resolutions, passed in 1751
an act prohibiting the issue of paper money in New
England, except in certain clearly defined cases.
This legislation was not extended to the other colonies until 1764.[1]

Notwithstanding unfortunate experiments of various kinds, the colonies were on the whole prosperous. Prosperity was probably more generally
diffused in New England and Pennsylvania than
elsewhere; but in every colony there were many
persons who could, according to the standards of the
time, command the material comforts and luxuries
of life. In the south the most substantial wealth
was probably to be found in Charleston; but a considerable number of the Virginian planters, though
often land-poor and in debt, were able to secure for
themselves luxuries of food, clothing, and furniture.
Such a man, for instance, was William Byrd. In
New England there were prosperous merchants, such
as Peter Faneuil, or Thomas Amory, who, after a
broad experience in various parts of the world, settled in Boston in 1719 and wrote of his new home,
"People live handsomely here and without fear of
anything." Philadelphia and New York also gave
to intelligent observers like the Swedish Kalm and
the English Burnaby the impression of comfort and

[1] 24 George II., chap. liii.; 4 George III., chap. xxxiv.

prosperity.   Burnaby, who visited Philadelphia in
1760, spoke of it with admiration, observing its substantial public buildings and its handsome streets.
A few years earlier Kalm wrote rather extravagant-
ly that "its fine appearance, good regulations, agreeable situation, natural advantages, trade, riches
and power, are by no means inferior to those of any,
even of the most ancient, towns in Europe." [1]

[1] Weeden, *Econ. and Soc. Hist. of New England*, II., 565 et
seq., 624 et seq.; Jones, *Present State of Virginia* (ed. of 1865),
28–31; Pinkerton, *Voyages*, XIII., 396, 456, 728, 736–739; Hart,
Contemporaries, II., §§ 23, 28.

CHAPTER XVIII

PROVINCIAL CULTURE

(1690–1740)

DURING the seventeenth century the pressure of material needs and the scattered character of the settlements prevented much development in the finer elements of civilization; and though New England showed a strongly idealistic spirit, her culture was narrowed by theological partisanship.

At the close of the century these unfavorable conditions were gradually changing and there began a period of substantial progress in civilization. The older communities were emerging from the hardships of the pioneer period; they were coming to have leisure and taste for intellectual pursuits, and becoming ambitious of larger opportunities for their children. The improved communications between different colonies were giving to their higher life some real community of interest, by weakening local and sectarian prejudices. The development of mercantile interests also helped to bring the backward or one-sided life of the colonies into vital contact with the main currents of European progress. In Boston, New York, Philadelphia, and

Charleston there were many men who had regular business connections with the Old World and from time to time found it necessary to cross the ocean.

Much credit must also be given to the royal governors. Francis Nicholson, for instance, while governor in Virginia, Maryland, and South Carolina, gave special attention to education, urging it upon the attention of his colonial assembly, and himself making contributions to the cause. When Yale College was founded, this zealous Anglican showed a surprising breadth of interest by contributing to its stock of books. So, too, his successor in Virginia, Governor Spotswood, was one of the chief patrons of William and Mary College.[1]

In New York and Massachusetts, Governor Burnet left an enviable reputation as a man of scholarly and literary tastes. In New York he had among his political advisers a rather unusual group of intellectual men, and during his residence in Massachusetts he was understood to be a contributor of essays to the *New England Weekly Journal*. Governor Dudley, whatever his faults may have been, was a "gentleman and a scholar" who kept himself in sympathy with the literary and scientific activities of his time.[2]

The Anglican church also exerted an important civilizing influence. The first two commissaries of

---

[1] Mereness, *Maryland*, 137; McCrady, *South Carolina under Royal Government*, 482; Trumbull, *Connecticut*, II., 30.
[2] Winsor, *Memorial Hist. of Boston*, II., 400, 435.

the bishop of London, Blair in Virginia and Bray in Maryland, are almost as well known for their educational as for their religious activities. The Venerable Society emphasized the educational side of its missionary work, and in many southern parishes the Anglican lay reader was the first teacher. In New England also the Anglican clergy were an important intellectual force, helping their Puritan neighbors by the stimulus of competition and preparing the way for a more tolerant practice.[1]

Perhaps the finest gift of the English church to the life of New England was the mission of George Berkeley, who lived from 1729 to 1731 in the vicinity of Newport. Dean Berkeley was the highest ecclesiastical dignitary who had hitherto visited the colonies, and was known already as a brilliant scholar. As the founders of Massachusetts had hoped to build up a "bulwark against Anti-Christ," so Berkeley saw in the fresh and youthful life of the New World a refuge for Christian and Protestant civilization. He desired to establish an American college under Anglican auspices, but the project was not supported by the English government, and he returned to England much disappointed.

Yet the time which Berkeley spent in Newport was not wasted. In a kindly way he used his influence against the sectarian spirit of New England

[1] Weeks, in U. S. Commissioner of Education, *Report*, 1897, II., 1380-1383.

Puritanism, and his sympathies were not confined within his own communion. After his return to England he gave generously to Yale College, both in books and in land, and he also contributed some books to the library of Hàrvard College. Through the stimulus of his intercourse and example he strengthened the intellectual life of the little colony where he lived, and his influence can be traced also in the founding of King's College in New York, 1754, under the leadership of his friend and disciple, Samuel Johnson.[1]

During this period there was substantial progress in the founding and development of educational institutions, and in the south the most important event was the founding of William and Mary College. Some subscriptions for such a college had been taken in Berkeley's administration; but little was accomplished until 1691, when the assembly sent commissary Blair to England with instructions to secure a charter. Blair appealed successfully to the queen and the king, and in 1693 came back with a royal charter, together with a substantial endowment from the royal revenues. From time to time this endowment was increased by grants from the assembly and by private gifts.[2]

[1] Tyler, in Perry, *American Episcopal Church*, I., 519-540; Weeden, *Econ. and Soc. Hist. of New England*, II., 546-548; Fraser, *Life and Letters of Berkeley*, II., chaps. iv., v.

[2] *Cal. of State Pap., Col.*, 1689-1692, pp. 300, 426, 452, 575, 693; Adams, *College of William and Mary*, 11-17; Letters of Blair, in Perry, *American Episcopal Church*, I., 116-119.

William and Mary College was thus founded under distinctly Anglican auspices and its close connection with the church continued throughout the
colonial era. Commissary Blair himself was its
first president, holding the office for fifty years; its
professors were generally clergymen in charge of
neighboring parishes, and emphasis was constantly
laid upon training for the service of the Anglican
church. About the college there was subsequently
built the capital town of Williamsburg, which, with
its double attraction of the college and the seat of
government, became a social centre of some importance. The college itself passed through many vi-
cissitudes; it was burned down in 1705, and, though
soon restored, it was described about 1724 by one
of its professors, the Reverend Hugh Jones, as "a
college without a chapel, without a scholarship, and
without a statute" having "a library without books
comparatively speaking; and a president without a
fixed salary till of late." In 1729 the faculty consisted of President Blair and six professors, including two in theology and two in the school of philosophy. Though its influence in the colonial era
was hardly comparable with that of Harvard, in
Massachusetts, it trained a large proportion of the
men who were to play conspicuous parts in the
struggle for independence.[1]

[1] Adams, *College of William and Mary*, 17–27; Jones, *Present
State of Virginia* (ed. of 1865), 45, 83 et seq.; *William and Mary
Quarterly*, VI., 176, 177.

William and Mary was the only college in the
south during the colonial era, and the demand for
higher education had to be met by sending young
men out of the colony either to England, or, occasionally, to one of the northern colleges. In the
richer families an education over-seas was, therefore, more common than in New England.

In secondary and elementary education the south
made some progress during the first half of the
eighteenth century. A "grammar" school at Williamsburg gave preliminary training in Greek and
Latin. In 1695 the Maryland assembly passed an
act for one or more free schools in which Latin and
Greek might be taught, but only one was established
under its provisions, the King William's School at
Annapolis. In 1763, Governor Sharpe declared that
there was not in Maryland even one good grammar-
school.[1]

South Carolina during the earlier years of the
eighteenth century passed a number of laws for the
encouragement of education. In 1711 the colony,
with the co-operation of the Society for the Propagation of the Gospel, established a school in Charleston; and a few were established elsewhere through
bequests by individuals or through the efforts of
societies.[2]

North Carolina was probably the most backward

---

[1] Mereness, *Maryland*, 137–145.
[2] McCrady, *South Carolina under Proprietary Government*, 510,
700; *South Carolina under Royal Government*, chap. xxv.

of all the colonies, but even here a few schools were
established during the first two decades of the
eighteenth century, chiefly through the efforts of
the Anglican church. The net results, however,
were small, and in 1736 Governor Johnston reproach-
ed the assembly with having "never yet taken the
least care to erect one school, which deserves the
name in this extended country." [1]

None of the southern colonies had a genuine pub-
lic-school system, but the deficiency in organized
education was partly made up by private instruction, which, in South Carolina especially, employed
a considerable number of persons during the latter
part of the provincial era. In that colony also something was done for the poor by the rich through the
institution of schools with free scholarships. [2]

Eight years after the incorporation of William and
Mary College another institution for higher education was incorporated in Connecticut. Yale College,
like its predecessors in Massachusetts and Virginia,
was founded under strongly clerical influences, and
was intended to be largely, though not exclusively,
a training school for ministers. Most of its promoters were Harvard graduates; but in Connecticut
there was a demand for a college nearer home, while
in Massachusetts many men felt that Harvard was
drifting away from the orthodox standards. The

[1] Weeks, in U. S. Commissioner of Education, *Report*, 1897,
II., 1380–1383; *N. C. Col. Records*, IV., 227.
[2] McCrady, *South Carolina under Royal Government*, chap. xxv.

act of 1701 incorporating the new college provided for a board of trustees composed exclusively of ministers.[1]

For the next seventeen years the college led an extremely precarious existence. A part of the instruction was given at Saybrook, but some of the students were provided for at various other places. Local jealousies made it difficult to fix a permanent seat for the college; but in 1716 the trustees agreed upon New Haven, and their decision was sanctioned by the general court. There was still some resistance, and in 1718 rival commencements were held at Weathersfield and New Haven; but by concessions to the disappointed towns the breach was soon healed. Meanwhile, donations were coming in from various quarters. Jeremiah Dummer collected a number of books for the college from friends in England; but the most important benefactor was Elihu Yale, a native of Boston, who, after receiving his education in England, became a prosperous East Indian merchant, and governor for the East India Company at Madras. In 1718, at the first New Haven commencement, the school was christened by its new name of Yale College, and in 1719 Timothy Cutler was made resident rector or president of the college.[2]

The college seemed at last to be definitely established; but it soon sustained a severe shock through the conversion of President Cutler to the principle

[1] Papers by Dexter and Baldwin, in New Haven Colony Hist. Soc., *Papers*, III., 1–32, 405–442.   [2] Dexter, *Ibid.*, 227–248.

of episcopal ordination. The trustees, however, proved equal to the occasion; Cutler was promptly deposed and a drastic rule was adopted excluding from the government of the college any one who might be tainted with "Arminian and Prelatical Corruptions." Yale College was thus more carefully forearmed against heresy than Harvard had ever been. Cutler's successors, Williams and Clap, both proved efficient administrators and safe theologians, and the college became prosperous and influential. Yale was the academic headquarters of thoroughgoing Calvinism both for New England and the middle colonies; and it trained the two great Calvinistic teachers of the period, Jonathan Dickinson and Jonathan Edwards, who became later the first two presidents of the college of New Jersey. Some of the secular leaders of the middle colonies were also educated at Yale, including such New-Yorkers as William Smith the historian and William Livingston the politician and later revolutionary leader.[1]

The enthusiasm of Cotton Mather and his friends for Yale was largely due to their consciousness of waning influence at Harvard, where there had long been a vigorous contest between liberals and conservatives for the control of the college. The Mathers desired a new charter in place of the old one of 1650, which should secure the doctrinal

[1] Trumbull, *Hist. of Connecticut*, II., 22 et seq.; Clap, *Annals or History of Yale College; Talcott Papers*, I., 6, *n.*, 58.

orthodoxy of the college. No act, however, which
the colonists could agree upon, was acceptable to
the crown or its agent the governor; until in 1707
the difficulty was solved by a short resolution declaring the old charter to be still in force.

The more liberal element in the church was
gradually increasing its representation in the corporation, and in 1707, with the help of Governor
Dudley, they elected John Leverett as president.
In 1717 the Mather influence suffered another severe check when two more ministers of the liberal
school were elected to the corporation. In 1722
the conservatives were strong enough to get through
the general court a vote which, by adding the resident tutors to the corporation, would have elimi-
nated the objectionable new members, but this
project was blocked by Governor Shute.[1]

These controversies between ecclesiastical fac-
tions, though petty enough in themselves, are his-
torically significant because they involve the important issue of academic freedom against ecclesiastical
control; and because the victory of the liberals made
the college for the future one of the strong human-
izing forces in New England life. In other ways,
also, this was a period of educational progress for
Harvard. In 1721 and 1727 the London merchant,
Thomas Hollis, established the first two professor-
ships at the college, one in divinity and one in nat-

[1] Quincy, *Harvard University*, I., chaps. iv.–xiv., passim, and
App.

ural philosophy. The latter chair was assigned, in 1738, to John Winthrop, a young graduate who during forty years of service was to be one of the best representatives in America of the scholar's life.[1]

Educational progress came more slowly in the middle colonies. The Quakers of Pennsylvania believed thoroughly in elementary education, but they cared little for the higher learning, partly because they had no clergy requiring special teaching. The first college in Pennsylvania was not founded until 1755, and then the chief mover in the enterprise was Benjamin Franklin, a transplanted New-Englander. Perhaps the most important Pennsylvania school founded before that time was the one established at Philadelphia in 1697 and subsequently known as the William Penn Charter School.[2]

In New York the presence of two distinct nationalities interfered seriously with educational progress, and, though there were schools in the province, they had a poor reputation. William Smith the historian, himself a native and prominent citizen of the province, wrote in 1756 that the schools were "in the lowest order." [3]

In New Jersey a law authorizing towns to levy taxes for the support of public schools was passed as early as 1693, and during the next half-century

---

[1] Quincy, *Harvard University*, I., 232–241, 398, 399, II., 25–27.
[2] Cf. Sharpless, *Quaker Experiment in Government* (ed. of 1902), I., 35 et seq.
[3] Smith, *Hist. of New York* (ed. of 1756), 229.

a considerable number of schools were actually established.   The educational leadership in New Jersey came largely from the Presbyterian church,
which had gathered to itself not merely the original
Presbyterians of Scotch-Irish stock, but their fel-
low-Calvinists from New England, Holland, and
Germany.   Largely through the efforts of Presbyterian ministers, the first charter of the College
of New Jersey was granted in 1746, three of the four
principal ministerial promoters being graduates of
Yale, and one of Harvard.   A year later, another
Harvard graduate, Jonathan Belcher, became governor of New Jersey, and through his efforts a new
charter was granted, which placed the college upon
a secure foundation.   Thus the higher education of
the middle colonies was in large measure the product of New England training.[1]   No other college
was founded in the middle region before 1750, but
the subject was already attracting attention, and
the next decade saw the founding of Columbia
College under Anglican auspices at New York, and of
the University of Pennsylvania at Philadelphia, the
freest from ecclesiastical control of all the colonial
colleges.

An important evidence of a developing civilization is the accumulation of private and public
libraries.   In the endowment of the early American
colleges, notably of Harvard and Yale, donations

[1] De Witt, in Murray, *Hist. of Education in N. Y.* (U. S.
Bureau of Education, No. 1.), chap. ix.

of books had played an important part. Gradually there developed in New England such considerable private collections as those of the Mathers and Thomas Prince. In the south the best-known private collection was that of Westover, in Virginia, which, when sold in 1778, numbered nearly four thousand volumes, collected largely by William Byrd, the contemporary of Governor Spotswood, and showing broad literary and scientific interests.[1]

Towards the close of the seventeenth century, Reverend Thomas Bray collected and sent to various places in America small libraries, made up largely, but not wholly, of theological literature. Most of these were in Maryland, but one of the most important was in Charleston, South Carolina, and there were three in New England. About 1729 the Society for the Propagation of the Gospel sent to New York a library of one thousand volumes for the use of the neighboring clergy. Generally speaking, little was done by the colonists to develop these collections, but in 1698 the South Carolina assembly appropriated money for the support of the library in Charleston, for which the distinction has been claimed of being the first public library in America.[2]

Of more importance as an indication of colonial

---

[1] Bassett, *Writings of William Byrd*, p. lxxxii., and App.
[2] Steiner, in *Am. Hist. Review*, II., 59–75; Smith, *New York* (ed. of 1792), 213; McCrady, *South Carolina under Royal Government*, 508.

initiative in this field was the public subscription library in Philadelphia founded by Franklin in 1731 and incorporated in 1742. Franklin tells us that "The institution soon manifested its utility, was imitated by other towns, and in other provinces . . . reading became fashionable; and our people, having no publick amusements to divert their attention from study, became better acquainted with books, and in a few years were observ'd by strangers to be better instructed and more intelligent than people of the same rank generally are in other countries." A somewhat similar movement resulted in the formation of the Charleston Library Society in 1743.[1]

The development of journalism is one of the most important social facts of this provincial era. At the close of the seventeenth century there was not a single newspaper published in North America, and even after the founding of the *Boston News Letter*, in 1704, fifteen years passed before it had any rival on the continent. During the next two decades, however, newspapers were established in Rhode Island, New York, Pennsylvania, Maryland, Virginia, and South Carolina. These were generally weekly publications, very imperfect in their reports of American news, giving considerable space to English court life and parliamentary procedure and to scientific or literary essays. Though often cautious

[1] Franklin, *Works* (Bigelow's ed.), I., 167–170; McCrady, *South Carolina under Royal Government*, 510–512.

about the expression of editorial views, they became important agencies of political controversy, and furnish to-day valuable sources of information upon numerous aspects of provincial politics.[1]

During the first half of the eighteenth century Boston was the chief journalistic centre in the colonies, and in 1735 there were five newspapers simultaneously published in the town. There Franklin began his career as printer and journalist by assisting his brother in the publication of the *New England Courant*. Papers of a much higher order were the *New England Weekly Journal* and the *Weekly Rehearsal*, afterwards continued in the *Boston Weekly Post*, which had distinctly literary aims and received contributions from leading ministers and laymen.[2]

During the seventeenth century the clergy were almost the only educated professional men in America. Lawyers were few and were regarded with suspicion, and there were few thoroughly trained physicians. During the next half-century there was a decided advance in all of these professions. The development of the Anglican church brought into the middle and southern colonies a few clergymen like Blair in Virginia and Garden in South Carolina, who had shared in the best educational opportunities of their time and yet were ready to spend their lives in the New World.

[1] Thomas, *Hist. of Printing* (Am. Antiq. Soc., *Collections*, VI.), II., 7–204, passim.

[2] Goddard, in Winsor, *Memorial Hist. of Boston*, II., chap. xv.

In New England the clergy lost ground relatively, but their best men began to show a broader spirit. At the beginning of this era the representative men were the two Mathers, especially Cotton Mather, who, though a man of great learning, felt it to be one of his chief functions to check the rising tide of innovation. With all his voluminous publications, he lacked the scholar's critical instinct. The men who succeeded him differed from him not so much in their formal statements of doctrine as in their more tolerant temper. Such a man was Benjamin Colman, one of the liberals whose influence in Harvard College was so much dreaded by Cotton Mather. "There are some practices and principles," he said, "that look Catholic, which though I cannot reason myself into, yet I bear a secret reverence to in others, and dare not for the world speak a word against. Their souls look enlarged to me; and mine does so the more to myself, for not daring to judge them." Yet Colman had misgivings about Yale College accepting Berkeley's generous gift of books.[1]

The most scholarly Puritan minister of the next generation was Thomas Prince, a graduate of Harvard in 1707, and for forty years pastor of the South Church in Boston. Prince found time to build up a large library and to write his scholarly though fragmentary *Chronological History of New England.*

---

[1] Tyler, *Hist. of Am. Literature* (ed. of 1879), II., 171-175; Tyler, in Perry, *American Episcopal Church*, I., 537.

In his dedication he enunciated principles of scholarship strikingly different from those of the *Magnalia Christi.* " I would not," he said, "take the least iota upon trust, if possible," and " I cite my vouchers to every passage." [1]

The progress of the medical profession was comparatively slow. One of the best-known and in some respects most intelligent of American physicians during this period was William Douglass, the author of an entertaining but not quite trustworthy historical and descriptive account of the colonies. Strangely enough, the sceptical Douglass opposed inoculation as a protection against small-pox, while Cotton Mather defended it. William Smith gave a gloomy view of physicians in New York about the middle of the eighteenth century, declaring that there were few really skilful ones, while "quacks abound like locusts in Egypt." South Carolina had a few physicians who showed not only practical skill but some capacity for scientific research. [2]

At the beginning of the eighteenth century lawyers were so few that even the most important judicial positions were often filled by men without specific legal training. This was true in the southern and middle colonies as well as in New England. In South Carolina, for instance, the first professional lawyer of whom there seems to be any

---

[1] Quoted in Tyler, *Hist. of Am. Literature*, II., 145 et seq.
[2] Smith, *New York* (ed. of 1792), 230; McCrady, *South Carolina under Royal Government*, chap. xxii.

definite record was Nicholas Trott, who came to the
province in 1698.

During the next fifty years there was a steadily
increasing number of trained lawyers, many of
whom, especially in the southern and middle colonies, had learned their profession in England. The
political leadership of the lawyers may be illustrated by such names as those of Charles Pinckney
in South Carolina, Daniel Dulany the elder, in
Maryland, and Andrew Hamilton in Pennsylvania,
all professional lawyers and all leaders in their respective assemblies. Even Massachusetts, where
the common-law traditions were weakest, was pro-
ducing some strong lawyers; among them John
Read, the leader among his contemporaries in the
profession; Paul Dudley, a student at the Temple
in London and afterwards attorney - general and
chief-justice of his native province; and Jeremiah
Gridley, who seems to have been a sort of mentor
for the younger lawyers of the revolutionary era.[1]

There are many evidences of increased refinement
and of genuine intellectual interests. It has been
said that the New-Englanders of the early eighteenth
century show little appreciation of the contemporary
literary movement in England; and it is true, for
instance, that the Harvard College library contained
few of the memorable books of the age of Anne.
Nevertheless, Franklin while a boy in Boston undertook to form his style on the *Spectator*, and the

[1] Washburn, *Judicial Hist. of Mass.*, 207–209, 211, 283–287.

newspaper essays of the period show clearly the influence of Addison and Steele.[1]

A wide-spread interest in natural science corresponded to the contemporary tendency of English thought; even Cotton Mather was interested in these studies, as were his contemporaries Joseph and Paul Dudley. Many Americans of that time were members of the Royal Society of London or contributors to its transactions, including the Winthrops and Paul Dudley in Massachusetts, William Byrd in Virginia, and the physician Lining of South Carolina. In Philadelphia the Quaker John Bartram won a European reputation as a naturalist; and there Franklin, in 1743, issued his appeal for the formation of an American philosophical society to stimulate and organize research.[2]

In some of the provincial towns there were considerable groups of cultivated people. With increasing wealth came a development of the æsthetic side of life, especially in domestic architecture and the furnishing of the house. The artist Smibert, who came to New England with Berkeley, left some portraits of representative provincial personages, which, like the later ones by Copley, indicate refined and comfortable standards of life.

Hugh Jones thought that while his Virginian friends were not much disposed " to dive into books,"

---

[1] Franklin, *Works* (Bigelow's ed.), I., 47; Goddard, in Winsor, *Memorial Hist. of Boston*, II., chap. xv.

[2] Franklin, *Works* (Bigelow's ed.), I., 480.

their "quick apprehension" gave them a "Sufficiency of Knowledge and Fluency of Tongue." During the second quarter of the eighteenth century the genteel public of Charleston was listening to lectures on natural science, paying good prices at the theatre to see such plays as Addison's tragedy of "Cato," and observing St. Cecilia's day by a concert of vocal and instrumental music. William Smith, writing of New York, gives the impression, confirmed by later writers, of a community which had some of the social graces, but was not very intellectual.[1]

Boston was thought by the Anglican clergyman, Burnaby, in 1760, to be "undeniably forwarder in the arts" than either Pennsylvania or New York. He considered their public buildings "more elegant" and observed "a more general turn for music, painting, and the belles lettres." The strict observance of Sunday was still a subject of comment by visitors, and the theatre was under the ban, but otherwise the Puritan discipline was much relaxed. Smith thought his own people of New York "not so gay as our neighbors at Boston," and in 1740 the Boston ladies were reported as indulging "every little piece of gentility to the height of the mode."[2]

In Boston and New York, as well as in Annapolis,

---

[1] Jones, *Present State of Virginia* (ed. of 1865), 44; McCrady, *South Carolina under Royal Government*, 492, 526–528.

[2] Smith, *New York* (ed. of 1792), 229; Burnaby, *Travels* (Pinkerton, *Voyages*, XIII.), 730, 738, 747; cf. Hart, *Contemporaries*, II., chaps. xii., xiv.; Winsor, *Memorial Hist. of Boston*, II., chap. xvi.

Williamsburg, and Charleston, English models were closely followed in dress and social practices, though it was observed in New York that the London fashions were adopted in America just as they were going out of use in England.[1]

Provincial society was growing richer, freer, more cosmopolitan in the eighteenth century, but it was felt by many to be losing in ethical and religious vigor. Significant as a protest against the prevailing tendencies of the time was the religious revival which had for its chief preachers Jonathan Edwards and George Whitefield. The "Great Awakening" may be said to have begun in 1734 with the revival in Edwards's Church at Northampton, in western Massachusetts. A short period of comparative inaction followed, but in 1739 the smouldering fire was fanned into flame by the passionate eloquence of Whitefield. The new revival spread through the southern and middle colonies and produced a powerful impression upon nearly all classes. Even the unemotional Franklin found it hard at times to resist the spell of Whitefield's oratory.

Gradually, however, the inevitable reaction came; for the movement was unwelcome not only to those who were tinged with the new secular spirit, but also to many who stood for the old ecclesiastical order. Thus Whitefield found among his antagonists the Anglican commissary Garden, of South Caro-

[1] *Journal and Letters of Eliza Lucas*, 6, 17; Jones, *Present State of Virginia* (ed. of 1865), 31.

lina, many of the leading Puritan ministers of New England, and the faculties of Yale and Harvard.[1] By 1745 the "Great Awakening" had largely spent its force, and to-day men question whether it really helped or harmed the cause of morals and true religion. Many of its leaders were men of no great significance in American life; and even Whitefield was not a man of commanding intellect or character.

One of these men cannot be so easily dismissed. Jonathan Edwards was not only a preacher of extraordinary power, trying to bring back his people to the hard but virile Calvinism from which they were gradually drifting, but perhaps the keenest and most original thinker America has ever produced. A graduate of Yale College at a time when it seemed on the verge of disintegration, he spent nearly all his life as the pastor of a small country town. Yet the great Scotch metaphysician, Stewart, said of him that in "logical acuteness and subtilty" he was not inferior "to any disputant bred in the universities of Europe "; and the German scholar, Immanuel Fichte, nearly a century after Edwards's death, expressed his admiration for the contributions to ethical theory made by this "solitary thinker of North America."[2]

This preacher and metaphysician was also a gen-

[1] Palfrey, *New England*, V., 1–41.
[2] Fisher, "The Philosophy of Jonathan Edwards," in *North American Review*, CXXVIII., 284–303.

uine poet. Like Dante, he used his imaginative
power in depicting the terrors of the world to come
for those who died unsaved, but he was also finely
sensitive to beauty in nature and in the world of
spirit. His record of his early spiritual experience
contains many passages of exquisite beauty. In
one of them he describes "the soul of a true Christian" as resembling "such a little white flower as
we see in the spring of the year; low and humble on
the ground, opening its bosom to receive the pleas-
ant beams of the sun's glory, rejoicing, as it were, in
a calm rapture; diffusing around a sweet fragrancy;
standing peacefully and lovingly, in the midst of
other flowers round about; all in like manner opening their bosoms to drink in the light of the sun." [1]

Edwards was born in 1703 and Franklin in 1706,
both before the close of the first century of English
colonization. The two men were alike in the keen-
ness and range of their intellectual interests, and
alike also in a reputation transcending the limits of
the provincial communities in which they lived.
In other respects they were as opposite as the poles.
In sharp contrast to Franklin, with his worldly wis-
dom, his unemotional temper, and his matter-of-
fact philanthropy, stands the great idealist Edwards,
who in his writings and his life probably approached
more nearly than any American before or since his
time the highest levels of the human spirit.

In 1743, while Edwards was absorbed in the

[1] Edwards, *Works* (Dwight's ed.), I., lvi.

problems of the Great Awakening, Franklin wrote his *Proposal for Promoting Useful Knowledge among the British Plantations in America*,[1] in which he urged that, " the first drudgery of settling new colonies " being " pretty well over," Americans might do their part in scientific and philosophical inquiry. Certainly his own achievements and those of Edwards might well have encouraged such a hope.

From these studies, however, Franklin himself was soon diverted by new and perplexing political problems. Already the final struggle was coming on for the mastery of the continent. Already, too, there lay beneath the obscure questions of provincial politics deeper issues which were to estrange the colonies from the mother-country and force upon them the great problems of government for a new nation. Thus politics rather than speculation became the absorbing interest of the next generation which saw the end of the provincial era.

[1] Franklin, *Works* (Bigelow's ed.), I., 480

CHAPTER XIX

CRITICAL ESSAY ON AUTHORITIES

BIBLIOGRAPHICAL AIDS

JUSTIN WINSOR, *Narrative and Critical History of America* (8 vols., 1884–1889), gives the most detailed account of the literature of this period, chiefly in vol. V.; but much important material has since appeared. Channing and Hart, *Guide to the Study of American History* (1896), is a compact and systematic collection of reference lists, in which, however, the topics are less developed for this than for the earlier period. J. N. Larned, *Literature of American History* (1902), contains useful descriptive and critical notes, mainly by competent hands. Charles McL. Andrews, *American Colonial History (1690 – 1750)*, (American Historical Association, *Report*, 1898), and his "Materials in British Archives for American Colonial History" (*American Historical Review*, X., 325–349, January, 1905), are serviceable accounts of printed and manuscript material. See also, Moses Coit Tyler, *History of American Literature* (2 vols., 1879; revised ed., 1897).

GENERAL SECONDARY WORKS

No comprehensive treatment of this period has yet appeared which represents fairly the present state of knowledge or the point of view of recent students. Of the general histories written during the eighteenth century, John Oldmixon, *British Empire in America* (2 vols., 1708; revised edition, 1741), and William Douglass, *A Summary, Historical and Political, . . . of the British Settlements in*

North America (2 vols., 1749, 1751), are still worth consulting, though neither is accurate. The most scholarly of the eighteenth - century writers was George Chalmers, whose works covering this period are *An Introduction to the History of the Revolt of the American Colonies* (vol. I., 1782; 2 vols., 1845), and his fragmentary *Continuation* (to 1696) of his *Political Annals of the Present United Colonies* (this continuation is in New York Historical Society, *Collections*, Publication Fund, 1868). Chalmers was a royalist official who had had experience in America, and argued that the colonists were during this period aiming at independence. Notwithstanding this theory, his careful study of the British state papers makes his *Revolt* still the best general account of colonial politics in the eighteenth century.

The accounts of the period by George Bancroft, *History of the United States* (last revision, 6 vols., 1888), and Richard Hildreth, *History of the United States* (6 vols., 1849–1852), are both scholarly, but defective on the institutional side and antiquated in method of treatment and point of view. The various volumes by John Fiske are fragmentary in their treatment of the eighteenth century, especially for New England, and lay special stress upon the picturesque aspects of politics and society. Another popular treatment is by Bryant and Gay, *Popular History of the United States* (4 vols., 1881, especially vol. III.), but neither this work nor Fiske gives an adequate view of general political conditions and tendencies. Justin Winsor, *Narrative and Critical History of America* (8 vols., 1888–1889), contains in vol. V. some learned and indispensable chapters, especially that by the editor on New England; but there is little account of general movements except on the international side. John A. Doyle, *English in America* (3 vols., 1882–1887), is as yet mainly confined to the seventeenth century.

GENERAL COLLECTIONS OF SOURCES

The most important repository of material relating to the colonies is the State-Paper Office in London. Abstracts of these papers have been published in the *Calendars of State Papers, Colonial Series: America and West Indies* (9 vols., 1860–1903); but the last volume so far published stops at 1696. Much of the remaining material has, however, been published by state governments and historical societies. Especially valuable for general colonial conditions are: the *Documents Relative to the Colonial History of New York* (14 vols. and index, 1856–1883); *Documents Relating to the Colonial History of New Jersey* (22 vols., 1880–1902); and *Colonial Records of North Carolina* (10 vols., 1886–1890).

Important contemporary documents are reprinted in Peter Force, *Tracts and other Papers relating principally to the Colonies in North America* (4 vols., 1836–1846), and in G. P. Humphrey, *American Colonial Tracts* (18 Nos., 1897–1898). Albert Bushnell Hart, *American History Told by Contemporaries* (4 vols., 1897–1901; vol. II. on this period), is representative both in the topics covered and in the narratives chosen to illustrate them.

INTERNATIONAL RELATIONS

The following histories of England covering this period are important for international relations: Leopold von Ranke, *History of England, principally in the Seventeenth Century* (6 vols., 1875); W. E. H. Lecky, *England in the Eighteenth Century* (8 vols., 1878–1890); Lord Mahon, *History of England, 1713–1783* (vols. I.–III., 1858); Earl Stanhope, *History of England, 1701–1713* (2 vols., 1872; also 1 vol., 1870); Carl von Noorden, *Der Spanische Erbfolge-Krieg* (3 vols., 1870–1882; published as vols. I.–III. of his *Europäische Geschichte in Achtzehnten Jahrhundert*), is the most adequate account of the War of the Spanish Succession and the underlying issues of commerce and politics. The lives, memoirs, and published papers of such statesmen as Marlborough, Bolingbroke, and Walpole should also be studied, together with the reports of debates, in William Cobbett, *Parliamentary History of England* (36 vols., 1806–1820).

For the colonial wars from 1689 to 1713, the leading
secondary authorities are: Francis Parkman, *Count Frontenac and New France* (1878), and his *Half-Century of
Conflict* (2 vols., 1892); Henri Lorin, *Le Comte de Frontenac* (1895); William Kingsford, *History of Canada* (vols.
II., III., 1888); S. A. Drake, *Border Wars of New England*
(1897). G. W. Schuyler, *Colonial New York* (3 vols.,
1885), is valuable for the New York frontier.

The principal English documents are in *Documents
Relative to the Colonial History of New York*, III.-V.;
vol. IX. contains translations from the French archives.
The important contemporary history of the border war-
fare is Samuel Penhallow, *Wars of New England with the
Eastern Indians* (1726; new ed., 1859). Cadwallader
Colden, *Five Indian Nations* (1727; good editions by J. G.
Shea, 1866, and G. P. Winship, 1904), is also valuable.
Compare, on this section, Reuben G. Thwaites, *France
in America* (*American Nation*, VII.), chap. xix.

RELATIONS WITH THE MOTHER-COUNTRY

For the relation of colonial policy to economic development see William Cunningham, *English Industry and Commerce in Modern Times*, pt. i. (1903). An old-fashioned
but substantial work is Adam Anderson, *An Historical and
Chronological Deduction of the Origin of Commerce* (4 vols.,
1787-1789). The best brief account of British colonial
policy is H. E. Egerton, *Short History of British Colonial
Policy* (1897), based in part upon the state papers. G.
L. Beer, *Commercial Policy of England towards the American
Colonies* (*Columbia University Studies*, III., No. 2, 1893),
is the most complete study on the commercial side.

Contemporary English opinion may be studied in numerous political tracts (see bibliography in Beer, as above);
in William Cobbett, *Parliamentary History of England*
(1806-1820); in *Journals of the House of Commons* and
Journals of the House of Lords. The statutes to 1713 are
in *Statutes of the Realm* (12 vols., 1810-1828); after that

date in Danby Pickering, *Statutes at Large* (109 vols. and index, 1762).

Louise P. Kellogg, *The American Colonial Charter* (American Historical Association, *Report*, 1903, I., 185–341), is an excellent essay upon British administrative policy, chiefly during this period, based largely upon the state papers in London. Other useful essays are: Eleanor L. Lord, *Industrial Experiments in the British Colonies of North America* (*Johns Hopkins University Studies*, extra vol., 1898); H. D. Hazeltine, *Appeals from Colonial Courts to the King in Council* (American Historical Association, *Report*, 1894); E. P. Tanner, "Colonial Agencies," in *Political Science Quarterly*, XVI., 24–49 (1901). For legal questions, Chalmers, *Opinions of Eminent Lawyers on Various Points of English Jurisprudence*, etc. (2 vols., 1814; also 1 vol., 1858), is of the first importance; it contains a number of official reports on disallowing colonial statutes. See also St. G. L. Sioussat, *The English Statutes in Maryland* (*Johns Hopkins University Studies*, XXI., Nos. 11, 12).

The documentary collections of New York, New Jersey, and North Carolina mentioned above contain important material on this subject. Especially valuable also are the following volumes of official correspondence: Robert N. Toppan, ed., *Edward Randolph* (5 vols., 1898–1899); the *Belcher Papers* (Massachusetts Historical Society, *Collections*, 6th series, VI., VII.); the *Talcott Papers* (Connecticut Historical Society, *Collections*, IV., V.); G. S. Kimball, ed., *Correspondence of the Colonial Governors of Rhode Island, 1723–1775* (2 vols., 1902–1903); *Correspondence between William Penn and James Logan* (Pennsylvania Historical Society, *Memoirs*, IX., X.).

Consult for subject-matter and bibliography of this section, Andrews, *Colonial Self - Government* (*American Nation*, V.), especially chaps. i., ii., xvii., xx.

POLITICS AND POLITICAL INSTITUTIONS IN THE COLONIES

H. L. Osgood, *The American Colonies in the Seventeenth Century* (1904), in the two volumes published, is limited to the proprietary and corporate colonies, but the royal provinces are to be considered in a third volume. Though dealing mainly with earlier conditions, these scholarly volumes constitute a valuable introduction to the study of political institutions in the eighteenth century. For the later period the student must depend upon monographic and documentary material.

E. B. Greene, *The Provincial Governor in the English Colonies of North America* (*Harvard Historical Studies*, VII., 1898), includes the royal and proprietary colonies, and gives special attention to the conflicts between the governors and the representative assemblies. The representative element in the constitution is considered in two careful monographs: C. F. Bishop, *History of Elections in the American Colonies* (*Columbia University Studies*, III., No. 1), is chiefly a summary of colonial legislation; A. E. McKinley, *The Suffrage Franchise in the Thirteen English Colonies* (University of Pennsylvania, *Publications*, *Series in History*, No. 2, 1905), is extremely detailed, giving more attention to causes and effects. Frank H. Miller, *Legal Qualifications for Office* (American Historical Association, *Report*, 1899, I., pp. 87–151), deals with another side of the representative system.

The following are useful accounts of particular provinces: [Edward] Long, *History of Jamaica* (3 vols., 1774), a good early description of a royal province; J. V. L. McMahon, *An Historical View of the Government of Maryland* (vol. I., 1831); [Benjamin Franklin], *Historical Review of the Constitution and Government of Pennsylvania* (London, 1759; reprinted in Franklin, *Works*, Sparks's edition, 1809), a partisan narrative. The best recent study of a royal government is W. Roy Smith, *South Carolina as a Royal Province* (1903); less successful, but useful, is C. L. Raper, *North Carolina* (1904); cf. E. L. Whitney, *Government of the Colony of South Carolina* (*Johns Hopkins University Studies*, XIII., No. 2, 1895). The best account of a proprietary province is N. D. Mereness, *Maryland as a Proprietary Province* (1901). W. R. Shepherd, *History of Proprietary*

Government in Pennsylvania (*Columbia University Studies*, VI., 1896), contains valuable material and shows thorough research, but is unfortunately constructed. Isaac Sharpless, *History of Quaker Government in Pennsylvania, 1682–1783* (1898, also 1902 as vol. I. of his *Quaker Experiment in Government*), is fair minded and suggestive.

CHURCH AND STATE

CHURCH OF ENGLAND.—J. S. M. Anderson, *History of the Church of England in the Colonies* (revised ed., 3 vols., 1856), is written by a moderate Anglican, largely from first-hand material, and, though old - fashioned, is still valuable. The most important recent history is W. S. Perry, *History of the American Episcopal Church* (2 vols., 1885); it contains some monographic chapters contributed by other writers, and important selections from the sources. Arthur L. Cross, *The Anglican Episcopate and the American Colonies* (*Harvard Historical Studies*, IX., 1902), is a scholarly monograph founded on manuscript as well as printed material dealing with the colonial jurisdiction of the Bishop of London and the attempts to establish an American episcopate. Bishop [William] Meade, *Old Churches, Ministers, and Families of Virginia* (2 vols., 1857, also, 1872), is a valuable authority on religious and social history. The most important documentary collections are: Hawks and Perry, *Documentary History of the Protestant Episcopal Church in the United States* (2 vols., 1863–1864), and W. S. Perry, *Papers Relating to the History of the Church* (5 vols., 1870–1878), containing documents for Connecticut, Virginia, Pennsylvania, Massachusetts, Maryland, and Delaware.

NEW ENGLAND PURITANISM. — See on this subject, H. M. Dexter, *Congregationalism as Seen in Its Literature* (1880); P. E. Lauer, *Church and State in New England* (*Johns Hopkins University Studies*, X., Nos. 2, 3); I. Backus, *History of New England with Particular Reference to the Denomination of Christians Called Baptists* (2d ed., 1871), valuable for the relations between the Congregational establishment and the dissenting bodies; E. F.

Slafter, ed., *John Checkley, or the Evolution of Religious Tolerance in Massachusetts Bay* (2 vols., 1897); A. P. Marvin, *Life and Times of Cotton Mather* (1892); Barrett Wendell, *Cotton Mather, the Puritan Priest* (1891), a brief but suggestive study, based largely on Mather's diaries. Important as illustrating religious feeling are: Cotton Mather, *Magnalia Christi Americana* (1702; best ed., 2 vols., 1853); and Samuel Sewall, *Diary* (Massachusetts Historical Society, *Collections*, 5th series, V.-VII.).

WITCHCRAFT.—For the abundant literature on this episode, see Justin Winsor, *The Literature of Witchcraft in New England* (American Antiquarian Society, *Proceedings*, X., 351-373, 1896). The most detailed study is in C. W. Upham, *Salem Witchcraft* (2 vols., 1867); but his treatment of the Mathers has been ably criticised by W. F. Poole, in *North American Review*, CVIII., 337-397. Important also are Samuel G. Drake, *Annals of Witchcraft in New England* (1869); and W. E. Woodward, ed., *Records of Salem Witchcraft, Copied from the Original Documents* (2 vols., 1864.)

OTHER RELIGIOUS BODIES.—See the various volumes of the *American Church History Series*, including bibliographical chapters and a final bibliographical volume. See also *Ecclesiastical Records, State of New York* (4 vols., 1901-1902).

ECONOMIC HISTORY

There is as yet no comprehensive economic history of the American colonies; but, for New England, William B. Weeden, *Economic and Social History of New England* (2 vols., 1890-1891), is a valuable storehouse of facts. Philip A. Bruce, *Economic History of Virginia in the Seventeenth Century* (2 vols., 1896), describes the initial conditions. Of the histories of particular colonies, Edward McCrady, *History of South Carolina under the Royal Government* (1899), is especially serviceable on the economic side.

SOUTHERN LAND ADMINISTRATIONS.—See J. C. Ballagh, *Introduction to Southern Economic History—The Land Sys-*

tem in the South (American Historical Association, *Report*, 1897), and the chapters on the subject in Mereness, *Maryland ;* Raper, *North Carolina ;* and Smith, *South Carolina*. There are two scholarly essays by J. S. Bassett: *The Relation between the Virginia Planter and the London Merchant* (American Historical Association, *Report*, 1901, pp. 551–575); and the introduction to his edition of the *Writings of Colonel William Byrd* (1901).

MANUFACTURES AND COMMERCE.—Some material may be found in the works of Anderson, Cunningham, and Weeden mentioned above; and in J. L. Bishop, *History of American Manufactures* (3 vols., 1867); but the printed material is chiefly in the documentary collections.

FINANCIAL HISTORY.—See the references in Davis R. Dewey, *Financial History of the United States* (1903), chap. i. The best general view of colonial currency is Charles J. Bullock, *Essays on the Monetary History of the United States* (1900). The most detailed study of currency and banking is Andrew McF. Davis, *Currency and Banking in Massachusetts Bay* (American Economic Association, *Publications*, 3d series, I., No. 4, and II, No. 2).

SYSTEM OF LABOR

On colonial slavery, see especially G. H. Moore, *Notes on the History of Slavery in Massachusetts* (1866); Edward McCrady, *Slavery in South Carolina* (American Historical Association, *Report*, 1895, pp. 331–373); Edward Needles, *An Historical Memoir of the Pennsylvania Society* (1848); Edwin V. Morgan, *Slavery in New York* (Americrn Historical Accociation, *Papers*, V.); and the following numbers of the *Johns Hopkins University Studies:* B. C. Steiner, *History of Slavery in Connecticut* (XI., Nos. 9, 10); Edward Channing, *Narragansett Planters* (IV., No. 3); Jeffrey R. Brackett, *The Negro in Maryland* (extra vol. VI.); J. C. Ballagh, *A History of Slavery in Virginia* (extra vol., 1902); Stephen B. Weeks, *Southern Quakers and Slavery* (extra vol. XV., 1890) The most scholarly treatment of the slave-trade and its regulation is W. E. B. Du Bois, *Suppression of the African Slave - Trade* (*Harvard Historical Studies*, I.). Important studies of white servitude are K. F. Geiser, *Redemptioners and Indented Servants in Pennsylvania* (supplement to *Yale Review*, X., No. 2, 1901); and two numbers in the *Johns Hopkins University Studies* : E. I. McCormac, *White Servitude in Maryland* (XXI., Nos. 3, 4); and J. C. Ballagh, *White Servitude in Maryland* (XIII., Nos. 6, 7). See critical chapter in Albert Bushnell Hart, *Slavery and Abolition* (*American Nation*, XVI.).

CONTEMPORARY NARRATIVES ILLUSTRATING SOCIAL CONDITIONS

For seventeenth-century narratives, see Andrews, *Colonial Self-Government* (*American Nation*, V.), 340–342. The footnotes in Henry Cabot Lodge, *Short History of the English Colonies in America* (1881), are still useful guides in this field. Many extracts are printed in Albert Bushnell Hart, *American History Told by Contemporaries*, II. (1899).

The following records of travel are noteworthy: Madam [S. K.] Knight, *Journal*, 1704–1705 (editions, 1825, 1865), a realistic account of contemporary conditions chiefly in New England; George Keith, *Journal of Travels from New Hampshire to Caratuck* (1706; reprinted in Protestant Episcopal Historical Society, *Collections*, I., 1851), records the missionary journeys of a zealous Anglican; George Whitefield, *Journal of a Voyage from London to Savannah* (2d ed., 1738, and numerous other editions of this and the continuations). For conditions at the close of this period, consult Peter Kalm, *Travels into North America* (in trans., 1770 and later eds.; reprinted in Pinkerton, *Voyages*, XIII.), written by a Swedish naturalist who travelled chiefly in the middle colonies during the years 1749 and 1750; Andrew Burnaby, *Travels through the Middle Settlements in North-America* (1775, and later editions; reprinted in Pinkerton, *Voyages*, XIII.).

Important contemporary descriptions of particular

colonies are John Callender, *Historical Discourse on the Civil and Religious Affairs of the Colony of Rhode Island and Providence Plantations* (1739; reprinted in Rhode Island Historical Society, *Collections*, IV., 1838); [Robert Beverley], *History of Virginia* (1705 and later eds.); Hartwell, Blair, and Chilton, *The Present State of Virginia and the College* (1727); Hugh Jones, *The Present State of Virginia* (1724; reprinted, 1865); William Byrd, *Writings* (1841; later eds. by T. H. Wynne, 1866, 2 vols., and J. S. Bassett, 1901), the observations of a cultivated man of the world. Much the most important personal records are Samuel Sewall, *Diary*, mentioned above, and Franklin, *Autobiography* (many eds. and in all eds. of his works). See also Eliza Lucas, *Journal and Letters* (Holbrook's ed., 1850), for South Carolina in the middle of the eighteenth century.

Good descriptions of social life founded on contemporary records are the numerous volumes of Mrs. Alice Morse Earle, dealing chiefly with New England, which are listed in Larned, *Literature of American History*, 70. See also articles on colonial life by Edward Eggleston (*Century Magazine*, 1883–1885), and the *William and Mary College Quarterly* (1893–). The numerous local histories, of which the best is Justin Winsor, *Memorial History of Boston* (4 vols., 1880–1881), are important for social conditions. See lists in Channing and Hart, *Guide*, § 23.

COLONIAL IMMIGRATION. NON-ENGLISH STOCKS

There is much monographic and antiquarian material on this subject, but no comprehensive treatise. For the Germans, especially in Pennsylvania, the best introduction is Oscar Kuhns, *The German and Swiss Settlements of Colonial Pennsylvania* (1901), which includes a good bibliography. Some important special studies are: Friedrich Kapp, *Die Deutschen im Staate New York während des Achtzehnten Jahrhunderts* (revised ed., 1884); various works by F. R. Diffenderffer, J. F. Sachse, and S. W. Pennypacker (titles given by Kuhns); G. D. Bernheim, *History of German Settlements in North and South Carolina* (1872).

C. A. Hanna, *The Scotch-Irish or the Scot in Great Britain, North Ireland, and North America* (2 vols., 1902), is unscientific but contains some valuable matter.   See also S. S. Green, *The Scotch-Irish in America* (American Antiquarian Society, *Proceedings*, X., 32–70, with bibliography).   C. W. Baird, *History of the Huguenot Emigration to America* (2 vols., 1885), deals chiefly with the seventeenth century. See also *Huguenot Papers* (in Virginia Historical Society, *Collections*, new series, V.).

On colonial regulation of immigration, see Emberson E. Proper, *Colonial Immigration Laws* (*Columbia University Studies*, XVI., No. 2, 1900); A. H. Carpenter, " Naturalization in England and the Colonies," in *American Historical Review*, IX., 288–303.

PROVINCIAL EDUCATION AND CULTURE

On the colonial colleges, the most scholarly work is Josiah Quincy, *History of Harvard University* (2d ed., 2 vols., 1860); the appendices contain many original documents.   For the founding of Yale, see Thomas Clap, *Annals or History of Yale College* (1766); papers by F. B. Dexter and Simeon E. Baldwin, in New Haven Colony Historical Society, *Papers*, III.; and W. L. Kingsley, *Yale College* (2 vols., 1879).   On William and Mary College, see H. B. Adams, *The College of William and Mary* (U. S. Bureau of Education, *Circulars of Information*, No. 1, 1887), which contains an extended bibliography; and various numbers of the *William and Mary College Quarterly* (1893–).

The reports and circulars of the U. S. Bureau of Education, though of unequal value, contain some valuable papers on colonial education.   See also E. W. Clews, *Educational Legislation and Administration of the Colonial Governments* (Columbia University, *Contributions to Philosophy*, etc., VI., 1899).

The best introduction to the study of colonial culture is

Moses Coit Tyler, *History of American Literature, 1607–1765* (2 vols., 1879; revised ed., 1897). Important also are Isaiah Thomas, *History of Printing in America* (best ed. in American Antiquarian Society, *Archæologia Americana*, V., VI., 1874); Stedman and Hutchinson, *Library of American Literature* (11 vols., 1887–1890); and A. B. Hart, *American History Told by Contemporaries*, II.

HISTORIES OF PARTICULAR COLONIES

A few essential books for this period will be given under each colony. For other critical estimates, see Andrews, *Colonial Self-Government* (*American Nation*, V.), chap. xx. NEW ENGLAND.—J. G. Palfrey, *History of New England* (vols. IV., V., 1875, 1890), is the most important single work on New England; it is based upon a wide range of printed and manuscript material and is not soon likely to be superseded. See also Weeden, *Economic and Social History*, mentioned above.

For Massachusetts, the most important history is Thomas Hutchinson, *History of Massachusetts Bay, 1628–1750* (2 vols., 1764, 1767; 3d ed., 1795), which is in part the record of a contemporary. The most useful documentary publication is the *Acts and Resolves, Public and Private, of the Province of Massachusetts Bay* (10 vols., 1869–1902). Besides the statutes there is much original material in the notes. Indispensable also are the *Collections* and *Proceedings* of the Massachusetts Historical Society. For New Hampshire, the standard history is Jeremy Belknap, *The History of New Hampshire* (3 vols., 1784–1792); and the chief documentary collection is *New Hampshire Provincial Papers* (7 vols., 1867–1873). For Connecticut, Benjamin Trumbull, *History of Connecticut* (2 vols., 1797; new ed., 1898), should be used with the *Colonial Records of Connecticut* (15 vols., 1850–1890), and the Connecticut Historical Society, *Collections* (9 vols., 1860–1903). For Rhode Island, the chief authorities are S. G. Arnold, *History of Rhode Island and Providence Plantations* (2 vols., 1859–1860; 4th ed.,

1899), and the *Records of the Colony of Rhode Island and Providence Plantations* (10 vols., 1856–1865).

MIDDLE COLONIES.—John Fiske, *Dutch and Quaker Colonies* (2 vols., 1899), is a general, popular account. William Smith, *History of New York* (1757 and various later editions), is valuable for this period. Of the numerous documentary collections the most important are the *Documents Relative to the Colonial History of New York*, already mentioned; the *Documentary History of the State of New York* (4 vols., 1849–1851); and the *Colonial Laws of New York* (5 vols., 1894). For New Jersey, see Samuel Smith, *History of the Colony of New Jersey* (1765), an unsatisfactory history, but containing many documents; and the *Documents Relating to the Colonial History of the State of New Jersey* (22 vols., 1880–1902), containing public records and important extracts from colonial newspapers.

For Pennsylvania, the most useful histories are Robert Proud, *History of Pennsylvania* (2 vols., 1797–1798), and those of W. R. Shepherd and Isaac Sharpless, already mentioned. The latter author asserts that "an authentic and impartial history of Colonial Pennsylvania is yet to be written." The chief documentary collections are *Colonial Records, 1683 – 1776* (10 vols., 1851 – 1852); *Votes and Proceedings of the House of Representatives* (6 vols., 1752–1776); the *Memoirs* of the Pennsylvania Historical Society and its *Pennsylvania Magazine of History and Biography;* and the *Statutes at Large of Pennsylvania* (vols. II.–VIII., 1896–1902).

SOUTHERN COLONIES.—For Virginia, the chief secondary authorities for this period are J. D. Burk, *History of Virginia* (3 vols., 1804–1805), and Charles Campbell, *History of the Colony and Ancient Dominion of Virginia* (1860). There are three interesting chapters, chiefly on social conditions, in John Fiske, *Old Virginia and Her Neighbors*, II. (1898). The principal collection of documents is W. W. Hening, *Statutes at Large, 1619–1792* (13 vols., 1823). See also the *Calendar of Virginia State Papers*, I. (1875); the *Virginia Magazine of History and Biography* (1893–); the

William and Mary College Quarterly; the Virginia Historical Society, *Collections,* especially vols. I. and II., containing the *Official Letters of Alexander Spotswood.* For Maryland during this period, the most useful secondary works are those of McMahon and Mereness already mentioned. The valuable collection of *The Archives of Maryland* has so far been confined mainly to the seventeenth century. Much important material is included in the Maryland Historical Society, *Fund Publications,* especially No. 34 (the *Calvert Papers,* II.).

The narrative history of South Carolina can be best studied in Edward McCrady, *History of South Carolina under the Proprietary Government* (1897) and *History of South Carolina under the Royal Government* (1899). The first volume is rigidly chronological, but the second contains valuable chapters on special topics. The older works by W. J. Rivers, *Sketch of the History of South Carolina* (1856) and *A Chapter in the Early History of South Carolina* (1874), contain many documents and should still be consulted. See also Smith, *South Carolina as a Royal Province,* already mentioned. For the narrative history of North Carolina, see F. L. Hawks, *History of North Carolina* (2 vols. 1857–1858), and on the institutional side, C. L. Raper, *North Carolina* (1904). The most complete documentary collection for the Carolinas is the *Colonial Records of North Carolina,* already mentioned. There is no similar collection for South Carolina; but important source material may be found in the *Collections* of the South Carolina Historical Society, still in progress, and in B. R. Carroll, *Historical Collections of South Carolina* (2 vols., 1836).

The best of the older histories of Georgia is W. B. Stevens, *History of Georgia* (2 vols., 1847, 1859); it shows extensive and scholarly use of the sources. C. C. Jones, Jr., *History of Georgia* (2 vols., 1883), though based in part on the older writers, shows also independent examination of source material, much of which is incorporated with the text. Among the numerous lives of Oglethorpe, the most important is still Robert Wright, *Memoir of General James*

Oglethorpe (1867); see also *Letters from General Oglethorpe* (Georgia Historical Society, *Collections*, III.).

The *Journal of the Transactions of the Trustees of the Colony of Georgia in America* was published in 1886, by C. C. Jones.   Important contemporary narratives are published in the Georgia Historical Society, *Collections* (vols, I.–IV., 1840), and in Peter Force, *Tracts on the Colonies.* Further bibliographical data are given by C. C. Jones, in Winsor, *Narrative and Critical History of America*, V., 392–406.

INDEX

341